Soar Like an Eagle, One Day at a time

A Portrait of an Alcoholic

A Novel

By

Sarah Ann Bray

ISBN: 0-7596-7310-1

This book is printed on acid free paper.

1stBooks – rev. 02/25/02

Dedication

To my Mom, who gave me life, love, and so much more.
And my children, who gave me a reason to go on.
To dear Miss Warren, who gleaned a spark and fanned it
Until it flamed.
And to you, God, for the gift and for the many times you
Carried not only my burdens, but me as well.

Thanks, and Love, S. B.

ILLUSTRATIONS   by SALLY BEHNCKE-

Chapter One

I am, I know, because at a distance, some faint feelings are trying to catch me. There is pain, but where? It refuses to settle in any one spot. The odors, unidentifiable, elude me. I'm not sure where that sound is, within me or somewhere else. I am here, but where is here?

Floating on billowing clouds that go on forever, they roll and toss me around as if driven by hurricane force winds. There's not even a breeze. Where will I land? Will I? I can't capture feeling, smell, or sound to know if they are mine. Please help me! I reach out, but fail to grip anything to stop my reeling. Not clouds at all, it's quicksand. I'm swimming up from a bottomless pit of boiling, certain death. Have to get air. There are fireworks in my head.

I clutch at the first thing touching my hand. What is it? I don't know. The pain is everywhere, my head, eyes, arms, face, and chest. Where is it all coming from? What's in my hand is soft, warm, feels soothing. A blanket. It smells like antiseptic. I know that smell. I'm getting closer.

I hear shuffling noises and voices in the distance. Can't understand them? A touch! No, fight back! Don't let them get me! Stop! Get away! Can't focus, are they calling my name? Can't let him catch me again.

"Where's Bobby?" If I shake my head, maybe I can evade this fog and find him.

"Bobby, Bobby, where are you?"

Shaking my head hurts. "God, where is Bobby?"

"Come on, Sarah, you're almost awake." A lady's voice, and she's talking to me.

My eyes hurt so badly, they won't respond. "Where is Bobby? I have to find him." Someone touches my face. My head jerks back. The hand was warm, but it hurt. I'm not ready for touching.

One eye flies open, but the other won't respond. She's in a white uniform, and I'm in an all white room. It all looks so bright. Maybe I'm dead. No, if I was dead it shouldn't hurt this bad.

"Where's Bobby?" I mumble.

"Well, you're finally awake. Who is Bobby?" the lady in white asked.

"My little boy. Is he here?"

"No, I've heard nothing about a little boy." She must think I'm hallucinating. Not to many fifty-year-old women have a small child.

"You've been asking for Bobby for over half an hour now. How old is he?"

"He's six. I have to find out where he is." The room keeps spinning.

She finally walks around the bed, in full view. I don't recognize her, but she looks like hell, like I feel.

1

"Who are you? Where am I?" I tried to move, but there were tubes everywhere.

"I'm an intern. I've been with you since they brought you in early this morning." She rubbed her eyes, yawned, then added, "It would be best if you don't try to move around too much. This is the hospital in Summit. You just came out of surgery."

My racing heart feels like it's about to tear a hole in my chest. "Please get me a phone. I have to find my little boy."

She's watching the monitors and must see how upset this is making me, so she finally hands me the phone. All the tubes really are making it difficult, but my shaky hands finally, after two screw-ups, manage to dial the right number. The phone keeps ringing. Of coarse, His Highness would still be passed out. He won't hear it right away, if he hears it at all. "Come on, damn it, answer the phone."

Finally he picks up the phone. "HULLO." He sounds very drunk.

"Carl, where is Bobby?"

"I guess he's in his room." He slurs. "Who is this?"

"It's me, Sarah." I said.

"Where in hell are you? I didn't know you were gone."

"I'm in the hospital, Carl, and I just came out of surgery. Will you please go check on Bobby?" I pleaded. "I have to know if he is okay."

I heard the clatter as he dropped the phone. It sounded like he either fell or knocked something over. Lord, I hope he doesn't try getting Bobby up. I held my breath.

After what seemed like an eternity, he came back on the line. "He's sleeping in his bed."

"Thank God." I gulped some air. "Please, Carl, go back and get some more sleep. I'll call you about noon."

Hanging up, I know he will pass out again as soon as he hits the bed. Bobby will be safe if Carl just lets him sleep, but I have to get him out of there.

The clock on the wall of my hospital room says it is only seven o'clock. He didn't pass out until sometime after three. Carl had started drinking yesterday with his friends and after they left the bar at ten o'clock, he really got with the program. At closing time he came in quietly and yanked me out of the living quarters for this beating. Usually, his bellowing wakes Bobby. Then my son has to watch his mom take her beatings. At least this time Bobby was spared.

I remember Carl throwing me at the pool table. His fist smashed my face several times. The last thing I remember was the corner of the wall in the hallway by the front door. When I hit that corner and collapsed, he must have thought I had enough. When I eventually came to, in a pool of my own blood, all was

2

quiet. I managed to crawl over and unlock the door, then to the phone, 911. That's all I remember until I awoke in this the hospital room.

The lady doctor took the phone. "Is your son all right?" Now she seemed truly concerned for Bobby.

"If you can call being alone with a father who is drunk and passed out all right, then he is. He's sleeping." All the sudden I knew I was going to vomit. She must have seen it coming and handed me the spit pan. "Sorry," I said, "anesthetics do that to me."

She mumbled, "That's a very common reaction." Then she handed me a tissue.

After thinking for a moment, "I can't believe they left him there. All of the EMT's and cops know we have a little boy. Why would they leave him with that animal?"

I must have been full of pain killers, and I drifted off. The next time I looked it was ten o'clock. The lady doctor had stretched out on the other bed in my room. Her radar was working well, she jumped up and started checking all of the monitors they had me fastened to. She could barely reach some of them. I would guess, at most, she was five-foot tall, and had one of the tiniest waists I've ever seen. She probably wears a size three and she looks like a kid. She came and sat beside my bed where we could talk.

Her white-blond hair haloed a caring face, softened even more by her haunting blue eyes. They looked better since she'd had some rest. "I've had a chance to read your file, Sarah. You've had some rough times in the past few years, haven't you?"

She didn't know how rough, or that only a small part of it was in that file. "Nothing quite like this, what are the damages?"

"Let me explain the tubes first," she said. "One is an I V, to give you some nourishment. One is oxygen. The big one in your chest is hooked to a pump. We're trying to inflate your left lung." Taking a deep breath, she continued, "You have seven broken ribs and a punctured lung. You also have a severe concussion."

I could hear the steady hum and gurgle of the pump, although I couldn't see it. "Well, it's no wonder I hurt all over."

"We didn't think you were going to make it through the night, and the entire team was here helping you. Your other lung started to give out." She slowly shook her head. "How long are you going to take this abuse?"

"I'm not going to lie any more." Every other time I had lied and taken the blame for all of my black eyes, cracked ribs, fat lips, and broken teeth. "I sure have walked into a lot of doors." I chuckled even though it wasn't very funny.

"You haven't been fooling Dr. Bradley. He's been writing 'Suspected Spousal Abuse' quit often in your file." She patted my arm. "That many injuries are not self inflicted."

She spoke so softly I dozed off. When I woke again, my head reeled. Carl is getting worse. This time I could have died.

Hey, it's twelve-thirty. I have to call and talk to Bobby. Maybe if I hear his voice, it will at least ease this pain in my heart. The doctor left the phone next to my bed so I dialed the number.

"Hello," Carl answered.

"Hi," I said reluctantly. "Can I talk to Bobby?"

"Just a minute," Carl answered. "He's eating."

At least he's taking care of Bobby, if he's eating breakfast. That's what you do at noon when you live in a bar. Carl didn't bother to ask how I was at all.

"Hi, Mommy, where are you?" Bobby asked.

"Hi, Sweetie, mommy doesn't feel so good, I'm at the hospital." I explained.

"Are you coming home?" He asked.

"I'm not sure when, Honey, but it won't be too long. What are you having for breakfast?" I asked, trying to get his mind off of me.

"Bacon, eggs." He said.

"And toast?" I asked. Just hearing his sweet voice brought on the tears.

"Yep, we burned the first ones, but these are good."

"I'd better let you eat while it's warm. I'll talk to you later, Sweetie, I love you." I had to get off the phone before I started bawling out loud.

"Love you too. Bye, Mommy."

Carl came back on the phone. I didn't want to talk to him, but I had to. I cleared my throat and asked, "Can you bring Bobby up here today?"

"He's to young to come to the hospital," he answered, in that tone of voice he used when he wanted to impress people on how smart he was. He usually came off sounding more pompous than smart.

"I asked already, Carl, and the head nurse said he can come to see me."

"Well, I don't want to see you at all, but I'll bring the boy."

"About two o'clock." I said abruptly, then wanting to cut the conversation short, I hung up. He doesn't want to see me? He just doesn't want to see the damage he's done. Who is this person? I've lived with him for fourteen years, and I don't know him at all. Maybe I did know, and just didn't want to admit it. My older children all knew, they tried to tell me, but love has a crazy way of glazing over a person's flaws, and Carl has more than a few of those.

The lady doctor entered the room and interrupted my thoughts.

"Hi, Sarah, how are you feeling after your nap?" She asked.

I chuckled, then flinched in pain. "Fit as a fiddle, if you'll unhook this stuff, I'm ready to leave."

4

"I can't do that. It takes at least four days on this pump to make sure your lung will stay inflated. Your head needs some time to heal too. Dr. Bradley will be in to see you when he finishes rounds. You know that he was here with you last night too."

"I didn't know," I replied, then asked, "Four days? What about Bobby? What about my work?"

"What if you hadn't made it?" She drove her point home.

After a moment of thought, I remembered something I was going to ask her earlier.

"Say, what can I call you besides lady doctor?" I asked. "You've spent so much time with me. I should be able to call you by your name."

"My name is Angela Long." She said. "Angie is fine, and I'm not a doctor yet. I'm only interning here for a few days. I live and work in Chicago, Illinois."

"Well, Angie, Bobby's coming to see me in a little while. Looking at this room through one eye is getting old. Bobby's sweet little face will be a welcome change. How bad are the damages?" I asked.

She didn't answer, but pulled the night stand over and slid it in front of me, before opening the compartment with a mirror. The mirror was small so I couldn't see all the damage at once. My right eye was black and swollen shut, my right cheek was all black and blue, my lips were all puffy and dark red, and I had several stitches over my left eyebrow. My fingertips followed my image. Even my own touch hurts. Not having my teeth was the most upsetting to me. Carl had broken my plate a week earlier during a previous beating. This is the third set he's had to replace. His fun is expensive. Then it dawned on me. Dr. Debrow, my dentist, has Saturday hours. His office is right acrossed from the hospital.

"Maybe Ilka would pick up my teeth, if they're ready." I said, not really to anyone, just a thought that came out of my mouth on its own.

"Who's Ilka?" Angie asked.

"She's my best friend, don't know what I'd do without her." I answered.

After I checked with the dentist, I dialed Ilka's number at work and told her what had happened, then pleaded, "Dr. Debrow says my teeth are ready if you could swing by for them. I look terrible anyway, but you know, I have always hated having to go without my teeth. Please, Ilka, could you?"

"Yes, and I know how you feel," she said. "I have someone here to watch the store right now. I'll take an early lunch hour, Sarah. I'll be there as quick as I can. Do you want me to pay for the work?"

"No!" I replied brusquely. "Tell them to send the bill to Mr. Carl Regent."

"Gladly." She said.

I laid the phone down, leaned back on my pillow, and took a deep breath. Twenty minutes later Ilka walked through the door, and caught me napping.

She gasped so loudly when she saw my face, that it woke me. "My God, Sarah, I had no idea it was this bad. How could he do this?" She had the look of sheer horror on her face as she came closer. Then she laid the small bag, containing my teeth, on the bed beside me and took my hand in hers. "I hope they threw the creep in jail."

"No, Ilka," I replied with a shrug of my shoulders. "As far as I know they didn't even talk to him. What's more, they left Bobby there with him. I still can't figure that one out." I squeezed her hand. "How can I thank you, Ilka?"

"You just get better, Sarah." She said. "I can't stay now. My lunch hour is almost over, but I'll be back after work. You can tell me all about it then." She gave me a very careful hug and then left, but the ever present smell of her perfume lingered.

A nurse came in and brushed the plate, then handed them to me. The teeth felt strange in my mouth after a week without them. I felt like a whole person again, hurting, but complete with teeth.

"That should make it a little easier eating your meals." The nurse said.

"Definitely. Now if you only had some kind of make up that would cover all my wounds I'd be in really good shape." I joked.

"Oh, I don't think Dr. Bradley wants any make up on your face. You have too many open wounds." She said very seriously.

"I was only kidding, you know." I chuckled. "I've never known any make up that would cover this mess, anyhow."

She removed my bedpan and disappeared into the restroom. Very efficiently she came back, replaced the pan in the night stand, fluffed my pillows and straightened the blankets on my bed before stilting out the door to answer another call light.

As I laid there thinking about the horror on Ilka's face, I almost called Carl back to tell him not to bring Bobby here. No, I have to see that he's okay. Will seeing me like this frighten him? Sure, but I need to see him for my piece of mind. God, I hate what this is doing to my sweet little boy.

I closed my battered eyes, tried to relax, and waited.

* * * * * *

It's two-fifteen. Where are they? My heart is racing. I'm imagining all kinds of terrible reasons why they aren't here yet. Then faintly, I could hear him. They must have just gotten off the elevator. There isn't any silence when Bobby's around. The sound of his high-pitched voice echoed all through the hospital corridors. Closer and closer I could hear him until…

6

Suddenly the door flew open and Bobby bursts in like a ray of sunshine, and Carl right beside him. Bobby's hair was all tousled and his eyes as big as pies. His face, as usual, was beaming with expectation.

"Mommy?" His expression went from one of a happy little boy to one I will never forget. He had the same look of horror as Ilka, and he clung tightly to his father's leg.

I didn't realize I was holding my breath until my lungs started to hurt, so I gulped for air. "It's okay, Honey. Come here." I held out my arms. "Mom needs a hug. That would sure make me feel better."

As soon as he heard my voice, he knew it was me, but still climbed on the bed like he was a little afraid of me. How could his dad be such an ass? I gathered him in my arms, then embraced him tightly. He felt so warm, wiggly, and familiar. For a minute I forgot the hurting. I only wanted to hold him. In my arms he was safe, or was he? Regardless, he was the best medicine in the world for me.

He put one tiny little hand on each side of my face, leaned back, and said, "What happened to you, Mommy?"

I looked at Carl for a split second, with my one good eye, then back to Bobby.

"Someone who doesn't like me beat me up, but I'll be all right. They're fixing all of Mommy's owies." I didn't want to lie to Bobby, but he didn't need me telling him his father had done this to me.

Carl stood by the door for a minute and then slouched over and sat on the other side of the room. He looked like something the cat wouldn't even drag in. Those damned double-knit pants should have been thrown out ten years ago, but they looked like he'd slept in them. Come to think of it, they were the same ones he'd had on yesterday. How could I or any other woman find this man attractive? He looked like he needed to sit. His mere presence made me uncomfortable.

The door remained open after they came in. It was visiting hours at the hospital. Just then, an elderly man and woman walked by in the hallway. It was Harold. A regular at our bar, and his sister, Dotty, who was a friend of mine. Harold did a double-take when he saw me in bed, stepped into the room, and asked, "What in hell happened to you, Sarah?"

Bobby piped up, "Some mean person beat my mommy up, Harol, but the doctor is making her better so she can come home."

Harold had seen me bloody and toothless before. He shot Carl a nasty look, took his sister's arm, turned and left.

Bobby had hopped down and was investigating all of the equipment around me. He had seen my face messed up before. Heck, he'd watched most of the beatings. He would have had to been deaf to sleep through Carl's bellowing. My

7

heart ached with love for my little guy. How long would it be before Carl hit him?

"You can look at it, Honey, but don't touch anything." I warned.

"I glanced in Carl's direction. I really didn't want him here, but no Carl, no Bobby. He wouldn't look me in the eye, never does after one of his nights of amusement. He's never admitted he beat me, and so, of course, has never had to say he was sorry.

Carl turned in my direction. He must have felt my eyes on him. "What the hell are you staring at? I suppose you're going to say I did this." He blurted out.

"I can't talk to you anymore, Carl." I said. "I needed to see Bobby, to make sure he was all right."

"He's all you think about anymore," he yelled. "How in hell am I going to run the place by myself, bitch?" He leaped up, lunged to the bed, and grabbed my arm where the I V was. Blood squirted all over the bed. Bobby started screaming. My heart was racing.

"Daddy! Stop!" Bobby was crying while he pushed on his father's leg, trying to protect me.

One of the nurses and Angie came running through the door. The nurse just stood with her mouth gaping, but Angie jumped right into action.

"I don't think so, Mr. Regent. You won't be doing that here." Angie warned. She held pressure to stop the bleeding, then repositioned the I V tube. Carl's size dwarfed her but he backed off. She was protective as a Pit Bull. Thank God.

"Bobby, come, give mommy a kiss and hug." I said with my arms outstretched. "I need to go to sleep now."

He scrambled back onto the bed. His crying had stopped, but there were still big teardrops on his cheeks. I wiped them off, then collected the last kiss and hug I'd have for a while, and nuzzled him in one of his kissy spots, the soft area under his ear. Bobby squeezed me hard around the neck.

"Bye, Mommy. I love you."

"I love you too, Sweetie. I'll see you as soon as I possibly can." I promised him.

As I watched Carl's drooping shoulders disappear through the door, I felt only contempt. I realized how much we both had changed since we bought that terrible bar. He's only a shadow of the man I fell in love with and married. He was handsome to me, once. He used to hold his shoulders high with pride. When his face broke into an eye-twinkling smile, my heart melted. He always had a good job, and was a good worker. We enjoyed gardening, fishing, and building together. He even tried to teach me how to play the guitar. I'm not musically inclined, but I always enjoyed listening to him play and sing. He has a very pleasant voice when he sings. The proximity of the liquor cabinet is all that's important to him now. He no longer walks tall. I've seen him smile recently, but not for me. He saves that for the other women at the bar. How could he have changed so drastically in such a short time?

I'm far from guiltless. Alcohol and I are not strangers. For Carl, I'm just a reminder of his first wife, Margaret. She drank way too much also, but I no longer wondered why she drank.

Without consent my eyes filled with tears. I've been holding them back too long. I thought our love would last forever, but now I know this chapter of my life is over. Been they're, done that. Bobby was my only concern right now.

Our baby sitter's mom, Vicky, might be a solution to my problem so I dialed her number.

"Hello." She answered.

"Hi, Vicky, it's Sarah," I said. "Sorry, to be so abrupt, but I have to ask a big favor."

"What is it, Sarah?" She sounded puzzled.

"Carl put me in the hospital and I'll be here for a few days. I know Bobby has stayed over with you in the past. Do you think you, Katy, and the other girls could stand having him around at your house, just till I get out of here?" Then I added, "I don't want Bobby to be alone with Carl."

"Sarah, that won't even be a favor. You know we all love Bobby. He can stay as long as he needs to. I can't believe Carl could be so violent. What do we need to do?"

"For right now, I'll talk to Carl. I'm sure he won't mind. He'll be running the bar alone, and Bobby and Katy will only be in his way. In his state of mind, I don't want them there with him. I'll tell Katy what to pack as soon as she gets off the bus. That is, unless Carl say's no. I'll call you back if he does. Can you pick them up?"

"What time?" She asked.

"About five-thirty? Katy can call you when she has things ready. Please, call me when they're with you, so I'll know they're okay." I pleaded.

"I will, Sarah, don't worry. Better give me the number where I can reach you." She added.

After I gave her the number, I laid the phone down and watched the clock. I had to stay awake now.

When I knew Katy would be at the bar, I dialed the number. This had to be worded just right so he wouldn't figure out, that he was doing me a favor. If he knew how crazy Bobby's being there was making me, he'd never let him leave.

"Hello."

"Carl, it's Sarah," I said. "You mentioned that you would be running the bar alone. I've come up with a partial solution, if it's all right with you. I know you'll have your hands full." In my mind I could picture what he might have his hands full of. He didn't even try to hide his infidelity anymore.

"So, what's your solution?" He asked.

"I talked to Vicky." I told him. "She said Bobby can stay with her and the girls till I get home." I figured saying anything about me ever possibly coming home, would detour his train of thought from my present goal. He had no way of knowing I was sitting here with my fingers crossed

"That's fine with me. I don't want them here under my feet anyhow," he said at last.

"Then, I'll need to talk to Katy for a minute. Vicky will be over to get them shortly."

He called Katy to the phone. I told her what to get ready, and when. Then I hung up the phone, and held my breath. At five-thirty-two the phone rang.

"Hello." I answered, praying it was Vicky.

"Sarah, the kids are with me." Vicky said. "Katy packed plenty of clothes for Bobby. He'll be fine here and we'll call often so he can talk to you. Don't worry about him any more."

"Thank God for you, Vicky." I said. "Bobby loves the way you and the girls dote on him. He likes to be the center of attention. Maybe that will help him forget how awful I looked when he saw me here in the hospital."

"Well, I haven't seen you, but having him here is kind of unique for all of us girls. Even Grandma likes it when Bobby is here. One little boy with six women to make over him is fun." She said.

"I hate to have to ask," I said hesitantly, "but you'll have to talk to the school bus driver, so he'll be aware of the change."

"I'll take care of everything. You get some rest, and get better. We'll talk to you later," she said before hanging up the phone.

I could breathe easily now. Getting Bobby away from that drunk was by far my biggest problem, and that was taken care of. A place to stay after my release, what we'll do for money, and transportation were all hurdles, I would have to face later. For now, I need to sleep.

*   *   *   *   *   *

Ilka came to visit for a few minutes every afternoon on her way home from work. She always brought two large carry-out coffees so we could have our coffee clutch.

"You know, Sarah, you're not the only one this has happened to." She said, not as a complete surprise to me. "Stan has done this to me, not as bad, but all the same... It seems as though booze brings out the caveman in most men." She stirred some creamer into her coffee and threw the plastic spoon away. "That can't go any farther than us, you know, what with Stan's job and all."

Angie Long walked through the door, dressed in jeans for her long drive home. "I wanted to come in and say Good Bye before I leave, Sarah." She turned toward Ilka. "It was nice meeting you, Ilka. You keep an eye on this girl. She's lucky to have a friend like you."

"Amen," I said. "If you give me your address, Angie, I'll drop you a line and let you know how I'm doing."

"I was hoping you'd say that." She winked as she slipped a card she had already written out into my hand, and kissed me carefully on the forehead. She said, "Good luck," and walked out the door.

"She's going to make a good doctor." Ilka said. "She is very compassionate. You were lucky she was here with you when Carl got so nasty."

"If that hadn't been such a disaster, it would have been funny, watching Carl back down from that little gal." I said. Then I looked her straight in the face. "I hate to go back to the same old subject, but I always had kind of thought you spoke to me from your own experience. You know you don't have to worry about it going any further, but Stan seems the type."

"It hasn't happened too often, but his anger is a frightening experience." She shivered with the thought. "I hate to run but Stan will be expecting his supper." The smell of her perfume was potent as she hugged me before leaving.

After she left, I kept thinking about her comment. She was protecting Stan the same way I had lied to protect Carl. The way my Mom had done for my Dad, and Grandma did it for Grandpa. Do all women lie or cover up to protect their abusers, the men they love, who claim undying love in return and then turn around and smack us whenever they see fit? Hiding behind booze to take out their frustrations on someone smaller than them is a cheap trick. I wonder if it really makes them feel superior. No other man will ever have that power over me, I vowed. I'll never again leave myself open to this kind of pain.

* * * * * *

On the forth day, Dr. Bradley came to my room. "I need to check the dressing on your chest." He listened to my lungs, removed the bandages, took hold of the tube, and yanked.

"Yeeooo!" I screamed. "And I thought you were a gentle person."

"Sorry," he said, "but if I took it out slowly, it would only have hurt longer. Your lungs sound good, Sarah. You'll have to take it easy for quite some time. Your ribs will be a long time healing, and a good jolt could puncture your lung again."

"When can I leave this nice, sterile motel?" I asked.

"I have to remove your stitches, sign some papers, and you're free to go." He told me with a smile.

"Thanks, Dr. Bradley. I wanted a chance to tell you. I've been going to A.A. since the first of April. I've had one setback, but that's a good day to start, huh, April Fool's Day?"

"Any day is a good day for that." He said. "Let me know how it's going. I want to see those ribs and have another listen to your chest in two weeks. Make an appointment with my office."

"You're the doctor." I quipped. "It feels good to stand on my own feet, but I'm a little shaky."

"Just take it slow, Sarah." He said as he turned to leave.

I said, "It is a relief to know I'm going h..." My voice trailed off. Where is home going to be?

After he left the room, I made a quick phone call.

*   *   *   *   *   *

By the time I was dressed a law officer was there to pick me up. It was Brent Nelson, who sometimes brought his wife out to our bar when he was off duty.

"Hi, Sarah," he said. "You look a little better than when we picked you up off the floor the other night."

"You were there? Maybe you can tell me why they left Bobby there with Carl?" I quizzed him.

"Now that you mention it, no one even gave Bobby a thought." He replied. "Sorry, but you were our main concern. It was a risky situation, you know. If we hadn't hurried, we might have had a corpse on our hands. Here, Sarah." He offered me his arm. "Just to be on the safe side. We don't need you on the floor again."

Upon reaching the bar, we found Carl in his usual state, passed out again. Only after raising an awful ruckus were we able to rouse him enough so Barry could serve him with a restraining order. This got his attention in a hurry. I made a quick retreat, to collect clothing for Bobby and myself, and my purse. I couldn't quit shaking. My legs had turned to rubber. As I listened to Carl start bellowing, telling the policeman what a no good "$%&" slut I was, it was clear, his filthy mouth was in royal form today. This time someone besides me had to listen to it. Barry was cool enough to let Carl rattle on.

"Let's get the heck out of here." I said to Barry.

It was a relief, for both of us, to hop back in the squad car with my bundles and leave Carl and his bar in a cloud of exhaust fumes.

Next, we drove to Vicky's to retrieve Bobby. He wasn't in any hurry to leave them, but he wouldn't let me put him down, so I knew he was ready to go with me. Our next stop was a motel on the main drag in Summit. Social Services had made arrangements for a two-week stay. It was Summits idea of a safe-house. I needed time to heal and decide what to do next.

Barry carried in our bags, said good luck, and left.

The room was just big enough for a bed, dresser, a black and white twelve inch T.V., and a bathroom you could almost turn around in. We had no food, no car, very little money, but we were safe. It started raining and according to the weather man on T.V., the rain was settling in for several days. We showered and curled up in bed to watch Gilligan's Island reruns and listen to the rain.

Bobby was sound asleep in no time at all. I reached over and shut off the television. I laid beside him listening to the rain and Bobby's deep, restful breathing. This was the answer to the prayer I had made at the hospital. It would take all the faith I could muster in the months to come. I was back to square one, with nothing, and a child to raise. My youth was gone. I was battling alcohol. Only with God's help, was I going too win this fight.

Chapter Two

The owner of the motel, a widow of about sixty, also worked afternoons for Ilka at the clothing store, so she was fully aware of our situation. She lent us an umbrella for the two block walks to and from school on Monday. For Bobby, this was an adventure. He didn't mind the downpour at all. The shops around the motel were mostly fast food, convenience stores and video shops. We stopped at a fast food place for Bobby's breakfast. On my return trip I stopped for a colossal cup of coffee and a couple plain donuts.

I plumped the pillows so I could sit and sip my coffee. No television today. I needed some serious thinking time. Time to sort out the mess I call "My Life." How had the alcohol, I had despised as a child, become the main hub around which my entire life revolves? My God given, artistic, talent has been on the back burner for most of the last thirty-seven years, and every other decent thing in my life right along with it. I sat back, shut my eyes, and let my mind drift.

*   *   *   *   *   *

The aroma of fresh baked donuts brought back memories of Mom's kitchen in Lancaster. I could hear a voice out of the past. Janie called to my little brother and I from the front porch. "Come on Sarah and Tag, Mommy's making donuts. Can't you smell them?"

The older home we rented on Tyler St. in Lancaster was really nothing special, but out in the side yard, under a huge maple tree, Daddy had built us a big square sand box with seats on every corner. This was where we could be found if we weren't eating or sleeping. There or in the barn, out behind the house, which daddy used for a garage.

"We'll be right there." I brushed the sand from my bare legs where it stuck, and from Tag's overalls.

"Hurry up, Sarah," Tag squealed as he jumped up and down in excitement. He was making it difficult for me to brush off his britches.

We arrived in the kitchen just as Mom was turning the first batch to brown the second side.

Tag squealed, "They smell good, Mommy, aren't they done yet?"

"Mmm, sure do!" Said Daddy, as he came through the front door. He was a Stone mason/Brick layer. His arms and face were covered with mortar mix that always made him look like a ghost, but accentuated his smile and his soft blue eyes.

"Hi, honey. I didn't know you were here. You must have finished early today." Mom said as she looked up at him and smiled.

14

"Yep, he answered. I've been laying up some flower bed surrounds for the Eberharts'. Work close to the ground goes fast. I thought on such a sunny day like this, we could head for the country and catch us a batch of frogs. But that can wait till we eat our fill of these donuts."

Walter Bray, born June 16, 1911

Grace Bray, born Jan. 9, 1912

"Sounds like fun. It's been a while since we've had frog legs." She commented as she brushed a stray black curl from her forehead with the back of her hand, then took the second batch out of the boiling fat and put them on a towel to drain and cool. They didn't lay there long. "I'll even pack a picnic lunch. Would you kids like a picnic?" She asked.

We were too busy, stuffing our mouths to answer. Our ear to ear grins were answers enough, but we did our best at bobbing our heads in agreement.

*   *   *   *   *   *

Later, Daddy got out the cane poles and tied them to his work car. He had cut the back out of our car and built a box to hold his tool chests. Us kids piled in the back and used the tool chests to sit on. Our water spaniel, Pal, jumped in too. Mom got in front with the picnic lunch and we were off to the country. Pal rode with her head and shoulders out so the wind could blow her ears out. It looked like she was flying. We bounced along country roads until we arrived at the stream Daddy had chosen today.

"All out," Daddy yelled. "We're gonna catch us some big old fat frogs." He took each pole and tied red yarn onto the hooks. "Everyone, climb the fence and head for the high bank, but no one goes near the edge til I get there."

Janie and I helped our little brother over the fence and made sure he didn't go near the water.

"I want to go first," Janie said. "I'm the oldest. I should be first."

"Okay, Janie, come on." Taking our hands and one at a time we'd sneak up really quietly and peek over the edge. When we spotted a frog, we'd slide the pole with red yarn out slowly and lower it over the frog. Snap! He was supper.

"We'll have to catch a bunch of these, they aren't very big, but they'll be tender."Daddy said.

By the time we had enough frogs for a meal, we were quite some ways down the creek. Daddy carried the poles and frogs so we could pick Mom some wild flowers. He whistled as we walked back to where Mom had the picnic ready. Even as little kids, we knew every river and creek in Grant County.

*   *   *   *   *   *

I was always up before the chickens. One Saturday Daddy said, "Sarah, get your little fanny up stairs and wake up your brother and sister. I don't have anything to do today so Mommy and I are going to teach you girls how to swim. We'd both feel better if you girls knew how."

"Where are we going?" I had to know some of the details so I'd know more than Janie. She was always first to know everything.

"Janie, Janie, Tigger," that was my nickname for Tag, "Wake up, wake up, Mom and Daddy are taking us to a swimming hole to teach us to swim."

Janie sat up in bed, and I started laughing.

"What are you laughing at?" She asked indignantly.

"You. Your hair is all messed up and you look funny." I poked fun at her. Janie and I were both pretty skinny. She was pretty and I was skinny. It did me good to have a reason to tease her.

"Well quit laughing at me and get Tag up. If you get him dressed, I'll make the bed."

Tag was already climbing out of his bed, and his hair was messy too, but he looked cute that way. Mom hadn't had the heart to cut his long blond curls off yet.

"How do you swim?" Tag asked.

"I don't know. I guess you get in the water and do a lot of splashing. Oh, wait a minute," I joked, "You do that in the bathtub all the time and your not swimming."

Janie laughed, "Mommy and Daddy are both good swimmers. I've heard them telling about swimming with Uncle Harlow and Aunt Evy."

Then I remembered, "Mom says to wear some old underpants. We have to use them for swimming. She doesn't want us ruining our good ones in the mud."

Janie and I changed into our oldest bloomers, grabbed Tag, and raced down the stairs.

* * * * * *

When we reached the creek Daddy said, "Come on Janie, you always want to be first."

He put her on his shoulders and she laughed and giggled until he walked out deep in the water and went under…

"I-e-e-e-e, glub, glub, glub."

When she came up for air, she started crying. Daddy held her close til she stopped sobbing. Once she settled down, he held her on top of the water and had her paddle her arms and kick her feet. Now she was laughing. When it was my turn, Janie got all excited, and jumped up and down.

"Don't open your mouth, Sarah." Jane screamed.

Well, I did the first time, but I learned better. The hard way. That seems to be my preferred way to learn everything. Neither of us really learned how to swim that day, but at least we had an idea of how it was done.

The bonfire Daddy had made warmed us as we got into some dry clothes, then we all made hotdogs and toasted marshmallows on sticks. We knew he always had his harmonica along and it didn't take too much encouragement to get him to play some Irish Ditties.

Tag climbed on Daddy's knee and when he started playing, and keeping time to the music, Tag bounced up and down squealing, "horsy, Daddy, horsy!"

When we piled back in the car, Pal was wet. She was a water spaniel and loved to swim, and wouldn't get out of the water until the rest of us climbed into the car. Us kids and Pal curled up under a blanket as the car meandered the county roads toward home. We were a family, Mom and Daddy, my brother and sister, and me. We belonged together. That's the way God intended us to be.

*   *   *   *   *   *

My Dad knew he could light up my world by saying, "Come on, Squirt, you want to go to work with me today?"

"Can I, Mom, can I?"

Mom knew I loved to go with him, and how I loved to watch him work, so she always agreed I could go.

"Come on, Sarah, I need a good helper today." This translated to mean he was working on a roof, building a chimney, where his tobacco and papers weren't close by. He had taught me to roll cigarettes, so I could send a hawk of fresh mortar with a cigarette along the side, up to him as needed. It fascinated me how he could throw a little mortar, chip the edges of a rock just right, and plop it into place. It looked like the rock needed to be exactly where he put it. I loved to watch him work and I'd go with him any day he'd let me.

These few, happy, memories of my father, I have kept locked away in a secret corner of my heart. They were like tiny diamonds hidden in a mine field, but as Paul Harvey always says: Now for the rest of the story…

*   *   *   *   *   *

Tag, Janie and I were in the sandbox when Daddy's car came bouncing up our street, turned in the driveway, and drove through the doorway of the barn. Us girls each took one of Tag's hands and were picking him right off the ground as we ran to the barn to meet Daddy. Our eyes were accustomed to the bright sunlight so the darkness in the barn was magnified. Daddy stepped from the car. As he turned to meet us, he kneeled down to our size. We all grabbed onto him and knocked him down in a pile of straw along that side of the car. The smell of mortar I was used too, but today another smell filled the air. It made my stomach churn. He wreaked of whiskey.

"Now you kids are in for it," he laughed, as his muscular arms pinned us down. He straddled all three of us with poor little Tag in the middle. Tag got the first whisker rub while Janie and I were getting tickled. Daddy's strength made it impossible to move. His fingers dug into our ribs so far it hurt. Then Janie and I got whisker rubs in turn as he tickled Tag. His whiskers were like a wire brush.

Tigger was the first to start crying. Tears came to my eyes, partly because of the pain, but mostly because he was hurting my little brother.

"Daddy, please stop." I whimpered.

"Oh, no. I've got all of you now." He said without letting up a bit. The rough ends of the straw were poking us in the back like needles.

"You're hurting Tag, Daddy." Janie squealed.

I felt like a trapped animal. He had my hands pinned down. I hated doing it, but he gave me no choice. I bit him.

He jumped back, and yelled. "You God damned little brats."

All of the sudden his attention was on his arm and his weight shifted. We squirmed free, pulling Tag along with us. Janie picked up Tag and we ran screaming toward the house. Mom had heard us yelling and we met her, face to face, as we rounded the corner of the house. She was frantic. She grabbed Tag from Janie's arms.

"What happened? Did someone get hurt?" she asked breathlessly.

"We didn't get hurt, Mommy." Janie said as Mom herded us up the steps and into the kitchen. "Daddy hurt us."

"Daddy smells like whiskey again." I managed. "He tickles too hard. Doesn't he know that hurts us?"

"Sometimes Daddy forgets his own strength." She said. "Especially if he's been drinking."

Tag's body was still shaking with each sob. Mom's eyes were wild as she tried to comfort Tag. He clung to her so tightly, he was shutting off her air. Tears filled her eyes.

We could hear Daddy's footsteps on the porch.

She handed Tag back to Janie and frantically pushed us through the stair door.

"Girls, take Tag up stairs and you all be as quiet as you can be. Don't come back down, no matter what. Try not to make a sound."

We climbed as fast as our legs would go. Janie was struggling. She wasn't used to carrying Tag up the stair steps.

Tag cried even harder now. He wanted Mommy. He was scared. Janie took Tag into the closet and they cuddled in a back corner on some old clothing. I kneeled by the floor register, barely breathing. Mom and Daddy weren't where I could see them, but I could hear everything. Daddy's voice was loud and his words were slurred together.

"Wha chu do witha brats?" He slurred. "One of them bit me."

He didn't know who did it? That was good for me.

"Walter, you get too rough with them." Mom pleaded. "They're only little kids."

"I don't know why I have to be saddled with the little brats anyway." He was using a lot of words I knew weren't nice. He didn't want us? Maybe my biting him made him hate us. Now what will we do?

I could hear sounds of silverware and dishes clinking together. Mom must be getting him his supper.

"Crash." It sounded like he broke a dish against the wall. Then another sound made my blood run cold. It was duller than a slap, but loud. Mom let out a moan and I knew he must have hit her. Then it happened again and I heard a loud thud like something hit the floor. All the sudden I could see Mom crawling through the living room door. Her face was bleeding. She staggered to her feet and locked the door.

"Bang, Bang, Bang." Daddy was beating on the door she had just locked Then he stomped away. Was he coming upstairs? God, I hope not. Then it got deathly quiet. I was afraid to breathe. I looked over at Janie and Tag, put my finger to my lips and went "Shhhh". Another door slammed, he must be in the bathroom. He stomped around a little while longer, then all was quiet. Mom had shut the living room light off so I couldn't see her anymore. Too much time passed, and I was afraid for Mom. It was getting dark and I was afraid to turn on the light. She had said not to come down, no matter what. Then I heard a familiar sound.

Z, chh, Z, chh, he was snoring. Thank you, God, for letting him go to sleep.

I could hear someone sneaking up the stairs. It was Mom. She was okay. I ran over and gave her a hug.

"Sh., kids. Your father's sleeping." She whispered. She handed us each a sandwich. Tag had fallen asleep so we slipped him into bed. "Be really quiet girls, eat your sandwiches, and we'll all crawl in with Tigger."

Daddy's snoring got increasingly louder so Mom turned on the night stand light. We quietly got into our pajamas. Mom's eye was swollen shut and both eyes continued to fill with tears, which she tried hard to hide from us. We eventually fell asleep all huddled together.

Sarah Bray, Just before W W II, born on Mom's birthday in 1936.

I grew up a lot that night. My Father had killed the only hero I'd ever had. He didn't have too much time for any of us from then on, but it made us that much closer to our Mom.

*   *   *   *   *   *

Sunday mornings were our special time with Mom. She always had us be real quiet getting ready for Sunday School so Daddy could sleep late. This Sunday was no different.

"I've got two pies made and dinner's in the oven," she whispered. "Everyone be real quiet. You girls will have to wear your snow suits on your way to Sunday School today. It's really cold out. Tag and I are ready whenever you are, girls."

"We're all ready, except for our stadium boots, Mom." I said as I laced my boots.

"It's a shame you have to cover your pretty dresses, after all that ironing." She grimaced.

"Everyone else will be bundled up too, Mom." Janie reminded her. We knew how proud Mom always was of our being dressed in freshly ironed frocks.

The square in down town Lancaster was all decked out for the holidays already, even though they were three weeks away. The Christmas decorations in the classrooms and church, and all of the carols they sang had us in a festive mood.

When we returned home, we opened the door and the smell of roast chicken filled the air. It must have gotten the best of Daddy too. He was up and had the table all set for dinner. For a change he even said grace before we ate our meal.

Still dressed in our Sunday best, Janie and I were cutting out paper dolls in the living room. Tag was mixing them all together so we cut some animals out of magazines for him to play with.

"You are a little pest, Tigger." I told him.

His eyes twinkled with mischief as he held the animals and announced, "More."

Daddy was sitting with his stockinged feet up on the footstool reading the Sunday paper and listening to music on the radio. Mom was cleaning the kitchen, and I was day dreaming as I watched my Dad. He had become very distant lately. That terrible night never ever got mentioned, but I thought about it every time he came home smelling like whiskey. I missed being close to him.

"We interrupt this broadcast to bring you a special news bulletin; The Japanese have bombed Pearl Harbor!" The announcement came over the airwaves.

Daddy jumped from his chair. "You kids be quiet. I want to hear the radio."

Mom came running in from the kitchen. "What did they say?" She asked anxiously.

"You heard right. Our ships were bombed in Pearl Harbor." Daddy said.

After a short time, he got in the car and left. Mom worked around the house but there seemed to be an electrical charge in the air, I had never felt before. We were too young to know what an impact this day would have on our lives.

Janie whispered, "Who are the Japanese?"

"I don't know any of what they said. Who is Pearl Harbor?" I only knew it had to be something bad, by the way our folks were acting. They both paced the floor a lot and never sat down. Daddy stared off into space a lot and could look right through us kids. We were definitely baggage he didn't want or need right now. Mom was nervous most of the time, like there was a black cloud hovering over us. I would have done anything for her, but what can you do when you're only six years old, you're in your father's way, and you have no idea what the fuss is all about.

* * * * * *

Next day, President Roosevelt came on the radio, "Yesterday, December Seventh, Nineteen-Forty-One, a date that will live in infamy, the United States of America was suddenly and deliberately attacked by naval and air forces of the Empire of Japan."

Radio broadcasting changed for quite a time after that. They used to play music by Kate Smith, Bing Crosby, The Andrew Sisters, Rudy Valley and the Connecticut Yankees, Perry Como, and a young singer named Frank Sinatra. They had stories like Baby Snooks, Amos and Andy, Great Gilder sleeve, The Shadow, and Inter Sanctum. Now it's all newscasts by Lowell Thomas, Edward R. Murrow, H. B. Caltenborn, and Walter Winchell. One by one they would interrupt the music and stories with news of the war.

Our family used to sit in the evening listening to stories or music. Since the war had started, no one had time to sit with us at all. Something we didn't understand was seriously wrong.

* * * * * *

Two weeks after World War II was declared, Daddy came home from work and announced, "I enlisted in the Navy."

"Oh, no, Walter." Mom sat down at the kitchen table, her face turned white.

Daddy walked over and started rubbing Mom's shoulders. "All of my brothers are enlisting too." He said. "The folks and I just talked to each of them and they all feel the same way I do. Harlow is the only exception. His family is too big, and he can do more good on the home front than he could do off somewhere fighting."

"How's that?" Mom asked.

"With his construction business." Daddy said. "There was talk at the tavern that they will be expanding the war plant, close to where he lives, in Illinois. He'd be a fool not to get in on that."

"There'll be enough going from your family anyhow." Mom said. "There are so many men gone from town already. It's starting to look like a ghost town. Walter, you work in construction too." She looked at him hopefully, "Can't you stay here and work too?"

"No! It's only gonna get worse. I'm going over to fight. We all have to make sacrifices."

I had been listening to them. When Daddy was around, I was almost afraid to talk. He had been very sarcastic lately and took to saying, "Kids are to be seen, and not heard." He got angry at the drop of a hat if we said anything to him, so we didn't. In fact, we avoided being around him as much as possible. I think he wanted to go to war to get away from us kids.

"What about the families?" Mom asked.

"Bernie, John, Alphie, Harry and Harlow are all bringing their families this weekend to see the folks. We'll know more after we talk to them about what they've decided to do." He continued rubbing Mom's shoulders as he talked. "We'll have to make room for some of them. It will mean a lot of extra cooking, Grace. Alphie and Leny can help too, but they don't have much room in their trailer. Mom and Dad have one extra room and a davenport. Oh, Heck, we'll make do, we're all family."

How could my Dad talk about family like it was something sacred? His own little family was scared to death of him. We had to weigh every word for fear he'd explode. I decided to keep my hands busy, my mouth shut, and my ears open, so I could find out what was happening.

"It's harder for your folks with no indoor facilities," Mom continued. "Your brother's families are used to things a little more modern."

"Hey, they raised seven of us and did all right."

"Your Mom had her hands full with all you boys and only one girl to help with chores. Is Genevieve coming too?"

"Come on, Grace, us boys all helped out too, and no, Gen can't make it. With a little two-year-old and the baby due any day, she doesn't want to travel this far." He put his hand to his chin and felt the two-day stubble. "Grace, there's something else we need to talk about."

That stubble on his chin reminded me of those awful whisker rubs. He hadn't done that since the war broke out. I personally didn't miss them.

"What do we need to talk about?" Mom asked.

25

"Not now." He whispered

He nodded in our direction and I knew us kids were once more in his way. I looked over at Janie and she rolled her eyes to let me know she was thinking the same thing. She had been listening too. We might have our differences but right now our world was like the cover on our old baseball. Once the laces start to break, it keeps coming apart more every day.

* * * * * *

Saturday morning our uncles started coming early. Alphie and Leny were the first to arrive because they lived here in Lancaster, and they had no kids to get ready, yet. Leny has been looking kind of chubby around the middle lately, like our neighbor lady who just had a baby.

"Come on in," Daddy said. "Gracie made fresh donuts and a big pot of coffee. Help yourselves. You're the first to get here."

They hadn't even finished their coffee when Harlow and Bernie walked in the door.

"Hi, everyone." They said, almost in unison.

Mom looked disappointed. "Where are Evy and Ruth?"

"The wives decided to stay home this trip. They figured you'd have enough people here without all the rug rats," Bernie said as he walked over and kissed Mom on the forehead.

Harlow said, "Since we live so close to each other, we decided to drive here together."

Bernie added, "We left long before daylight and only had one flat on the way. We didn't have a spare. It was lucky we had a patching kit along. That coffee smells awfully good, Grace. Got a couple of cups for some weary travelers?

Mom got up and filled a cup for each of them. She was sitting close to the coffee pot.

"Thanks, Gracie." Uncle Bernie said

"Hi, Alphie, Leny," nodding to each of them. Harlow asked, "How's married life?" He grinned. "From the looks of you, Leny, it must be agreeing with you."

Aunt Leny's face flushed. She knew the Bray boys well enough to know they loved to tease.

The kitchen was getting full of grown ups, so Janie and I took Tigger to the living room. I can't remember ever seeing all of the Brays together at one time. This would be a day I'd not soon forget.

* * * * * *

We kept busy staying out of the grownups way. Aunt Leny and Mom came into the living room with us so the men could talk war. This was the first time I'd seen Mom sit down for days, and I couldn't let the opportunity pass. I plopped down beside her. Janie did the same thing on the other side. She put her arms around us. She smelled so good. Not perfume, just the familiar smell of Mom. Her freshly ironed dresses always smelled like the combination of Fels-Naphtha and starch. Janie and I held her around the waist, our arms entwined like ropes. We weren't going to let go until we had to. Aunt Leny started right in talking.

"Grace, we have a full size hide-a-bed, so if it's okay with the guys, beings they came alone, Harlow and Bernie can stay with us. John and Char have always been thick with you and Walter. And all of your kids have been very close too. You'd probably enjoy having them here with you."

"You've given this a lot of thought, Leny." Mom said. "But, that should work out fine. Janie, Jenny, and Sarah can sleep in the girl's big bed. Tag and Jerry will both fit in Tag's bed easily. That just leaves Harry. I don't think he will mind bunking out to the folk's. It will give him a chance to visit with Mom and Dad. I can imagine how shaken they are by all this war talk."

"That takes care of the sleeping arrangements. I wonder how the guys are coming on who's going where in this terrible war. Are you staying here with the kids, Grace?"

"Well, Walter told me last night. He wants me to go to work at the war plant in Illinois. Down by Harlow's, you know. Maybe even stay with Harlow's family." Mom said. "He says we can save the money for a house of our own."

"How about the kids? Will you take them with you?"

My mind jumped to attention. Ya, Mom, how about us? I'm anxious to hear your answer. What are you going to do with the little brats?

"Walter thinks they should stay with his folks." Mom said. "That would help all of them keep their minds off the war, at least a little."

Oh great, I thought, we are getting dumped on Grandma and Grandpa Bray.

"What will you do with your furniture?" Leny asked. "You wouldn't try to keep the house here too, would you?"

"No, we'd probably store it somewhere. You know, Leny," Mom said as she untangled from us girls and started to get up, "we'd better get some food around for all these soon-to-be servicemen."

Janie, Sarah, and Tag

After the two women went back to the kitchen, Janie and I went to the front window to watch for Jenny and Jerry. Janie put her arm over my shoulder. This wasn't her normal behavior. She must be feeling like I do. At least we were more important than the furniture.

* * * * * *

Uncle Harry came through the front door with a big smile for everyone. Janie, Tag, and I ran to get a hug. He smelled so good, always did. He hugged us, stood up straight, and saluted his brothers.

"Say hello to one of the newest members of the Merchant Marines."

"Hey, Buddy, about time you got here," Harlow said. "What did you do, just stop and enlist along the way?"

He never had a chance to answer. Another car pulled in, out in front of the house.

It was Uncle John, Aunt Char, Jenny and Jerry. Janie and I went flying out to meet our cousins. At last, there is someone our age. Now all the brothers were together except for Virgil, who had died during the depression, trying to hop a ride on a train.

It was cold outside and the grown ups were spilling over into the living room, so all of us little people went upstairs to play. It had been several months since we'd seen Jenny and Jerry. We used to be together all the time when they lived closer. I helped Jenny hang up their coats and then put my arm around her shoulder.

"I wish you lived closer, Jenny," I told her. "We need someone we can feel close too. The grown ups only want to talk about war all the time."

"I know!" She answered. "My dad says he's going to the army. We probably won't see him for years."

"Will it be that long?" I asked.

"Yes. Dad says he will be gone for four years." She answered. "That's how long they have to sign up for."

Janie was in deep thought, "I'll be in seventh grade by then," she said, her eyes as big as I'd ever seen them. "Daddy won't be here to see us grow up."

"Tigger will even be in school. Wow!" I said as I looked over at Tag and Jerry, playing tinker toys without a care in the world. "He'll be big before we see Daddy again."

I didn't say it out loud, but I don't think our Daddy cares. Tomorrow in Sunday School I will say a prayer for all of my uncles and for Daddy. I also want to ask him not to take our Mom away too. He has to know how much us kids need her. Maybe during war, kids don't count.

*   *   *   *   *   *

Aunt Char, Leny and Mom baked pies, made bread, and cooked everything they could get their hands on. This family could really eat, and talk…Kids didn't stand a chance for any attention here, so we gave up and kept ourselves busy playing and staying out of the way.

Grandma and Grandpa Bray walked down to our house after lunch. Grams couldn't stop herself from crying when she saw all of her boys together for this reason. She has always been such a strong person, and kind of reserved. I'd never seen her cry before. She made the rounds, hugging each of her boys like she didn't want to let go. They all had tears, too. She and Grandpa finally sat down at the table and had a bite to eat and a cup of coffee. Mom remembered to serve Grandma's coffee with a cup and saucer.

Grams always poured her coffee into the saucer, a little at a time. Then drank the coffee from the saucer, the way she had learned in Germany as a girl. She smiled at Mom.

"Thanks, Grace."

Grams looked worried. She said, "All that will be left in Lancaster are young boys, old men, the ailing, and us women."

Harry asked, "Is it really that bad already, Mom?"

"Yes! With all this war talk, and the men all leaving, people are really at loose ends. They're locking doors that haven't seen a key in years." Gram said, "I've heard tell there are window peekers around. Makes a body wonder who you can trust."

The five of us kids just kind of squeezed in between grown ups whenever we got hungry. No one seemed to know we were there at all.

Grandpa, Daddy, and a couple of the other guys left to get some beer. They came back with three cases. With all these Bray men that wasn't too much beer, but the more they drank the louder they talked.

It was getting late and I hadn't talked to Mom since lunch time. She was over on the other side of the kitchen talking to Grandma and Aunt Charlotte. The only one of the three that was paying any attention to her kids, today, was Grandma Bray. I needed my Mom now.

"Mom!" I said, loud enough, I thought, to get her attention. She must not have heard me, just kept right on talking.

"MOM!" I yelled. She heard that! She stopped talking and hurried over to the stair steps.

"What do you want, Sarah?" She asked impatiently.

I said. "Tag and Jerry are already asleep, Mom. Is it all right if Jenny stays with Janie and me?"

"Sorry, honey," she apologized, "we lost track of time. Yes, you girls go to bed, I'll get you up in the morning for Sunday School." With that, she turned and walked back over by Grandma.

No kiss tonight. We were like toys shoved back on the top shelf of the closet. Still loved, but for the time being, forgotten. I climbed the stairs.

"We are all supposed to go to bed." I told the other girls.

As we cuddled under the blankets, the drone of the grown ups talking was like soft music or rain on the roof. My last comment before I fell asleep, fell on already deaf ears.

"Sure would be nice if someone would remember to come up and kiss us good night."

*   *   *   *   *   *

We hurried home from Sunday School.

"You girls are just in time for breakfast." Mom met us at the door like she always did.

Everyone was back to our house and some were getting ready to leave for home. While I ate my eggs and toast, I picked up bits and pieces of their conversation.

Uncle Bernie was going to the Marines...

Alphie was going to the Navy...

Aunt Leny was moving out of the trailer, but...

She was moving into our house...

Aunt Char, Jenny, and Jerry were staying where they live, close to where Uncle John will be stationed and close to Aunt Char's Mother...

The three of us were going to be living at Grandma and Grandpa Bray's.

*   *   *   *   *   *

By the end of the week Daddy was gone to the Great Lakes Naval Station. Mom had a job at the proving grounds in Illinois. She has to start work next Monday morning. Leny moved into our house so we didn't have to store our furniture.

Us kids were packed up and then taken to Grandma and Grandpas. In the past two weeks our world had been torn apart and scattered in the wind. At five years old I was learning that war is 'Hell'. All anyone can do is hold on to loved ones that are close enough to hold on to, and pray that everything turns out okay. I bawled like a little baby when Mom drove away.

*   *   *   *   *   *

Taking both hands to smooth back a few loose strands of grey hair to the bun on the back of her head Gram said, "Girls, we don't have any closets, so your clothes will have to be kept folded and put away in the bureau drawers. You're the tallest, Janie, so you take the top drawer. You take the middle one, Sarah, and you can both put your little brother's things in the bottom one." Then she added, "You know where the hooks are out in the kitchen to hang your coats."

"What did you do with Alphie's model airplanes?" I asked. The room had always had wooden airplanes hanging down from the ceiling. Alphie was the youngest of her boys, and his hobby had been building model airplanes.

"I packed them away when I learned you kids were coming to stay." She answered. "I'll give them to Alphie after the war is over."

"How come Alphie didn't go into the air force, Grandma?" Janie asked. "He always liked planes so much."

Gram smiled, "Alphie's always looked up to your father, so when Walter went into the Navy so did he." She had a far away look in her eyes, then she snapped back, stood up, and said, "I'll be in the kitchen fixing supper." She disappeared through the curtains hanging acrossed the doorway

Janie and I unpacked the boxes of clothes, into drawers that smelled like moth balls, while Tigger looked at a picture book. I could also smell the kerosene stove, so she must be heating dishwater. When we finished with our clothing, we hustled out to the kitchen. The sun was shining in the long row of windows on the back wall of the house. The teakettle was making the windows steam over. In some places' droplets were running to the bottom. Gram had lots of very healthy house plants. The plants and the steam made her kitchen look something like a greenhouse. Her canary, Pretty Boy, was singing loud and shrill, in a continuous medley.

"He sure does sing a lot, Gram." I had my nose right up to the cage and it didn't slow down his singing at all.

"Yes, this is Pretty Boy's favorite time of day, when the sun shines in on him. Sounds happy, doesn't he, Sarah? He doesn't know there's a war on," she commented sarcastically.

Grandpa came in the back door. He looked tired as he hung up his coat and hat. He didn't say a word, just washed his hands, dried them on the circular towel, and sat down at the table, ready to eat.

"You girls can help put the food on the table," Gram said.

We each grabbed the full bowls and did what she asked.

Our Grandparents didn't talk during meals so us girls tried to do the same. I had heard my Grandfather say many times, that kids should know their place, but Tag chattered on constantly.

I noticed that the meat plate had one piece of meat for each of us, and one extra. I knew without asking that it was for Grandpa. He held his knife in one fist and his fork in the other. When he was chewing his food, his fists rested, one on each side of his plate with knife and fork pointing straight up. You just knew, if you reached for that last piece, you weren't going to get it.

After supper Gram stacked the dishes on the back side of the table and put the dishpan and the rinse pan on the front side. Then she put boiling hot water from the teakettle in each one and gave us a warning.

"You children should never touch this teakettle. It's usually very hot." She added, "Now. You can pump some water from the cistern to cool the dishwater down a little, not too much though. It needs to be hot to get the dishes clean."

"Can you drink cistern water, Gram?" I asked.

"It probably wouldn't kill you, Sarah, but no, it's rain water caught by the eves troughs and saved in the cistern for washing and scrubbing," she answered. "Being soft water, it's especially good for washing your hair. It makes hair soft and shiny." She added. "If you're thirsty, you should drink from the water pail."

After we finished the dishes, we helped Gram feed her chickens and bring in a fresh pail of drinking water from the pump in the garden.

"Well, girls," Gram said, as she sat down the pail, "The only chore we have left to do, is bring up some canned food from the cellar for tomorrow's meals."

The cellar! That sounded ominous. Neither Janie nor I had ever been in Gram's cellar, or any other cellar. We looked at each other with some hesitation.

"Do Janie and I have to go down there?" I asked

"You can stay behind me if you like, but yes, I need some help, girls."

The cellar door at their house was outside. It had two big doors you opened like a book, braced them with two-by-fours, so you didn't break the hinges, and walked down a set of steps to another regular door. We hid behind Gram as we ascended the steps. She opened the door. We waited on the bottom step as she groped through the darkness for the light cord. The musty odor of the room mingled with the earthy smell of fresh dug potatoes and the pungent aroma of onions. The dampness and chill, made goose bumps stand out on my arms.

She pulled the cord and light flooded the room.

"Wow," I said breathlessly. "You have enough food down here to feed the whole town, no wonder you raise such a big garden."

"You like my root cellar, Sarah? It's a lot of work, but we never have to go hungry."

"I didn't know this was under your house." I said in wonder. The quiet of this tiny world under Gram's house intrigued me. It was a whole other place to explore. Why had the word 'cellar' always frightened me? There was nothing down here to be scared of.

Gram handed Janie a jar of canned meat, and me a jar of applesauce. She gathered her apron, filled it with potatoes, and we started back to the kitchen.

It was little steps for little people. Grandma Bray had made us feel helpful, and at the same time, I had conquered my fear of the cellar. Had we only been here one day? Gram had taught me so much already. Maybe this wouldn't be so bad after all.

*　*　*　*　*　*

Grandpa and Tag were in the living room, sitting by the potbelly stove. As we walked in, Gramps asked, "Can I get you girls to rub my knees with liniment?"

"Sure, Gramps," Janie said, "just tell us how."

He pulled up both pant legs and handed Janie the open bottle. "Just put a little in your hand and rub it on my knee. Sarah can do the other one," he instructed.

I recognized that smell. I always smelled it when Gramps was around. I like it, but, this close it made my eyes water. As we rubbed, he laid his head back and the deep wrinkles on his tanned, leathery face seemed to relax. When we finished, he pulled down his pant legs, put on his left bedroom slipper, and put both feet up on the stove rail to warm his knees. He held the right slipper in his hand. I thought he had a sore foot or something.

Grandpa said, "If you children would like, and you can find a story book, I'll read you a tale as a reward for all of your help."

We hurried and found the new book Mom had gotten us about <u>Black Sambo.</u> Janie and I pulled chairs as close as we could to Grandpa's rocker. Tag scrambled onto Grandpa's lap. As Gramps read, he seemed to enjoy the story as much as us kids did. When he finished, he shut the book with such enthusiasm, we knew he was done reading.

"Grandpa," I said. "I've been wondering. Why do you always just hold that one slipper in your hand?"

His face almost broke into a smile as he answered. "If you kids do something you're not supposed to do, you won't have to wonder about it anymore, Sarah." That was all he ever had to say. The ground rules were laid.

Shortly, we were all dressed in flannel night wear, cuddled under the feather tick on our bed. Tag was in the middle. The heat he radiated kept Janie and me both too warm, but at least we were together. All the anxiety I had felt about Mom and Daddy leaving was falling away. If you can't be with your own folks, I guess Grandparents are the next best thing.

*　*　*　*　*　*

Gramps worked in the woods all day and usually came home by way of the tavern. If we met him a block from their house, by the West End Store, and he was in a good mood, [drunk] he would slip us loose change for some candy. Sometimes we felt guilty taking the money, but it was his own fault for getting in that shape. I remember one evening in particular. Janie and Tag weren't around so I met him all by myself, and he handed me fifty-cents, saying...

"Here, Sarah, get some candy for you and your brother and sister."

Yeah, right! Licorice ropes were five cents each. The other kids weren't around, so I gorged my skinny little body on the black delight. After a short time, I didn't feel so good, so I headed home to lie down. I puked black licorice all over a new feather tick, Gram had worked hard to finish. Everyone was mad at me. After that day, even the smell of licorice would make me ill, but Janie never missed a chance to wave it under my nose. Once again, I had overdone on something I liked, and really made a mess of things. It wasn't the first time, and probably wouldn't be the last.

Some day, maybe I'll learn to control my habit of over indulging on things I like, and then hating myself afterwards.

*   *   *   *   *   *

One day in the Spring, I had been helping Gram in the garden for hours, and needed a cool drink of water and some to splash on my face. As I came around the corner of the house, I stopped dead in my tracks. The cellar doors start to come up and a head protruded from between them. The hair stood up on the back of my neck and my heart started racing. It must be a window peeker or maybe something worse. I stalked closer, like a cat, as silently as possible. I picked up the two-by-four usually used to hold the cellar door, braced my feet, and swung as hard as I could.

"Crack." The head disappeared, and the doors slammed shut.

"Gram," I screamed. My knees were shaking so badly. I had to drop to the ground.

She came running. "What happened, Sarah?"

When I caught my breath, I answered the best I could. "Someone was coming out of the cellar doors. I hit him on the head."

She helped me up, but I hung tight to the two-by-four. She bent to open the doors.

"Don't Gram!" I screamed, "He might hurt you."

"Hush, Sarah," she said sternly, "He might frighten a small girl. Let's see how he'll deal with me." With that she pulled both doors up and let them fall open. Without the two-by-fours, it almost pulled the hinges lose. She let out a gasp, then started down the steps and kneeled over the man lying there.

I sneaked closer, where I could see him clearly. When I recognized the dark leathery face, I dropped the two-by-four and gasped, "Is he dead, Gram? Did I kill Grandpa?"

"No," she replied, "but he has a big goose egg on his head. The fool doesn't think I know all the places he hides his bottles."

"Can I do anything to help, Gram? I asked

"Yes. Run and get his liniment," she answered. "I don't have any smelling salts, but a good whiff of that stuff should bring him around in no time. Hurry on now, Sarah."

My heart was already racing, but I ran as fast as my legs would go. Finding the bottle in the drawer of the buffet, I grabbed it and started back outside. The screen door slammed behind me, my foot hit a clump of grass and I fell head over heels on the lawn. The liniment stayed clutched tightly in my hand, luckily. I scrambled to my feet and hurried to where Gram was still leaning over Grandpa.

"Here, Gram." I handed her the bottle.

She unscrewed the cap and waved the open bottle directly under his nose.

"Cough, cough," he was starting to come around. As he put his hands under himself and tried to sit up, Gram whispered to me.

"You had better make yourself scarce, Sarah." She waved her hands, shushing me away.

I ran back into the kitchen. Seeing the cistern pump reminded me of my original intent. My legs weren't shaking anymore, but I was sweating something awful. I gave the handle of the pump a couple of stokes. The cool water trickled immediately into the wash basin. Dipping both hands in, I splashed water onto my face and back over my sweaty braided hair. That felt so good, I scooped more and held it to my face. I could finally hear them coming, so I dried my face quickly on the towel and lit out for the bedroom. I had no idea how long I'd have to hide out. A good thing I had a tablet I could draw in.

I could hear Grandma getting my Grandpa comfortable in his chair. Holding my breath so he couldn't hear me, I tried to hear what they were saying.

"You just sit here, Henry, and I'll get a cool cloth for your head." Gram said.

Grandpa said some words in German I couldn't understand. Probably just as well. Then Gram walked out of the room, only to return shortly, then leave again. As she left, she said.

"That should keep the swelling down a little. I have to go now and prepare supper."

I could hear Janie, Tag and Gram talking from the kitchen. The plates and silverware clinking told me Janie was setting the table. I ventured a peek through the curtain at Grandpa. Oh no! He saw me.

"Come here, Sarah." He said.

I couldn't tell from his voice, how mad he was, but I was scared to death. I walked slowly out of our bedroom and edged close to him. He reached out and grabbed my arm and pulled me closer yet. I thought I would pee my pants. Just then he put both hands on my waist and lifted me onto his lap. He looked straight into my tear filled eyes before he pulled my head over so it rested on his shoulder. After a couple of seconds his chest started heaving up and down. He was laughing. Yes, he was laughing and I was crying. I jerked my head back. Never having seen my Grandfather laugh before, it puzzled me why he would suddenly do it after being beamed on the head. Maybe I knocked him goofy.

"Why are you laughing, Grandpa? Doesn't your head hurt?" I asked.

"You bet it hurts, Sarah." He put his hand up and rubbed the knob on his head. "You swing a mean two-by-four. The scared look on your face just tickled my funny bone, I guess."

"You aren't mad at me?"

"No, Sarah, I'm not mad." He said as he shook his head. "You did just what you should have done if there had been a real intruder. I won't have to worry quite so much, if I know you're here, guarding the homestead. Now you go and dry those tears and let's see if your Grandmother has supper ready."

Every once in a while when we all thought Grandpa was sleeping in his rocker, his hand would go to his head and he'd start to chuckle, mostly to himself. Don't get me wrong, I was never proud of knocking him silly, but I did give him a reason to laugh.

*　　*　　*　　*　　*　　*

With each one of my uncles that went into the service for their country, my Grandparents received a red and white flag with a gold star in the center to hang in their window. They now had five and you could hardly see out of the living room windows anymore.

Gram read the bible a lot and went to church every Sunday. She made sure we got to Sunday School. We were Methodist. Gram liked Reverend Vincent's sermons. I think he was at our church forever. I held onto my Sunday School papers for dear life. Paper was getting harder to get and it was all I had to draw on.

All the uncles and my dad wrote letters to their folks almost every week. Gram would read them aloud at night while Janie and I took turns brushing her long hair. Some of the letters were cut up because the government was fussy about what the men wrote home to their families. They censored all the mail by cutting out any part that was objectionable. Some letters were reduced to shreds. This brought on some of Gram's favorite German words.

Mom called every Sunday right after lunch when she knew we'd be in the house. It was the highlight of our week. Six weeks after Daddy left, he got his papers and shipped out on a battleship to fight in the war. Mom decided to stay in Illinois and worked until spring. Gram and Gramps were so good to us. Gram taught me to knit, crochet, and sew, and we loved to sit and listen to her play the piano. She played by ear, and could play any tune we could hum. None of that means much when you are little kids, homesick, and miss your folks so badly. We all looked forward to springtime.

$$* \quad * \quad * \quad * \quad * \quad *$$

"Mom!" I screamed.

"Mom." Janie echoed.

"Mommy." Tigger squealed.

"She's here, Grandma. Mom's home at last." I hollered at Gram.

We all ran out to the car and swamped her when she got out. Our hugs and kisses didn't seem to be enough. I wanted to hold her so tight she could never leave again. Mom started crying and I noticed she was holding onto us just as tightly.

"I've missed you kids so much, I'll never leave again." She smoothed down us girls' hair and ran her fingers through Tag's curls. "This world is so messed up and confused right now that I'm not going to pull our family apart any more than it already is. I'm home to stay." She promised.

"Are you all done at the plant, Grace?" Grandma asked as she walked toward us. Harlow came around the car, and she forgot all about her question to Mom.

"Harlow!" She cried. "I didn't know you were driving Gracie home." She put her arms around her son and held onto him while she unloaded a whole mess of bottled up tears. Then she let go, straightened her shoulders, dabbed her eyes dry with her apron, and asked, with as much dignity as she could muster, "You gonna stay around for supper?"

"Yes, Mom," he said, "and breakfast too, if you'll have me. In fact if you can find room for me, I don't have to be home until Sunday night. Just so I can get some rest and get my crew working Monday morning."

Mom grabbed her suitcase from the car and the four of us disappeared into the bedroom. We had a lot of catching up to do. Grandma and Harlow went to the kitchen where I'm sure Gram would be preparing a special supper.

We all starting talking at once so Mom had to settle us down. "Hush, you have to talk one at a time so I can hear any of you. I want to hear all about what you've been doing, but there's no hurry. I'm not going anywhere."

With her assurance that she wasn't leaving again, we were able to tell her all of our adventures. Janie took delight in telling her about the licorice and how I had knocked Grandpa out. I think Mom always knew if any of us were going to get into mischief, it would be me. I seem to have a talent for jumping into everything headfirst, to heck with the consequences. Tag hung onto her like a leech. I guess Janie and I didn't realize how much he needed Mom. He was still her baby. I remember being a little jealous of all the attention she gave him.

Mom broke up the party by saying, "Let's go see if there is any coffee." We all piled for the kitchen. Gram brought Mom some coffee and then poured small cups for Janie and me. Tag never left Mom's lap.

"It's a day to celebrate girls." Gram said. "You're finally going to be a family again."

Mom had tears again but she managed, "Mom, I don't know how we'll ever be able to thank you. I'm going to give you some money. I know it won't be enough for all you've done."

"I want you to keep your money and put it toward that house you and Walter have always wanted." Gram said. "That will mean more to me than any amount of money. Besides, Henry and I enjoyed having the children here with us. They filled the gap in our lives after all of our boys left for the war."

"Thanks, Grandma." Mom said. "We'll make it up to you somehow."

I couldn't tell if Grandma was really being completely honest, or if she was saying that to make Mom feel better. It made me feel better, anyhow, knowing we hadn't just been burdens.

The next few weeks were busy for all of us. Gram was spading her garden so it would be ready for spring planting, Janie and I were finishing with our last days of school for the year, Tag and Pal were busy helping Gram, and Mom was walking all over town trying to find the right house for us to live in. Once we went down to see Aunt Leny and the new baby at our old house. She had been buying furniture with her allotment checks so she'd have some when we took ours. Her baby was a newborn and slept most of the time, so he wasn't much fun for us. Grandpas' knees still hurt every night, but he quit being so grouchy once Mom got back. She even got away with teasing him about the bump on his head. He'd smile at her with the same twinkle in his eye that Daddy and Tag had when there was mischief in the air. I knew that twinkle well.

*   *   *   *   *   *

"I found our house." Mom said. "I made the down payment and we can move in as soon as I get it cleaned up and we want to. What do you say kids, you want to?"

We were so excited. We fired one question after another. She answered as many as she heard in the Malay.

"The house is on the Bee Town Road, it has three bedrooms so Tag can have his own room, it's only three blocks from the South School instead of the eight you've been walking, and it has a big garden. That will be our first big project, kids," Mom said, "planting the garden. A very big Victory garden."

Mom cleaned, painted, wallpapered, and we moved in. There were lots of closets in the new house so Mom could hang up our dresses after they were all starched and ironed. Janie and I still shared our room and our big bed. Tag loved his smaller room, because it had all his toys and no girl stuff, but he still liked to sneak in and pester us. We had a bathtub and an indoor toilet. We soon made friends with the neighborhood kids, and Mom renewed a friendship with one of the ladies from our old neighborhood. Anne Mae's husband was away fighting too. They had so much in common, they were good company for each other. Anne Mae had a girl and a boy about our ages. Nancy, a year older than Janie, was a tall, slim, blond who was really into dolls. She had her room all cluttered with them. Gary was a year ahead of me in school. He had his own bike, but wouldn't share, even with his sister. We spent most nights together, alternately at their house or ours. Seemed like there was safety in numbers.

Our lives were somewhat back to normal except for Daddy being gone. Things were good. The only fighting now was quibbling between me and my siblings.

They say still water runs deep. When the absents of his boys all off fighting in different theaters of war proved to be too much, Grandpa leaned over his rifle, pulled the trigger, and took his own life.

Chapter Three

"Have a good day at school, girls." Mom said. "Make sure you shut the door tight, so Pal can't push it open to follow you."

We could hear Tigger crying as we started for school, but Mom had assured us that he only cried until he found something to distract him.

"It sure doesn't take us long to get to school now, does it, Janie?" I asked. "We no sooner leave the house and 'woops' we're at school."

"I like living closer." Janie said. "Do you like school this year, Sarah? I saw your teacher, and she's really old."

"She is old, and she's an old maid, but I like her." I told Janie. "Her name is Miss Warren, and she lives right over there." I pointed out a big, square, grey house we could see in the next block. Janie put her eye along the side of my arm to see where I was pointing.

"Really?" She asked.

"Yeh," I said, "she only has a little over a block to walk to school. She has a bad leg so it's nice she doesn't have far to walk." Then I asked. "Do you like your new teacher?"

"She's all right." Janie said, "I don't know her very well yet, but she's really young."

"Is she married?" I asked

"No. She's engaged." Janie explained. "Her fella is in the service, so she doesn't know when she will get married."

"Here come your friends, Janie, so I'm gonna run ahead." I said. "See you after school."

"Bye." She turned to wait for the girls that were yelling and waving at her.

I was long gone. Janie and I had different taste in friends. Those uppity girls weren't my choice. I'd rather walk alone, but my long skinny legs don't like to walk. It seems, they only know one speed, as fast as possible. I ran all the way to school and up the school steps. You can't run in school so I put my coat and lunch in the coatroom and walked into Miss warren's classroom.

"Good morning, Miss Warren." I greeted my teacher.

"Sarah, you're here early," she said. "Do you want to help me?"

"To do what?" I asked.

"Those bookshelves over there need dusting and rearranging." She said as she pointed at the large shelves in the corner. "They are really a mess. You always do such neat work. You' ll have to take everything off, dust, and put things back neatly."

"Sure I can." I agreed. I started the task, but the shelves didn't look that bad to me.

41

As other kids arrived they would say good morning to Miss Warren and go to their desks or stand in groups talking. A red headed girl, Beverly, came up close to me.

"Teachers Pet." She whispered.

Was I? Is that why Miss Warren always had things for me to do? Doesn't she treat all the kids this way? During the next few days I paid more attention. She was nice to everyone but maybe Beverly was right. Miss Warren and I seemed to have a special bond. After that I would stay after school occasionally and we'd talk.

One day she said, "You probably don't know it, Sarah, but I taught your father many years ago."

"Was he smart in school?" I asked.

"He could have been," she said, "but he was always too busy getting into mischief. He spent many hours sitting in the corner." Then she chuckled. "The punishment never helped at all."

"Did you like him?" I asked.

"Sure I did, Sarah." She answered. "I liked all of the Bray children, but your daddy had something special. He was artistic, like you. I saw if right off."

"I love to watch him work." I said.

"I've seen some of the work he did while he was working with the C C camps." She said. "Beautiful work. You should be proud of him."

"Have you seen the bath house at the swimming pool?" I asked. "I know he did that."

"Yes," she said, "and some that are similar at other towns around here also."

"Mom told us about that." I said. I've never seen those. Then I added, "I hope he gets home soon."

"I hope all the men and women get home safe and sound." She said. "It doesn't really sound like it will be soon though? Are you children and your mom doing okay?"

"Sure we are." I bragged. "Mom is working at Tabber's Food Store while we're at school, and Tag, my little brother, likes it at the baby sitters' cause there are lots of other kids there for him to play with."

"Sarah, I have some odd pieces of paper I don't need. Would you like to have them to take home?" She asked.

"Would I ever, Miss Warren. Paper is so hard to get now." I said. "Mom brings me home any clean wrapping paper she finds. I love to sit and draw, but you already know that."

After that, she made sure I had a piece of paper to take home each night. Some had lines but I didn't care. When the school year was over, I told her, "I'm gonna miss you, Miss Warren."

"I'll miss you too, Sarah, but you can always drop by my house anytime." She offered.

"Really? Thanks." I replied. She was treating me almost like a grownup.

I didn't see her during summer vacation except from a distance. When school started again, I dropped by her room quit often just to talk. She never failed to give me paper as I left, always encouraging me to keep drawing.

*   *   *   *   *   *

One day, as Janie and I arrived home after playing with friends, Mom was all excited.

She said, "Anna Mae is taking us for a ride tomorrow, kids. We're going to look at a car."

"We're gonna have a car of our own?" Janie asked. She always looked surprised when Mom did something gutsy.

"Sure, why not? We have to live even if your dad is gone for a while." She said. "Every time we go to see my mother at Mt. Hope, we have to catch a ride with somebody going in that direction."

"The rides over there aren't that bad," I said, "but those rides home with Tony at two in the morning... I hate to be woken up from a sound sleep." Then I asked, "can I have more cookies, Mom?"

"Help yourself, Sarah," she answered impatiently. Then she continued. "That's when mailmen have to travel, and Tony has never minded our riding back to Lancaster with him. Our company helps him stay awake too. But, I'm sure it won't hurt his feelings, not having to wait for me to load you three sleepy heads into the car."

"Are Nancy and Gary coming along?" Janie asked.

"Of course," Mom said. "They go wherever their mom goes, just like you kids do."

Next morning we all climbed in the car when Anna Mae and the kids got there. The trip to the other side of Fennimore seemed like a long ride. Tag rode on Mom's lap in front. If any of us kids had been fat, the four of us couldn't have fit in the back seat. Mom took the car she was looking at for a test drive up and down the farm road where it was at.

"Looks okay to me." She said to the owner. "Can you do any better on the price?"

"Well...Well..." he looked surprised that a woman would haggle on the price. "I guess I could come down another twenty-five. I know things are tough and you have your hands full with the kids."

"Thank you." She paid the man, he gave her some papers, and us kids jumped in the back seat of our shiny black, thirty-seven, fleet back, Ford.

"You girls sit with Tag between you and make sure he sits still. Here, Sarah, hold on to my purse." She said as she handed me her purse. "It's been a long time since I've driven, but here goes."

The plan was for us to follow Anne Mae back to Lancaster, to make sure we didn't have car trouble, and just in case one of us had a flat tire. We started down the road.

Mom and the fleet back Ford

Slam! Mom had apparently not tried the brakes before. She tested them now, and all of us kids ended upside down on the floor of the back seat with the contents of her purse all over us. We weren't hurt, just surprised. We all busted out laughing.

"Sorry, kids," she chuckled, "the brakes work." She knew we were all right because we were laughing. "Just shovel all that stuff back in my purse. None of you got hurt, did you?"

We made it home with no further excitement. We were so proud of that shiny car, but we had to leave it sitting out because our garage was full of clutter.

"We're going to have to clean the garage, kids." Mom said, "but not today."

*   *   *   *   *   *

It was September, second, nineteen forty five. The weather had been exceptionally pleasant that fall. For a change there weren't any of our friends around so Janie and I were taking our time walking home from school.

"Do you ever wonder what Daddy looks like now, Sarah?" Janie asked.

"Sometimes I can't even remember what he looked like before." I answered. "It's been three... almost four years since we've seen him. We weren't very big when they dropped us off at Grandma and Grandpa Bray's house. That was the last time we saw him."

"Gosh! That was forever ago." Janie said.

When we reached the house, Mom met us at the door and she was beaming.

"The war is over, girls." She said happily. "Daddy will be coming home soon"

Janie and I looked at each other and said, almost in unison, "We were just talking about him."

"We've almost forgot what he looks like, Mom." Janie said. "And Tag was so little, do you think he remembers Daddy at all?"

"It won't take long to get reacquainted once he gets home, girls. You don't look like the little kids he remembers either." She reminded us. "You girls are both almost as big as me now."

I laughed, and said, "Mom, you only stand five-two. It doesn't take much to be as tall as you."

She gave me a friendly swat with the towel she had in her hand and headed for the kitchen, where Tag was having cookies and milk.

Mom wore herself out for the next few weeks cleaning, scrubbing, polishing and re-polishing.

Everything had to be shipshape before Daddy got home.

When we received word of his arrival time we piled into the car and drove down to Dubuque, Iowa, where his train was to come in at seven o'clock in the evening.

The depot was full of uniforms of every description, soldiers, sailors, marines, Wacs, Waves, and nurses. They all carried suitcases or had duffle bags slung over their shoulders. It was wall to wall people on the train platform.

"Where is he, Mom?" I asked.

"Just keep looking. He'll be here somewhere." She was trying hard to keep us all together in this crowd. People were shoving and pushing something terrible

"There," Janie yelled, "he just stepped off the train." She took off running, as fast as she could with this crowd, with Tag and me and Mom right behind her.

45

When he saw us, he threw down his duffle bag and kneeled down for a group hug for us kids with kisses for all. Gosh, he's handsome in his uniform.

"You kids have grown up while I was gone," he said. "Why didn't you wait for me before you did that?" Then he laughed and roughed our hair.

Daddy was home, just like I remembered him.

Dad in his uniform

Then he grabbed Mom, and gave her a long kiss. He held her tight for the longest time. Then we all heard him say, even though he was trying to whisper. "Why in hell did you bring the kids with? I thought we could celebrate a little tonight."

"Walter, they're not babies anymore. They've been missing you for a long time. I couldn't disappoint them."

She could see the tears welling up in our eyes, and she looked as miserable as we felt. I felt unwanted. He not only didn't want us here, but now he was mad at Mom. Oh, yes Daddy was back, just the way I remembered him.

The three of us huddled under a blanket in the back seat, and all those old fears came flooding back. It took almost two hours to reach Lancaster and he never even spoke a word to Mom, all the way home.

When we reached home, he tossed his duffle bag down. Nosey little Tag was anxious to see what was in it so he started trying to open it.

"Stay the hell away from that." Dad grabbed the car keys and slammed out the back door. We heard the car start, and he was gone. Tigger ran up to his room and hid under the bed.

Mom said, "You kids might as well go to bed. Looks as though our big celebration is over." Us girls followed her upstairs so she could do something with Tag.

We all assured Mom how much we loved her. Tigger was quiet for a change, too quiet. He had been too young, probably, to remember this side of Daddy. Janie and I tried to get his mind off of what had just happened, by reading him his favorite book until he fell asleep. Mom laid down beside him and listened too. It was just the four of us again.

When we finally went into our bed, Janie asked me, "Did you ever think of this side of Daddy while he was gone?"

"No, I didn't. All I ever thought about were the good times." I said. "Why did we forget how mean he can be?"

Janie said, "I don't know, Sarah. It's like they took someone who was already mean, taught him how to kill, and sent him home to us. Now, I guess, we're the enemy."

"Well, Janie, he's not going to hurt me anymore. I don't even like him. I still love him, but I don't like him."

We only caught a few brief glimpses of his good side after that. He took us picking roadside asparagus a couple of times. He took us kids to Shriner's Park and taught us to shoot his twenty-two rifle. One Sunday Mom actually talked him into going to church with us. I was scheduled to receive a bible, complete with my name in gold, for five years of perfect attendance in Sunday School. Reverent Vincent was presenting it, himself. I think Daddy was proud of me that day. But he never said so.

*   *   *   *   *   *

One day Daddy returned home early from work. As usual he was covered with mortar mix, but I could tell from his walk that he had been to a bar.

I was along the side of the garage helping Tigger lift his big, white, rabbit from the wagon, back into its cage. Tag loved to take his bunny for rides in his <u>Red Flyer</u> wagon. The rabbit was almost as big as Tag and he couldn't lift it high enough to get it into the door of the pen. It was almost in when Daddy snuck up behind me and slipped his arm around my waist.

"I gottcha now!" he slurred. "You can't get away now."

"Don't." I yelled as I pushed the rabbit through the opening.

Tag hooked the lock. He looked like he was ready to cry. "Daddy, please, don't hurt Sarah." He pleaded.

Daddy didn't stop though. As he wrestled me to the ground, I set my jaw. I was determined that he wasn't going to get the best of me. He was in for a fight.

He tickled, and it hurt, but I showed nothing. I just laid there quiet.

He gave me a whisker rub that stung and made my face burn. No reaction.

He got angry. The tickling got worse. I felt nothing but contempt. The harder he tried the less I felt. Finally he gave up, got to his feet, and gave me a shove that sent me rolling. When I finally came to a stop, I got slowly to my feet and walked nonchalantly over and put my arm around Tag.

I had won this round. He now had a taste of Sarah's will power. Me too, and I liked the feeling. Learning the secret to overcome pain was exhilarating. It was a secret I would never forget.

*   *   *   *   *   *

Daddy was angry. He stomped off to the car, and without even cleaning up, got in and drove away. I had an uneasy feeling in the pit of my stomach that we hadn't seen the worst of this day.

After he left Tag and I went in the house and relayed to our Mom what had happened. She was preparing supper, so she kept busy. I noticed she was nervously watching out the window for Daddy's return. We were all dished up and in the process of eating when she saw him coming.

"Here he comes, kids, and he is really drunk tonight. Please don't do or say anything that might aggravate him. Just go ahead and eat your supper."

We sat still at the table as he staggered into the house and headed for the bathroom. Our bathroom had two doors, one from the kitchen side and one from the folk's bedroom. When he finished, he neglected to unlock the kitchen side. He went out the bedroom side, through the bedroom, and flopped on the couch in the living room.

We ate our supper in complete silence. Even Tag was quiet. Daddy started snoring before long, so we all breathed a little easier.

Our newly acquired, yellow, kitten, Puff, went scooting acrossed the floor like a shot and straight into the living room. We froze for a moment and then, as quiet as we could, peeked in to see where the kitten had gone. Puff jumped onto the arm of the couch by Daddy's feet. His feet could always clear your sinuses. The kitten took one whiff, let out a screech, jumped straight into the air, and took off running.

We all broke out laughing.

Daddy leaped from the couch and chased us into the kitchen. I lost track here of what happened to Janie and Tag. I got my first beating that night, and he showed no mercy for Mom.

Then he headed for the bathroom. Finding the door locked, he started swearing.

"&)(%^#$#$%" He doubled his fist and shattered the door from top to bottom. Splinters of wood flew everywhere.

We huddled in the corner of the kitchen with Mom, fearing what might happen next. We heard him puke several times, then a loud crashing sound and silence.

"Don't any of you move." Mom said. She snuck over quietly and peeked through the shattered door.

He had passed out on the floor of the bathroom, in a puddle of his own vomit.

When his snoring grew loud, we slipped up the stairs with an armload of paper bags, packed our clothes and quietly left the house.

I may have won my battle earlier in the day, but Daddy won the war.

Chapter Four

Like four homeless waifs, we knocked on the Smyth's door in the middle of the night. Their house was dark and we hated waking them. A light came on and Mrs. Smyth opened the door.

"What in the world! Grace?" Mrs. Smyth exclaimed. "What are you and the kids doing here, bag and baggage?"

"Walter finally went too far…" Mom choked up and couldn't say anymore.

"Well, get inside here." Our neighbor said. "You don't have to stand out in the chilly air."

We stepped in and sat down our bags.

"Look at you. Did he do all this?" She asked in amazement, before she ran warm water over a towel and started dabbing at our cuts and bruises. Clifford and I heard Walter shouting earlier. We thought he had settled down when it got quiet."

"No," Mom said. "We've just been waiting til he was sound asleep so we could get out of the house. He was like a wild animal tonight. He lost all control. I have to get the kids away, where he can't get at them. Beating me is one thing, but not the kids."

"He must have the car keys or you'd already be long gone." Mr. Smyth said as he buttoned his shirt.

"They're in his pants pocket and he's sleeping in them." Mom said. "I wasn't going to take a chance on getting him started again. Do you know anyone who could give us a ride to Mt. Hope? I'd go to Anna Mae's but she and her husband are having their own problems. We wouldn't help by showing up in the middle of the night."

"You know our son, Dan, he sees this all the time at the clinic." The older lady said. "His women patients come in looking like you do now, some a lot worse, and do you know what? They lie for the bastards that did it to them."

I couldn't believe she said that. In the three years we've been neighbors, I've never heard her swear. She and Clifford were just sweet old people who love to work in their garden, which happened to be right next to ours.

"Let me give Dan a call, but first, you kids go in and lay down on the couch." She said as she directed the way. "I'll get a blanket. Children shouldn't have to go through this kind of nonsense." We huddled together on her couch. Mrs. Smyth covered us and it felt good. Tag dozed off. It was way after his bedtime. Janie and I were much too shaken to sleep.

Clifford made some coffee for Mom and had a cup with her.

Mrs. Smyth hung up the phone, and turned to Mom. "Dan says our grandson, Bob, is home studying tonight. He won't mind giving you a ride to your mother's. Young people like any excuse to drive, or to get out of studying. He'll be here in thirty minutes." Then she asked Mom. "Did you call your mother, Grace?"

"I didn't want to take a chance on waking Walter." Mom said. "Could I, please, use your phone? I'll call her now before she gets too sound asleep." She smiled at the elderly couple. "It's only my neighbors I like waking up after they're asleep for the night."

She went into the kitchen to use the phone and spoke to grandma so quietly that we couldn't hear.

When she came back, she announced, "Mom says she'll be waiting for us, girls. Everything will be all right. I won't ever let him hit any of you again."

It sounded great. Mom had the best of intentions. We all knew that if Daddy got angry enough she was no match for him.

*　　*　　*　　*　　*　　*

Grandma Leigh's house in Mt. Hope, WI

Mom must have carried us in and put us to bed. When I woke, the sun was shining and I was still in my clothes. I climbed out of bed and went down to Grandma's summer kitchen.

"What time is it?"I asked as I rubbed my bleary eyes.

"It's noon, honey." Mom said.

"Wow, no wonder my heads all messed up." I commented. "I always get up so early it's still dark out."

"I thought you might be a little disorganized. It's all right, Sarah, we've all had a rough night." She assured me.

"Did you sleep yet, Mom?" I asked.

"No," she said, "Grandma and I have been talking."

"Your face looks awful, Mom. Why don't you go, and crawl in with Janie? I warmed the bed for you." I joked.

"Thanks, Sarah. I think I will. Okay with you, Mom?" She asked

"Sure, Grace, go ahead." Grandma said. "Sarah and I have lots to do after she has a bite to eat." Grandma said.

Grandma's younger dog, Teddy, was sitting on her black leather davenport. He was so excited with all the company. He was wagging his entire body, instead of just his tail.

"Hi, Teddy." I sat down and petted him.

"You better come and have some lunch, Sarah." Grandma said.

I changed seats to the table where she had a sandwich and milk ready for me.

"Gram, why does my dad do this to us?" I asked.

"The drinking drives him crazy and he can't think straight. When your dad wakes up today, if he already hasn't, I'll bet he can't remember what happened last night."

"Thanks for the sandwich, Gram. Your homemade bread is so good. What are we gonna do now?" I asked.

"Oh, just my chores." She said "We have to pump water for the ponies, pick up the eggs, and fill the wood box."

"Before I do anything, I have to make a trip to the outhouse." I said, crossing my legs in agony.

"Well, get to it then." She said, shushing me toward the door.

While Gram and I did the chores, Teddy trotted along sides. Flash, her old dog, was content to lie on the doorstep, sunning himself and watching us.

"All finished but the wood, Sarah. Want me to teach you how to chop kindling?" She asked. "I'll do the big chunks first. You go sit over there on the steps with the dogs so I'll know you're out of the way of my axe."

She chopped enough wood for the night and then showed me how to chop splinters off the big blocks for kindling.

Mom had supper going when we walked in with our arms full of wood.

"This is a pleasant surprise, Grace. I don't have to make supper tonight" Gram smiled.

"I'll do anything I can to make it easier for you, Mom. I just appreciate having a safe place to come with the kids." Mom said. "Walter called when you were outside and I told him I can't do this anymore. We're done. He wasn't very happy."

"Don't let him get to you, Grace," she said. "He wasn't worried about your happiness, was he?"

"You're right, Mom, but it hurts. I love him so much." Mom said.

"And he loves the bottle." Reminded Grandma.

*   *   *   *   *   *

The announcer on the radio said, "And now, The Grand Old Oprey"

I had been awake for quite some time, but didn't know if anyone else was. I got out of bed and went down to the kitchen.

"Hi, Gram, I love that program." I said. "Country music is my favorite. You must like it too, huh?"

"Yes, I do, Sarah. When I get up every mourning to make bread, the country music keeps me company." Grandma said.

"That must be why I like to get up so early. I get that from you." I said earnestly.

Teddy was jumping around, wanting attention. Flash wagged his tail, but that's all the interest he showed.

"You make bread every morning?" I asked.

"Yes, it gets my day started right." She replied. "Making bread is my therapy. If I'm mad about something, I take it out on the bread dough. The more I pound it, the better I feel, and the better the bread turns out."

My Grandfather died before I was born. He and my oldest uncle died of Diphtheria. My Grandparents had a big family. Mom was the oldest. I had two aunts and two uncles who were married and had families of their own. My aunt Shelly was the youngest and still lived with Grandma. She was in high school.

Each day we became more used to having two families, living as one. Aunt Shelly was more like a big sister than an aunt. After supper we would play cards, read or make popcorn. If it was hot, we'd take the chairs outside and listen to the wind in the big pines. There were five of them in the front yard. If it rained, even in the daytime, I liked to lie in bed. With no insulation and a tin roof overhead, the rain was like a symphony, soft and low as it tickled the tin. An afternoon repose was the usual result. Here, we belonged and were loved. Grandma made us all feel good. Even if she had nothing, she was willing to give you her share. We all thought this tranquility couldn't be invaded. We were all wrong.

* * * * * *

We ran into the house, "Mom, Daddy's here. What should we do?" Janie and I said almost in unison.

"Just stay in the house, kids." She warned.

He slammed into the house without knocking. He was out of place here. Grams' house was peaceful and quiet. He was loud and obnoxious.

The smell of whiskey immediately filled the room. Gram shooed us into the living room.

He started slapping Mom around, cursing her, then slapped her again and she hit her head against the refrigerator. Gram came out of her bedroom with a shotgun and pointed it right at Daddy.

"Stop it, Walter." She said. "You leave my house, right now. Leave Grace and the kids alone. And don't think I won't shoot. You've done enough damage to your family."

He hurried out the door, after a few choice words for Grandma, ran down the drive, jumped in our little black Ford, and left. Mom was left holding her jaw.

"Is it broken, Grace?" Gram asked.

"I don't think so," Mom said, "but it pops every time I move it. You see now, Mom, how he is when he's drinking?"

"I can't believe how he's changed." Gram shook her head. "You and the kids can't go back to that. You stay here as long as you need. We'll manage just fine."

We did too. I went to forth grade in Mt. Hope. The walk to school was close to a mile, but Janie and I never minded. Aunt Shelly never walked with us. She could walk so much faster. At least that's the reason she gave. There was a creek along the way and we liked to dawdle. In the winter we never ran out of snow forts to build on our way home, when we knew the fire was waiting to take the chill out when we finally got there. Mt. Hope didn't have a kindergarten so Tag would have to wait and start school next year in first grade. This Grandma taught Janie and me more on the sewing machine. We both made skirts that we could wear to school.

During the summer we canned things from the garden, dried corn and fruit. We raised two pigs that we butchered in the fall. All that meat was kept frozen in the locker plant at the Lansing Store. Gram had lots of chickens and eggs. What more could you ask?

Spring came and school was over. Mom's divorce was final, and she found a house for us in Fennimore, and a job in the next block so she would always be close by.

Chapter Five

I don't know if it was thinking about my father or the damage Carl inflicted that was making my head ache, but I needed to take a pain pill. I had just enough cold coffee to wash it down with. I'll have to admit when I started this journey, searching for a reason why alcohol was the constant theme in my life, I had my doubts, but...

Through all of the memories, I now realize it was there from the start, through no choice of my own. It was lurking around every corner. Each generation of the Bray family had succumbed to it. Why should I be any different? Even the experience with black licorice was a warning sign of an addictive personality.

In Alcoholics Anonymous they tell us, 'get rid of the old baggage'. When you clean closets, the first step is to pull everything out and look it over. Then decide what to discard. So far, I've only made a small dent in my closet, but, I can't stop now. I need to get all the baggage out. Who knows, maybe I can even find little Sarah Bray's will power in here somewhere.

Medication relieves most of the pain inside of my battered head, but the actual healing needs more time. The wounds are still very visible, and no medicine can heal the pain of betrayal.

For right now, I need food and a hot cup of coffee...Now, where'd I put that umbrella?

*   *   *   *   *   *

I stood in a pay phone, protected from the rain, but not the dampness, and talked to Ilka while I ate my lunch. She invited Bobby and me to come to her house for supper. She's even coming to get us so we won't have to walk in the rain. Her husband, Stan has to work the night shift. She and I will be able to talk my problems into the ground. We always do. I've never been to her house though. I met her at the clothing store, where I thought she was just a clerk. Turned out she owned the store. Talking to her was as easy as throwing down a shot of brandy. Dropping by to talk with her each time I shopped for the bar was my salvation. Carl made me account for every minute I was gone, so I'd pick up something for Bobby each time I visited her shop. Turns out she's the only true friend I have in this north country. All the so-called friends from the bar, the ones I've waited on for eight years, are giving me the cold shoulder since I started going to meetings. They treat me like a traitor.

Now I have a fresh cup of coffee and have plumped the pillows once again, on with my quest... Where was I now? Oh yes. Mom was about to tell us about our new house in Fennimore.

*　*　*　*　*　*

Janie pouted, "Do we have to leave our friends again?" There's that look again. She knows just how to pull Mom's heart strings. "Can I call Mary Adele and Jean and tell them I'm moving?" Janie asked.

"Sure you can, Honey," Mom said, "but don't forget, they'll always be your friends. You can see them whenever you come to visit Grandma. Please, wait until we finish talking."

I had made fiends too, but none so close as Janie had. Tag could care less. We were both excited about moving to a new house. It would be a treat not going out in the cold and dark for you know what.

"You all know." Mom said. "I have to go to work. There are jobs in Fennimore that I can handle. We won't be living alone in our new house. I'll be renting out rooms to help make the house payments."

"Who's gonna live with us, people we know?" I asked.

"We don't have to know them, Sarah." She said. "Most of them will just be there to sleep, but we will need to share the bathroom."

Tag scowled, "You're sure it's an indoors one?"

Mom laughed. "Yes, I'm sure. No more cold outhouse or scratchy catalog pages. We'll have three rooms downstairs," Mom persisted, "One will be my bedroom, the others, a living room and the kitchen. You kids will have your own big bedroom upstairs. You'll have to share the room for now, but you'll each have your own bed."

"Good, Tag is so warm when he sleeps, he drives me right out of bed," I said as I roughed Tag's hair.

"Quit it, Sarah, you're not that much bigger than me." He had that devilish glint in his eye.

"I know it. You're going to school this year. You'll be taking lunches like Janie and me."

He puffed out his chest and flexed his muscles. He was a terrific little brother. I sure wouldn't trade him off.

"No more sack lunches." Mom said, "Our new house is half a block from school. You can all come home and have lunch with me."

Tag's face started glowing when Mom said that...

Janie asked, "How many people will there be in our house?"

Rolling her eyes up in thought, Mom said, "Let's see, there are the Hall's and their two children. That's four. The Fultons, they have a boy about Sarah's age.

They run a restaurant and don't get in until late. All they do at the house is sleep."

"That's seven. Is that all?" Janie asked.

"No." Mom sighed. "There's another bedroom that's empty right now, but a young couple is interested in renting it. That's nine."

Janie's expression changed. "That makes thirteen, with us. It'll be like living in a hotel. Daddy won't come around with all those people there."

"That's good thinking, but don't count on it. I want you kids to be very careful. When he's drinking, he doesn't know what he's doing." Mom put her arm around us girls and Tag laid his head on her lap. Teddy and Flash just sat and wagged their tails.

"Let me finish telling you about the house... Oh, heck, you'll see it tomorrow."

Janie said, "I'm going to call the girls now, Mom."

"Will we still have to carry wood? I'm getting to be a really good wood chopper." I bragged.

"No, not anymore, Sarah, the house has a coal furnace instead of a pot bellied stove."

That big old coal furnace soon became a thorn in Mom's side. When we moved in, we found out that we had a female rat and her litter living in our basement. We sat out poison. The kind where they try to find water after they eat it. That way they won't die in the wall and stink. The young ones died right off, but that big Mama took a while. Mom happened to go to the basement when it was in the throes of death and she swears it attacked her. After that Mom was jittery about standing down there while the fire got started. She tried to hurry the process by tossing in a small can of kerosene. 'Whomp', soot went all through the house, and all over Mom. She looked so funny when she sputtered up out of the basement. A five-foot-two, black troll, with her hair and eyebrows singed off muttering to herself. The only part still white was her eye balls and her teeth. We didn't dare laugh. It really wasn't funny. We'd no sooner get the house cleaned up and she'd do it again. The house was a major cleaning job. She, on the other hand cleaned up quite well, with enough pumice soap and lots of shampoo.

Dad came quit often, most of the time when he was drunk. He had been ordered to pay support, but didn't very often. When he did send something, he'd show up a day or two later and want it back, and give us a bad time in the process.

If we thought Dad was due for a visit, we'd sneak home from school the back way and hide in the bushes' til we knew it was safe.

An older lady moved in. One day she met us at the back door.

"You kids get in here with me. Your father was here earlier and he's very drunk."

When we walked into the kitchen, the first thing we saw was a butcher knife sticking in the wall.

"I don't even want to think what he planned to do with that knife," she said, and kept us in her room with the door locked.

Another time, drunk, he was determined to take Tag with him. He said Mom could keep us girls. He chased us around the block with our own baseball bat, while we tried to protect Tag. Drink was driving Dad crazy. What would happen next?

*　　*　　*　　*　　*　　*

Tag and I had our bikes disassembled out in the garage, so I headed there right after school. Mom was hanging clothes on the line.

"Is Tag out here, Mom?" I asked.

"I didn't see him," she said, "but I just came up with this load of clothes. What are you two up too?"

"Gotta see if we can get the tires back on our bikes." I answered. "We took them off to tighten the spokes. They were getting wobbly."

Just then we heard a loud thump in the garage. She followed me to see what had happened. As we turned in the door, she let out a scream. My Dad had hung himself but he was still kicking. I screamed too, I guess, but we got under him and tried to lift him up. The men from the machine shop came running, when they heard us scream, and managed to get him down. He had used baling wire around his neck and it had cut in all the way around. They had a hard time getting the wire off. By now he was having convulsions. It took six men to carry him into the house and hold him down. Someone at the shop had called for a doctor. By the time they got him in the house the doctor was there. He gave Daddy a shot of something, and he soon settled down.

The doctor said, "If it swells inside, like it's swelling outside, there's nothing more we can do."

A week later while sitting in school, I started shaking and couldn't quit crying. My teacher carried me the half of a block to our house. The doctor told Mom it was an emotional break down. I stayed home the rest of that day and the next one too. A small patch of hair on my head turned grey, overnight.

Dad lived through it. Not long after that he was sent to prison for a year. I thought it was Mom's fault, but the state put him there for back child support. We had been on welfare while living at Grandma Leighy's. Mom never told us that. The year he spent in prison we didn't have to live in fear. In the forties, we were considered from the wrong side of the tracks because our Mom was a divorcee.

We lived in ultimate disruption for about three years. Some people came, others left, and with each change our room arrangements did, too. It was all worth it though, by the time I was ready for high school, we were the only ones living there and the house was almost paid for.

* * * * * *

At first she didn't tell us. Mom had been seeing the local stock buyer, Warren Lund. We suspected she was interested in someone when she started coming home later than usual.

"We're having company for dinner tomorrow, kids." Mom said.

"You mean we finally get to meet your boyfriend?" Janie smirked. "We know about him, Mom. Are you sure you want to be with another man that drinks?"

"Come on now, kids, you know I drink now and then too."

"Mom, we're not babies anymore." I said. "If you like him, that's what's important."

"Good, because he's asked me to marry him and I accepted." She confessed. "We were going to tell you tomorrow." That was more than we had expected to hear.

Life with a stepfather was different, but he was a nice person, treated Mom well, and being a stock buyer kept the freezer well loaded. Mom didn't have to work so hard anymore.

* * * * * *

During high school Jane had several boyfriends, but none she was really serious about. She liked to be with her girlfriends, get all fancied up, and go out dancing. Then she met Brad Barlow, a boy from Melford. He had been out of school a couple of years, so, to me, he was more man than a boy. Jane had been seeing him exclusively since they met, about a year ago. Brad enlisted in the army, and was sent to Germany where he was an M P. (Military Police) She wrote him almost every day, and was saving her wages from working for furniture. She still liked to go dancing with her friends, though. One day when she was busy primping… I was laying on the couch watching the new twelve-inch television set, Warren had bought for us, when Tag snuck in.

He whispered in my ear, so Janie wouldn't hear. "Let's play a joke on Janie."

"What are we gonna do?" I whispered back.

"When she finally gets done in the bathroom and goes upstairs to dress, let's lock the door." He said quietly.

Innocently, by all outside appearances, we sat watching television.

"Don't you love television?" I asked Tag.

"I spend too much time watching it, but it was nice of Warren to get it for us." He replied.

"I remember two years ago, when the first one came to Fennimore. Darlene and I went down town on Saturday night to watch it in the window of the Home Appliance Store. It was a re-e-eally big deal." I said, trying to mock Ed Sullivan.

"Sh… here she comes." Tag whispered.

We waited till she got upstairs to her room and wasn't paying any attention to us. Tag reached over and closed the lock on the stair door as quiet as he could, and went back to watching the television set. When we finally heard her feet on the steps, we were giddy with anticipation.

"Thump." …the door wouldn't budge. She had hit the door with her full weight expecting it to swing open. She couldn't help hearing our laughter.

"&%$*()#"&" She knew more of those words than I gave her credit for. After about five minutes of listening to her verbal abuse Tag grinned at me.

"Sarah, you get over by the front door and make sure it's open." He said. "When I unlock this door, we're gonna have to run like hell."

Jane charged out like a mad bumble bee. Our legs must have looked like windmill blades, but we escaped, and didn't come back home til we knew she was gone with her friends. Next day we caught heck from Mom, although, I suspected she even chuckled about it when Jane wasn't looking.

Grandma Lieghy passed away that year, and for a short while Aunt Shelly lived with us. They said Grandma died of pneumonia. I felt that she just plain wore out. Warren purchased Grandma's land to graze cattle on. All of the buildings were ram shackled, except for the house, and it wasn't in too good a shape. While my Aunts and Uncles were going through Grandma's things, they found my old tattered bible and returned it to me.

During high school I worked for Corina, at the same place where Mom worked. Because of my age I couldn't serve drinks, but I worked in the kitchen and served food. I'd always had soft teeth, lots of toothaches, and dentist bills, so I needed my wages and tips to pay for them. The man that owned the supper club and also tended bar was like a surrogate father, while I was at work. When he knew I had a toothache, he would bring a shot of brandy back to the kitchen.

"Now, don't drink it, Sarah," he would say. "Just hold it in your cheek to deaden the pain."

This allowed me to work nights I would have spent at home in pain. It was, nevertheless, my first taste of alcohol.

*　*　*　*　*　*

The memories so far, have been painful, exhausting, or hilarious, depending on the source. Mostly it feels like it's tearing my heart out, and the tears have flowed freely. Regardless, it's lightening the load to get them out and shake the cobwebs loose, but I'm ready for a break.

It's two-thirty now. By the time I slosh through the rain, over to school, Bobby will be waiting for me. I'd better get a move on.

Bobby was waiting by the front door of the school. He asked. "Can we stop for a malt, Mommy?"

"Not today, Honey," I said. "Ilka invited us over to her house for supper. She is coming in a little bit to get us. We have just enough time to polish your nose and change clothes before she gets here."

As we walked Bobby never missed one puddle. It was a good thing he had another pair of sneakers to wear. What is the magnetism between little boys and puddles? It seemed like only yesterday he was a baby, dependent on me for almost everything. Now here he is making his own choice to splash water all over me. As we entered the driveway of the convenience store Bobby stopped and looked me in the eye.

"Mommy, can I call and say Hi to Daddy?"

It was then I noticed we were standing right beside the pay phone. The restraining order was for Carl to stay away from me, not Bobby. I guessed it wouldn't hurt anything if Bobby wanted to talk to his dad.

"Okay, Honey, I'll put in the money and dial the number for you."

He talked his little boy chatter for about five minutes while I tried hard to keep the umbrella where it would do the most good at keeping us dry, although I was already soaked.

Finally Bobby held the phone out to me. I thought he wanted me to hang it up. "Mommy, he wants to tell you something."

I didn't want to talk to Carl, but I also didn't want to put Bobby in the position to have to tell his father that. I took the phone like one would take the head of a venomous snake.

"Yes?" I said.

"I just wanted to tell you, that the only thing I did wrong the last time, was that I didn't finish the job, Bitch." Then he slammed down the receiver.

I stood there for a minute looking at the receiver in shock and disbelief. It hadn't been just the booze. He knew full well what he was doing when he beat me. The slamming down of the receiver reminded me of my Grandfather closing our story book. It was over, done, ka-put. Good, now I know for certain and I can get on with my life.

*   *   *   *   *   *

61

"Your home is beautiful, Ilka, and you have so many nice things." I was especially looking at the china cabinet full of figurines and fancy clocks.

She noticed where I was looking and said, "The Royal Dalton and Hummels came with me from Germany. I've only added a few pieces since I've been here. The old ones mean a lot to me because they remind me of home. I don't think I'll ever get back to Germany."

Her entire house had a certain elegance, and she fit right in.

The cartoons on her big color T. V. kept Bobby occupied so the two of us could talk after we ate our meal. She was also a good cook. That probably doesn't help her weight problem.

"How are you really doing, Sarah?"

"Being put in a small motel room, confined by my battered condition, and this constant rain is a bitch, to tell you the truth." I exclaimed.

"I hate to hear you sound so negative." She frowned.

"I'm not though." I said. "I've made up my mind. I can't do anything too physical, but I can use this healing time to figure out, why I am, where I am, today."

"He put you there!" She almost shouted.

"That's not what I mean, girl." I said. "What I'm talking about... Put it this way. You fell in love with Stan while he was stationed in Germany, you married, you returned to the United States, and to Wisconsin. You then had a son and have a business to run. You're here... kind of a straight line. I on the other hand have lived here all my life. From as far back as I can remember, I've hated alcohol. Instead of my life going in a straight line, like you, somewhere along the way I got lost. Alcohol went from being a hated enemy to being the center of my life. I need to find out how it happened. I need to stay away from alcohol. I need my life back. I need to draw the pictures I see in my head. I need to hold Bobby close so he's safe..." I took a deep breath. "Dear God, I'm a needy person."

"Right now, you're tired, and need some rest...Then she grinned. Sorry, didn't mean to add to your 'need' list. Let me take the two of you back to the motel so you can get some sleep."

"No." I said. "Right now I need to help with the dishes."

"Oh, fine." She said seriously. "Now I have a needy person helping me with my chores." We both laughed as we cleaned up around the kitchen. It was good to be with someone who made me laugh.

We reached the motel and Bobby and I both thanked her for the nice supper.

"We could do it more often," she said, "but when Stan is home, I don't think you'd be that comfortable."

"That's fine, Ilka. Right now I don't care to be around any man, specially when I know what Stan is capable of. Did I tell you that I have to be in court tomorrow at two, for our preliminary hearing? I'm not looking forward to it. Just looking at Carl will be hard."

"You can do it, Sarah. Just keep your chin up. The judge will be able to see from your face what that man has done to you."

After she left, I started the shower for my little guy. Having always taken baths before, even this was fun. He was asleep before I finished my shower, and I wasn't far behind him. Next morning was an exact duplicate of the day before and I soon found myself alone again in the motel room with my large cup of java, where I needed to be. I wanted to go back to continue where I left off. High School, I believe.

*   *   *   *   *   *

High school, oh yes. Ron Reamer came to mind like a flash, not unlike the first time he entered my life.

Early in the day, while making a store run for my Mom, I bumped into Jerry. He was your typical boy next door, and we had been good friends for years.

"Hi, Sarah, whatcha been up to this summer?" He asked.

"Working, mostly." I said. "How about you, Jer? Got your wheels yet?"

He grinned from ear to ear. "You bet, last week. I got my license the first time out, so Dad bought me a car." His face lit up, and he said. "Hey, how about you find a date for a friend of mine and we'll make it a foursome at the drive-in movie tonight?"

"Who's the other fella?" I asked.

"You probably don't know him." He said. "He's a boy from over by Melford. His name is Ron Reamer. Can you get a friend?"

"I probably can." I replied. "What movie's showing?"

"The Blob." He answered. "Ever hear of it?"

"Who hasn't?" I joked. "Give me a call in an hour or so, I'll see what I can do. I gotta get this stuff home to Mom."

"I'll call." He waved as he jumped into his car.

I called Donna Rewey. She had a bout with Polio a couple of years ago, but was back in good health now. She agreed to a blind date so long as I would be there.

Jerry and Ron pulled up in front of our house at seven-thirty, in Jerry's new, old, car. They honked and I ran out and jumped in front with Jerry. "Nice car, Jer." I commented.

"Thanks." He said. "Sarah this is Ron."

"Hi." I turned to the back and caught my breath. I was sitting in front with a friend and Donna had a date with the handsomest boy I had ever met. We picked Donna up and I was dying of envy. Lucky for me, they didn't hit it off.

Two nights later Ron was my date. I was completely smitten. Fennimore was building a new high school. Behind the building site, after dark, was an excellent lover's lane. One night we got caught in the rain and made huge ruts in the mud before we got out. After that they blocked the drive when the workers finished for the day. By then he had stolen my heart and my innocence.

One night, after work, some friends asked me to come along to Melford for burgers. We entered the café, and ran smack dab into Ron and a strange girl. Ron spotted me and came right over.

"Sarah, come outside for a minute." He asked. Totally confused, I followed him.

"Please, don't make a scene." He said. "The girl I'm with is Lillian. I got her pregnant and we're getting married next month. I'm sorry as hell."

I couldn't say anything. We had been going together for two years, and this was the last thing I expected. I turned, walked to the car, got in and locked all the doors.

My friends were kind enough not to mention his name on the way home. They dropped me off and I'm sure it was a relief to them to be rid of me. My bad mood was spoiling their fun. I found a bottle of aspirin and took them all. Then went right to bed.

Sometime in the early morning, I awoke wringing wet and my skin felt like slime. Trying to be quiet, so as not wake anyone. I left the house in a stupor. I needed some air, badly. Nothing looked right, but it was all where it was supposed to be. It was me who wasn't right. I was flying above the wires watching a skinny young girl walking the streets hour after hour. I was having an out of the body experience, or I was just plain, crazy. By daylight, I felt halfway normal, only my clothes were soaking wet and I was chilled clear through to the bone.

Returning home, I ran our old claw foot tub full of hot water and soaked until the water was cold, my skin looked like a prune, and I was starving.

"How stupid can you be?" I said to myself.

"What?" Mom was standing behind me as I raided the fridge.

"Sorry, talking to myself, Mom." I really felt stupid.

"Did you get an answer?" She asked.

"No. But I need to talk to you, Mom." I told her what had happened, all of it. It all just poured out and then it was over. On with my life.

*   *   *   *   *   *

Brad finally came home from Germany and he and Janie were married. She was a beautiful bride in a street length, white dress and hat. She had been working in Madison since she graduated, sharing an apartment with friends.

After the wedding they moved to Madison. Tag and I were used to Janie being gone by now, but this made it seem a whole lot more final. She was all grown up and gone. Even though they came home to visit on week ends often, it was never the same. Jane was a married woman now, while Tag and I were still kids. We were even closer than ever, but even our interests were changing. We were growing up.

*   *   *   *   *   *

Daddy was living in Madison now. We hadn't seen much of him since he returned from prison and Mom had remarried. He never did. I had been to see him in Madison a couple of times before. He still drank, but not when I was there. It had really been hot lately and I'd been working too many hours, so I gave him a call.

"Hi, Daddy, how would you like some company this weekend?"

"Sure, honey." He sounded pleased. "How are you getting here?"

"I checked the train schedule. It arrives in Madison about two in the afternoon." I said. "If it's easier for you, I can catch a bus to your place. You are living in the same place, aren't you?"

He laughed. "I'm still there, but I'll meet you at the West Washington Street Station at two. Bring your swim suit. I'm working at a home on Lake Mendota. These people are millionaires. They have a private beach and I know how you love to swim. They're away on vacation, but they won't care if we swim. I do every evening."

"I'd like to buy a new one. That's all the shopping I want to do." I said. "I'm anxious to see you, Daddy, it's been a long time."

"See you Saturday then, Sarah. I love you." He said.

"Love you too, Daddy, bye." I hung up.

When I arrived in Madison, Daddy was there waiting for me.

"Yo, Sarah." He hollered as soon as I stepped from the train.

I ran down the platform and gave him a big hug. He handed me a piece of paper. It had two or three things scribbled on it.

"What is this?" I asked.

"Oh, it's just a list I made of things you might like to do while you're visiting me."

"I forgot. It's the week end. You won't be working. I won't get a chance to see what you're doing now." I said with a pout.

"You'll get a chance to see it tonight. I live only five blocks from the lake where I'm working. We can walk over this evening and take a dip in the lake, if you'd like."

"That sounds great." I said. "I really want to see what you're doing now."

"Check the rest of the list and find something we can do this afternoon." He said. "It's such a nice day. The zoo might be fun."

As we climbed into his old station wagon, I asked.

"Can we pick up some hot dogs so we don't have to think about supper?"

"You really are a chip off the old block, Sarah." He smirked. "That was my idea right from the start. Guess the acorn doesn't fall too far from the tree after all."

"You know Daddy," I said, "Miss Warren always said you and I were a lot alike."

"Miss Warren? Did you have that old biddy for a teacher?" He asked. "She used to make my life miserable. She had me in the corner more than I ever sat at my desk. Picky, Picky, Picky."

"According to her, you were a mischief maker, Daddy. Anyhow, she was my favorite teacher while you were away fighting. She always encouraged me to follow my art." I said. "She bragged about your work too, almost like she had a hand in it. Did she push your talent too? Be honest now."

"Maybe your right." He said. "Some of the things she taught me have stuck in my head to this day."

"Isn't that what teaching is all about? She was a good teacher. I never sat in the corner once." I bragged.

We reached the Vilas Zoo and found a vendor where we picked up hotdogs. We walked as we ate, ending up at the monkey cage. Finding a bench right in front of the monkeys, we sat finishing our lunch and laughing at the antics of the little primates. Then we jumped back into the wagon to head for the square. I still needed a bathing suit, and that was by far the best place to shop.

He drove, next, to his rooming house where we changed into our bathing suits. We put our clothing on over the top of them til we got to the lake. This part of Madison was nice. The majestic Elms were like umbrellas sheltering each street. We walked slowly, enjoying the shade and the company. He even introduced me to some acquaintances we met along the way.

"There is the house I'm working at, Sarah." Daddy said.

The house was a mansion, built out of brick, with rock trim. It was larger than Fennimore's library. Sure enough, the back yard ended at the lake.

"Is that where we're going to swim?" I asked, pointing at the beautiful landscaped shoreline.

"It's not only where we are swimming. It's where I'm working right now." He said. "See the new rock walls on the terracing? That's your old man's handy work."

"Can we go down close, so I can get a better look?" I asked.

"We'll have a rough time swimming up here," he joked, "so I guess we'd better go down to the lake."

I looked over and he had that mischievous twinkle in his eye. Even though he was poking fun at me, it was nice to know even a small part of the little mischief maker was still around.

As we walked toward the lake, I asked him. "Are you happy, Daddy?"

"I enjoy my work, Sarah." He said. "As for the rest of my life, I guess I'm as happy as I deserve to be."

I could see that the twinkle was gone, so I didn't ask any more questions. I stood on the pier, slipped my outer clothes off, then slipped slowly and carefully into the water. Daddy took a run and did a cannonball right beside me. I got drenched, if I wanted to or not. We swam and cooled off for over an hour, then dressed and headed back to his room.

That night we played double solitaire until we were tired enough to sleep. The roll away his landlord gave him, for me to use, was not very comfortable so I was awake most of the night. He snored peacefully away in his big bed. As soon as daylight came I ran acrossed the street to the donut shop for donuts and coffee. I had to be at the train station in about two hours, so I had to wake him.

"Come on, Daddy." I shook his shoulder, "Wake up. We don't have much time."

"You don't have any heart, Sarah." He growled. "At least your Mom used to let me sleep on Sunday." He crawled out and disappeared into the bathroom.

I couldn't resist the door he had opened for me. "Do you ever regret the way things turned out for you and Mom, Daddy?" I hollered in at him. "I have this dream of being a mother eventually, if I ever find the right guy, and some day celebrating a fiftieth anniversary."

He came out of the bath all spit and polished. "We all make our own choices, Sarah. Take your sweet time making them. The hard part is living with your choices afterward." He gulped his coffee. "We had better get going, or you'll miss your train."

On the way he pointed out several fire stations and other buildings he had done the work on.

Daddy still did beautiful work, and he knew I'd rather watch him than go shopping. He still loved all of us. He was just never able to battle the booze. Even though he made good money, except for his room and food, it all went for liquor.

As the train rocked slowly Westward, toward home, my last thought was of my father sitting in a pub with his cronies, making up for lost time, the time he had spent with me. Seemed to me like Daddy had made some very sad choices.

Chapter Six

Jake Cullen came skating at the rink one night with a group of my friends from Mt Hope. I remembered him from years ago, but he wasn't a kid anymore. He was tall and handsome. My heart raced when he asked if he could walk me home. Tag, who was working most nights as skate boy, gave me the high sign when he saw us walk out together. We only lived kitty-corner from the rink, but it took him an hour to walk me there.

From that day on we were almost inseparable. Dancing was one of our favorite pastimes, but by far, not the only thing we had in common. Jake had graduated last year, so when he wasn't working, his time was his own. The warm days were much too nice to waste sitting in school. My grades weren't even close to the top 10 percent, so a few absent days wouldn't hurt anything. I skipped to go hunting and fishing with Jake. Mom was working and the principal had a hard time confirming the excuses I wrote for myself but signed her name. When the time came for me to get my drivers license, Jake lent me his car. From then on I drove it more than he did.

Jake and I were in love. All of our friends and family knew that. We knew that. But we had one big problem. Jake liked to drink and I didn't. We broke up at least once a week over his drinking. I didn't want to take a chance of ending up like Mom had with Daddy.

One night we were all dressed up for a night of dancing. There was a big party on the outskirts of Mt. Hope. Everyone was having a few beers before heading out to the 'Checkerboard' in Prairie du Chein.

Jake handed me a can of beer. "Come on, Sarah." He said. "Don't be such a prude."

Is that what he thought I was? That wasn't what I wanted. All I wanted was to be part of his life. Maybe one beer wouldn't hurt

I had a couple, three, maybe four beers, and being my first, they hit me hard. The trees started spinning and everyone was talking slow and fuzzy. This wasn't any fun at all and I thought I was going to get sick…I was sick… I managed to get behind a car before I puked, but I got it on my dress. Now I was going to smell like vomit. Oh, shit.

"Let's go dancing," someone yelled from behind a '48' Chevy.

"Where the heck are my keys?" Jake asked.

"Here, I have them," I said. "But, I don't think either of us should drive."

"Give them to me, Sarah. Oh, hell. Keep them. I'll ride with someone else." He jumped in another car, full of his friends and away they drove.

I had been driving his car a lot recently, but I knew I couldn't drive now. The guest room at his house was mine to use when I stayed over. Next morning, when

I finally woke up, I couldn't remember a thing. My brand new, beaded, moccasins were on the floor with both front ends shredded. I must have walked to his house from the country and drug my toes all the way. Jake's car was still in the country, but I couldn't tell you why. My coming out party, and I had all the signs of an alcoholic in the making. I had blacked out on my maiden voyage.

Why did I do that? Well, it won't happen again. I promised myself. I felt like I had really let myself down, and it didn't happen again... Not til the next time. After that, my time was spent dragging myself to school in the daytime, and partying at night. I still worked, but only because I had to. Mom and Tag had busy lives of their own, so I don't think they even noticed that the real Sarah had disappeared, and been replaced by someone I didn't even know or like. I still drew pictures occasionally but the passion to do it was gone. I loved Jake, of that I had no doubt. If he was going to be part of my life, then so was drinking. The choice had been mine, right or wrong.

*　　*　　*　　*　　*　　*

Tonight Tag's class was graduating from eighth grade. I had made up my mind to spend this night with my younger brother and let Jake do whatever he wanted.

"Hey, Tigger, do you and Jack want a couple of cute dates for tonight?" I asked. Jack was Tag's best friend.

"What?" He asked with a puzzled look. I hadn't spent time with him for ages.

"After graduation, you wanna go out with me and Darlene?" I repeated the invitation.

"Where are we going?" He asked. I could tell he thought I was pulling his leg.

"To the drive-in first for burgers, fries, and shakes. Then we'll drive around and go from there. It's more fun if you don't plan too much." I said.

"You payin?" He asked, with that mischievous grin.

"Yes, brat." I shot back.

Warren, Mom, Tag and I walked the half block to the ceremony. Grade school had now been moved into the old high school building. Fennimore was actually talking about tearing down the old grade school building. In my opinion, there was too much history in that old building. It should be made into a museum. Anyhow, the service didn't last long, and we soon walked back home, joined now by Tag's friend, Jack.

Darlene was driving for our big date. We both got gussied up for the occasion. When she arrived, I told her. "Wait till you see our dates, Dar. Suits, ties, and hair all slicked down. They are excited about going out."

"Let's show them a really good time." She giggled like a teeny bopper.

"What do you have in mind?" I asked hesitantly. "Nothing too daring, I hope."

"Na, they're younger than the kids at our hang out so let's take them there, and make them feel like part of the gang. We can dance to the juke box. They'll have a good time and if we have the urge we can still sneak a smoke. Okay?" She had been thinking ahead.

"SH... here they come."

When they walked in, I planted a kiss on Tag and Jack's cheeks.

"You guys look so handsome tonight." I complimented them. "You should wear suits more often."

"Sure," Tag said, as he wiped my kiss off of his cheek and tried to pretend that he didn't like it. "I'd look sweet over at the machine shop dressed like this. Gramps and the other guys would love that. I get teased enough because I'm a kid. What would they do if I showed up in a suit?"

"They'd probably love you, like I do," I couldn't stifle the grin. "Or...give you a worse time than ever."

We jitterbugged til my legs were weak, and it was closing time. We dropped Jack off, and when we finally arrived home Mom was waiting for us at the door.

"Where in the world have you kids been until this hour?" She asked frantically. "I was worried."

Tag didn't say a word. He made a beeline for bed, leaving a trail of dress clothes in his wake.

"We've been out on the town, Mom." I explained. "Darlene, me, and a couple of real gentlemen."

It had felt good, spending a night with my little brother, and friends. There had been no thought of drinking and we had a ball. Why was my life in such turmoil? I had dreamed for so long of finally growing up. Now that I was almost there, the transition from being a kid to being grown up was more painful every day. Like Daddy said, we all have to make our own choices...

And then we have to live with them.

*　*　*　*　*　*

Now it was my graduation day. Because I had gotten stupid earlier in the year and dropped out of school, I wasn't certain if they would sign my diploma. I had wised up and gone back to school after six weeks, but I took on a real battle. I had, not only my daily schoolwork, but piles of make-up. Now was the day, and I still hadn't finished bookkeeping, my worst subject. At six in the morning the phone rang.

"Sarah, it's the school." Mom called up to wake me.

"Be right there." I yelled down.

When I answered the phone, it was exactly the person I expected.

"Sarah, Mr. Grey here. You need to come to school," he said. "You have only today to finish this work. It should have been done two days ago, but I'll give you today to finish it, out of the goodness of my heart." Then he chuckled.

"Okay., Mr. Grey," I said. "I'll be there in half an hour."

"You'd better plan on the entire day." He said. "These last five chapters are do or die for you."

"See you as soon as I can get there." I said, then hung up the phone.

I grabbed some clean jeans, fresh blouse, and socks. I had a quick sponge bath and ran the six blocks to the new high school. While catching my breath, I checked my other classes. I made the grade in all of them, some just barely. Some of my teachers probably passed me because I drew their maps and charts for them. Mr. Grey would make the difference if my diploma was signed or not. There wasn't much drawing to do in bookkeeping.

"Good morning, Mr. Grey." I said sheepishly.

"Good morning, yourself, Sarah, sorry I had to call you so early," he apologized.

"That's Okay. This mess is my own fault." I said. "I'm glad you called."

I sat at the table with books spread all over, and my brain on the verge of busting. He couldn't know how I hated bookkeeping. After watching me struggle for three and a half hours, and explaining the same principles' of bookkeeping over several times, Mr. Grey grabbed an armload of books and test papers.

"I'm going to the library to grade these papers, Sarah," he said. "If you need any more help, the answer book is here on my desk." He winked at me and walked out, closing the door behind him.

It took me almost two hours just to copy all the answers. I didn't dare get them all right. No one would ever believe that.

* * * * * *

I met Miss Bonita, my Home Economics teacher in the hall.

"I'm so glad you came back to get your diploma, Sarah." She said with a big smile.

"Me too. I don't know what I was thinking," I said. "Cross your fingers, for me, that it's signed when they give it to me."

"You're not sure?" She asked in amazement. "Graduation is in four hours."

"Yes, I know, and no, I don't know. The office girl just told me, if the teachers' have signed, I made it. If not…Well," I said, "all I can do now is pray."

"You have your life figured out either way, don't you?" She asked with a peculiar grin.

"Yes, but after all this," I said, "I'd like to get my diploma."

"Well, good luck tonight. We're all going to miss your drawings." She remarked as she walked down the hall.

"Thanks," I shouted back to her. "I need all the luck I can get."

I was all dressed in my cap and robe when Jake pulled up to take me to school. He came in the house carrying a big box and handed it to me. After unwrapping four boxes, each one smaller, and stuffed inside the last one, I finally found a ring box. Inside was a beautiful diamond. My emotions were wound so tight today, this was the last straw, I started bawling.

"I didn't want to make you cry." Jake comforted me. "Will you wear my ring?"

*　*　*　*　*　*

The class was milling around in Long Hall, while friends and family filled the gymnasium. I was flashing my new diamond around when Miss Bonita came up to me.

"Now this is a surprise." She said. "All of us teachers thought you had gotten married when you dropped out."

"Fooled you." I said with a grin. Now I understood the weird look she had given me earlier.

My class marched into the gym to the tune, "Ceremony," and took our seats on the stage. Our class was the largest to graduate in Fennimore, the second class from the new high school. The Baccalaureate, Valedictorian, and Salutatorian speeches took forever. It was probably my imagination. Everyone else knew their grades.

Finally it was time for the diplomas. It won't be long now. They started with the A's…finally… They announced my name…"Sarah Bray."

I walked to the front, got my sheepskin, and returned to my seat. The student in front of me hid me from the audience, so I slipped my diploma from its cover, and sneaked a look, and started to laugh out loud. The entire class knew my situation and they all laughed too. One by one, our laughter turned to tears. Parents were crying too. This show of raw emotion disrupted the proceedings, but we were closing the cover on a big part of our lives. When we walk out the doors tonight, we won't be coming back, accept to visit. We <u>all</u> graduated.

Chapter Seven

Having all of my top teeth pulled really put me in a slump, but they were too soft to save. I was working days at a restaurant on the square in Lancaster. My boss couldn't juggle the schedule to let me have any time off, so I'd been working with a black and blue, puffy, face, while I was getting used to my false teeth.

Three months ago I threw Jake's ring at him when I found out he gave some girl a ride home from a dance, while I was working. He called constantly, assuring me that I was the one he loved. I finally relented and the ring went back on my hand.

Jake's mouth dropped open when I told him the news.

"Do you have any ideas, honey? We don't have any money saved yet... Jake! Say something."

"It's a little late to think about that now," he said. "Let's just get married. We planned too anyhow."

We had talked about marriage but never imagined that it would be this soon. I'm going to move out of my Mom's house, right into being a mom myself. I had envisioned maybe doing something with my art. Possibly even go to art school if I could find a way.

"I guess I'm still a little in shock over the news." I said as tears filled my eyes. "Sorry, seems like all I do any more is bawl."

"Christmas is two weeks off, Sarah. If we can make arrangements fast enough, let's be married then." He said. "The relatives will all be home for the holidays, anyhow."

"Really?" I asked. Now the tears came for real. "At least I'm not too badly out of shape yet."

Jake put his arm around me. "Your so slim, Sarah, no one will ever know. This isn't the wedding we planned on, but at least we'll be married."

"Do you really think we can do it that soon?" I asked.

"We'll never know til we try," he said. "Come on, hon., cheer up. We have a lot to do."

The next two weeks were run, run, run. We ran to the courthouse for the license, the doctor for blood tests, the minister about the church and ceremony. We talked to Jake's cousin, J.B. and her boyfriend, Chad, about standing up with us. And we talked to Mom and Warren about our plans

Mom's smiled cautiously and said, "I'm glad you decided to do the right thing" That made Jake feel a little better. He had been nervous about talking to my Mom. Even though he was like one of the family by now, my being pregnant was a shock to her. Janie had at least been married before she got pregnant.

73

Warren, always the businessman, offered another suggestion. "Your grandmother's house has been sitting there empty for a couple of years now, and it needs lots of work, but it's fixable. If you kids want to do the work, I'll furnish the material, and you can live there rent free. I know it's not modern, but it would be a roof over your heads and ...," he chuckled, "it's affordable."

Mom added, "Why don't you give Janie a call, you're both the same size. If she agrees, maybe you can use her dress and hat for your wedding. I know you're on a tight budget."

"Good thinking, Mom, I'll call her." I agreed.

Janie said I could use them, she would even have them cleaned and bring them down when they came for Christmas.

The engagement ring Jake gave me for graduation came with a matching wedding ring, so we found one to match for him. His suit was fine. On Christmas Eve, he remembered how bad his dress shoes looked so he had to make a last minute run to Prairie. The next mourning we were all set as soon as regular church service was over.

Of course we were nervous during the service, but it didn't help that I kept hearing giggling going on behind me. The giggling from the crowd, made Jake so nervous, he tried to put the ring on the wrong finger. After we kissed and walked down through the church I couldn't wait to find Mom and find out the reason for the laughter.

"It wasn't you they were laughing at, Sarah," she said, "but one lone fly wanted to keep landing on your shoulder. On that white dress it really showed up like a sore thumb. He must have come back a dozen times." She gave us both hugs. "Congratulations, Mr. And Mrs. Cullen."

*　　*　　*　　*　　*　　*

The weather was too cold to think about the repairs to the house, so we accepted an invitation to stay on the farm with Jake's aunt Marie and uncle Dale until it got warmer. They weren't that much older than we. Their two little toddlers would give me some practice with children. During our stay with them, Jake hunted so many rabbits that Marie and I decided to can the meat. I didn't know how many shades of green a person could turn until I did just that, when she let the steam off of the pressure cooker.

Spring came and new life was evident everywhere. There were baby calves, baby pigs, a new colt, and buds were popping out all over. I wasn't getting sick at every strange smell anymore, and was no longer crying all the time. It was time to get to work on the house, so we loaded up with scrub pails, rags, brooms and other items we needed and walked through the door of Grandma's old house to get started.

Jake's teeth were chattering. "How do you heat this place? It's to cold to work until we have some heat."

"Grandma always had a wood range in the summer kitchen and a pot bellied stove in the living room. She never heated the parlor unless company was coming. I don't think we should try to heat the summer kitchen."

"Then what do you plan to do?"

"Being's there isn't any plumbing anywhere we can put our stove and refrigerator (everything we had, was cast offs' from the family) in the room that used to be the living room and the parlor can be our living room." I was getting uncomfortable. I wasn't used to the extra weight around the middle. "We'll need a space heater for the parlor," I said. "I already found a wood range for the kitchen. That will furnish enough heat for the bedroom too."

"Where did you find a range?" Jake asked.

"I saw an ad on the bulletin board at the grocery store." I replied. "They only wanted thirty dollars."

"We'll be able to swing that," he said. "I'm sure a space heater will be expensive, though."

Jake had been used to spending his pay checks for beer, guns, ammo, and fishing equipment. Living at home, he never had to pay for food, clothing, rent or any other bills. Having to take responsibility for paying bills would be a shock to his system.

"The rent is free. We should be able to afford a heater." I shot back at him.

We moved the wood range in. It took three men and a horse, but once it was up and working it felt nice and cozy. It was all the heat we needed for now. Oatmeal cookies from that wood range were the best, and became a daily ritual. I scrubbed, painted, hung curtains and cooked. Jake replaced broken window panes, cleaned weeds from the yard and even did some stump removal. Warren had the large maple and all of the pines cut down two years ago, for fear they would come down in a storm and hit the house. With no shade the house got hot in the afternoon. That was a good reason for me to nap. Naps got more frequent as I grew bigger.

By going to auctions, I was able to find most of the things we needed for our home. Two of my treasures were a wooden high chair and an antique baby cradle. They cleaned up really well but I wanted to give them a fresh coat of paint. My problem was not knowing weather to use shades of pink or blue.

Jake spent lots of his evenings in town drinking with his buddies. Most of the time I was content to sit by the wood stove, listening to the snap, crackle, of the fire and drawing pictures.

Sometimes I would just sit in my rocker and daydream about the new baby. I did so want to be a mommy, a good mommy, like my mother and grandmothers.

*   *   *   *   *   *

On August, ninth, nineteen-fifty-five, our son was born. Arron John Cullen weighed seven pounds, six ounces, and he was perfect. Mom and Warren were at the hospital almost before I got back to my room. Jake was so proud, and he couldn't sit still. He must have made a dozen trips between my room and the nursery. Each time his face was beaming. I had no doubt he would be out celebrating tonight with his pals, passing out cigars.

"Did you have a hard labor," Mom asked?

"No, thank goodness. I asked Dr. Shields not to give me any anesthetic." I told her. "I wanted to be awake to see my baby come into the world. My ability to will away pain has never let me down in the past, and it worked this time too."

"You were lucky, Sarah," she said. "All of you kids were long, hard, childbirths."

"But, you're so tiny, Mom," I argued. "I'm a lot taller and built differently from you. Dr. Shields said I could have a thirteen pounder with no more problems than today."

"Ouch, that would hurt." She winced.

"Well, I wouldn't have missed it for the world. Isn't he a doll? Now I'll have someone around to keep me company." I laid my head back on the pillow, then I remembered..."Could you call Daddy and let him know he has a grandson?" I asked.

"No." She said. "You and Jake will have to do that yourselves. I don't want to get him started again. A call from me, might be all it takes."

"I'm sorry," I apologized. "I shouldn't have asked. He probably won't come down here anyway. Do you have any idea where he is now?"

"You can find out from Grandma Bray." She said. "I hear he stays with her sometimes."

"That's a good idea," I agreed. "I can tell her the news too."

After they left, I rang for a wheel chair, grabbed some change, and wheeled down the hall to the pay phone. It gave me another chance to peek at my baby boy.

"Hello." Grandma Bray answered.

"Grandma, it's Sarah. I have some news for you and Daddy. Do you know where he is?"

"Not right this minute," she said, "but he's been staying here. He should be home for supper anytime now."

"Well, tell him I just had a little boy," I bragged. "We named him Arron John. This is Daddy's first grandson."

"Oh, Sarah, I'm happy for you. Where are you?" She asked.

"In the hospital at Boscobel." I told her. "If he doesn't make it down here, I'll be staying at Mom's for a week. I don't want him to come to Mom's house. After that week, I'll be home."

"Are you still living in your Grandma Leighy's house?" She asked.

"Yes, but remember, I won't be home for the next two weeks." I reminded her.

"I'll tell him," she said, "but you know he doesn't have a car."

"I know," I said, "but he always finds a way when he wants too badly enough."

"Congratulations, Sarah." She said before she hung up.

The time flew by at Mom's. Lots of friends dropped by to welcome Arron. Mom wanted me to stray longer, and it was tempting with all the modern facilities, but I wanted to get home. Jake and I had our own family now.

*   *   *   *   *   *

I bustled around getting settled back in. It was so quiet and peaceful out here in the country. I didn't realize how much I missed it. Carrying water to launder cloth diapers would get me back in shape in no time. Arron slept most of the time. I was nursing him so I didn't have to mess with formula. Life was good and I was glad to be home. In no time I was even back to my daily oatmeal cookies.

"Bang, Bang," Someone was pounding on the door. I had fallen asleep in the rocking chair, and the knocking startled me awake.

"Just a minute." I shouted, trying to get my bearings.

"Washa godda keep da damned door locked for?" The voice slurred.

Oh, my God, it's Daddy and he's drunk. I wished I hadn't said anything and I could just let him think I wasn't home.

I opened the door. "Daddy, why did you come out here like this? You're drunk."

"You called me. Wanted me to come and see your kid." He staggered and almost fell. "Well, here I am." He looked terrible. He had lost a lot of weight and the wrinkles covered his face and his once strong and muscular arms.

"Come on in." I said reluctantly. "I have some coffee made."

"I don't want no coffee." He growled. "Where's the kid?"

He wasn't alone. The man sitting behind the wheel of the car, was wasting no time. He was draining the bottle of whatever it was they were drinking.

I begrudgingly opened the bedroom door. I didn't want him near my baby, but I figured he would leave once he'd seen 'The Kid'. He stubbed his toe and went flying, sprawled over the baby, cradle, and all. My motherly instinct kicked in. I pulled him up and got him away from the baby. Arron didn't even stir. A shove got my Dad back to the kitchen and I closed the bedroom door.

"You need some coffee, Daddy." I insisted.

"I don't want no damned coffee." He swore. "Come here. I always wondered what kind of a piece you'd be. You're big enough now. You've been around the block and know what a man wants."

My God, my dad had actually thought about me that way. The thought made me sick.

"It's just the booze talking, Daddy." I said with disgust.

He grabbed my arm and tried pushing me down on the couch. He was so drunk, that I was able to get free of him, leaving him laying there like a wet mop.

"Stop it, Daddy." I pleaded. "Think what your doing."

"Stop it, hell." He said. "I haven't had a woman for months now. Come here." He reached for me again.

"You get out of my house." I ordered.

"You think you're big enough to make me?" He sneered.

I wasn't sure of his strength, or mine. He was so drunk and wobbly, he didn't look like he could punch his way out of a paper bag, but I knew he was normally very strong.

"I'm gonna try." I spit back at him with determination. I pulled him up and gave him a shove toward the door. He almost fell, but stopped short by holding onto the door frame.

"Get out." I ordered. Giving him one final shove, I sent him sprawling onto the cement landing outside of the summer kitchen door. Quickly, I slammed the door and locked it.

"And don't come back." I screamed. "I never want to see you again."

He struggled to his feet and swayed back toward the house. He doubled his fist and put it through the glass in the door, sending glass flying all over me. A couple of large pieces stuck in my arm.

"You probably ain't no good anyway, whore," he yelled as he turned and staggered to the car.

I slipped back through the next door and locked it too. This door had no glass, but I wasn't sure how good the lock was. I watched through the window and my tears as they drove away. My body was shaking so badly now, and my legs wouldn't hold me. After quite a time I managed to wrap my arm and make it to the phone, to call Mom. She and Warren would be right out. I knew Jake was driving truck out of town and I wouldn't be able to reach him. I cleaned the shattered glass from the floor, and noticed something shiny where Daddy had fallen. His harmonica was laying there, broken into two pieces. One of the few nice memories I had as a child, was my father's mouth organ, and the Irish ditties we all loved to hear him play on it. From this day forward it would be a reminder of the shame I felt for my father.

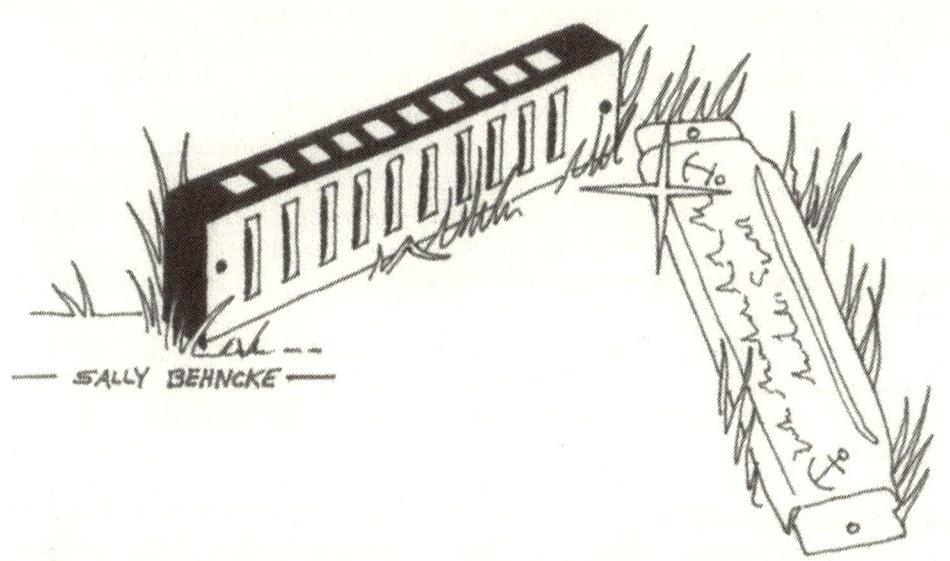

Dad's harmonica after Sarah threw him out of her house

Chapter Eight

During the next few years, we moved to many different towns, many different houses, most with no indoor facilities. Rent was cheap and Jake could hang onto most of his paychecks to buy whatever he wanted.

We moved to Blue River when Jake started driving semis. The apartment we rented was upstairs of an older house. It at least had water, cold water, and a toilet, though we had to share that with the people from downstairs.

On February, eighteenth, nineteen-fifty-seven when I went to the hospital for the birth of our second baby, Arron went to Mom's. Cyle Duane was a big baby, with a mischievous twinkle in his eye. I knew that twinkle well. Upon leaving the hospital, I spent three days at Mom's to get my strength back. Arron couldn't seem to get enough of his baby brother. I was feeling fine, so Jake and I took our two boys and headed home.

We climbed the long stairs with all our bundles and Jake unlocked the door. Duke, Jake's hunting dog, shot out between our legs, almost knocking me and Arron and the new baby down the stairs. When I looked in, I couldn't believe what I saw.

"My God, Jake," I grimaced. "Has Duke been in here since I went to the hospital?"

"I completely forgot about him." He said. "I was in such a hurry to get to your Mom's every night, and I didn't even stop here."

"You haven't fed him? No wonder he tore the place apart. You had better go catch him. He'll probably be into garbage cans to find something to eat. Poor Duke must be starving."

Jake hurried out to find the dog, leaving me with the kids, to handle the mess. There wasn't a clean spot in the entire apartment to lay down the baby. Duke had torn our beds apart, and defecated everywhere. The content of the waste basket was torn to shreds all over the floor. Even the roll of toilet tissue from the bathroom was shredded. The window by the couch was broken out. He must have been trying to escape. A jump from that window would have killed him.

Finally, kicking things aside with my foot, while cradling the baby in one arm and holding onto Arron with the other hand, I cleared a place on the floor to spread a blanket. I laid the baby down and quickly grabbed Arron's arm...

"Honey," I ordered. "You sit here by your little brother and don't touch anything."

Snatching the broom, I swept up the broken glass and the litter. The bedding got piled in a corner and I remade the beds. Now I could move the baby.

Looking out the window, I could see Duke was back on his chain by the doghouse and he had been fed. Jake was nowhere to be seen. He was no doubt at the bar next door.

When he finally came home, he was snookered. I couldn't talk to him. I wanted to strangle him.

"Not gonna talk to me, huh?" He garbled.

"I'm just glad I'm not your dog." I said snottily. The rest of the night we were silent and he left for work the next morning without a word. It was a great homecoming.

My body, which even during pregnancy, could never be considered anything but skinny turned into a rack of bones. The children's welfare had never been a problem, nor Jake's. Taking care of myself was another matter. Pneumonia caught me unaware every time I turned around. I was in the hospital for a week with a bad case when Dr. Shields said...

"You know, Sarah, you're pregnant again." He said it as if he was giving me bad news. "Now you had best take better care of yourself. You've already had as much penicillin as your body will take. I'm going to write a prescription for multi vitamins that I want you to take religiously. You have a nice little family, which will soon be bigger. They need you."

Dr. Shields might have thought my pregnancy was bad news, but I didn't. My dream had always been to be a mommy. Now I would have three, the same as my Mom. Maybe this one would be a little girl I could sew frilly dresses for. This gave me a reason to get better.

On October, twenty-first, nineteen-fifty-eight, Laurie Carol made her debut. She was my tiny, blonde haired, blue eyed, Puddin. I had my babies, and they were my life. As long as they had food to eat and a place to stay warm, Jake could do whatever he wanted with his money.

*   *   *   *   *   *

Trout fishing is what Jake did with most of his free time during the summer. He was late getting home. I was starting to suspect that he had stopped off for a beer with the guys and forgot where we lived, when the car pulled in.

He came in all excited. "Honey, how would you like to have a place of our own? A big place that you can fill up with babies if you want."

"For heaven's sake slow down." I said. "Sit down and eat while supper is still hot. We can talk while you're eating. Where is this place?" I asked

The peaceful Big Green trout stream in Werley

"Okay, Okay," he said breathlessly. "You know that big old store building at Werley? You've seen it. It's been sitting there empty for a few years now. The old man that owns it must have been in a nursing home. He passed away recently and the family wants to sell it."

I remembered it. I had often wondered why it was sitting empty. "It's awfully big for a house, don't you think?" I asked.

"I was thinking maybe we could open a bait shop." He said, with his mouth full. He swallowed and then continued. "With all the fishermen that go fishing on the Big Green and down on the Wisconsin River, it would be the ideal place to sell bait."

"What in the world got you thinking about this?" I asked.

"I ran out of bait." He chuckled.

"Wouldn't it be cheaper to just go get some more bait?" I laughed with him.

"Supper's good, Hon." He complimented me. At the rate he was gulping it down, I don't know how he could tell how it tasted? "You know how many people fish in that area." He continued. "You've been with me when we could hardly find a spot to drop a hook in the water. I think it would work. Let's go take a look."

I had my doubts, but I could be wrong, so I said, "Fine. I'll call in the morning and set up an appointment."

We looked the place over from top to bottom and with the help of an old family friend, made arrangements to purchase it. I'd never dared dream about a place like this. It had seven bedrooms, as it used to be the hotel in Werley when the narrow gauge railroad ran through there. There was indoor plumbing, a living room, dining room, big kitchen and an open stairway, besides the store itself. Wow! By the time we signed the papers, Jake had added carry-out beer to what he wanted to sell.

"The first thing we have to do is talk to the town chairman to see about a liquor license." I said. "Without a license, all of our plans would be in for nothing."

"You kids have a good idea," the chairman said, "but you'd better get a 'class B' license."

"Why a 'class B'?" Jake asked.

"Just in case someone pops a top on your property," the man explained, "you won't be in any trouble."

From that point on Jake was on a roll. This license allowed us to actually open a beer bar. I wasn't fond of the idea, but Jake was elated. He was going to own a bar. Word spread quickly, and he was somewhat of a celebrity amongst his friends.

The old building was in remarkable shape for having sat empty for years and it wasn't long before we moved in. The living quarters had a screen porch crossed the front, where you could sit and enjoy the peaceful country days.

"The quiet down here reminds me of your Grandma's old house." Jake said.

"Yes, but don't go through the screen door. The mosquitos in Werley are the size of birds. It makes me wonder if they could carry off the kids."

From the porch you could see the Big Green trout stream running the length of the valley, crossed by a picturesque bridge. The banks were mostly willows, with a worn spot here and there where some fisherman had spent his time. The only thing to disturb the serenity was an occasional passing car or the bawling of the Holstein herd on the other side of the creek. The serenity didn't last long.

I took care of the kids and the bar all day and then help tend the bar at night. We had a neighbor girl, Patty, come in to watch the kids after supper, til they fell asleep. During the day, if I got busy, they were on their own to get into mischief. And, we did get busy. All the farmers in the area liked to play euchre, so the bar took off like a shot. If they weren't in the fields or milking, they were in Werley playing Euchre. After months of this I was worn to a frazzle.

"Jake, this isn't going to work. The kids need someone to watch them. When I get busy, there's no way for me to leave the bar, and worrying about them is turning me into a wreck."

"I've noticed you have an awfully short fuse lately," he said. "We can get Patty to come down more often. Schools almost out, so we'll ask her." Then he dropped an unsuspected bomb. "I've been thinking of quitting my job anyhow. The bar's doing well enough now to support us."

Patty was a good helper and that really made a difference. She was glad to get a summer job so close to home. I missed being the one who was watching my children, but at least they weren't getting into any trouble and weren't in any danger.

Jake was another can of worms though. With all the <u>free</u> time he had now, he could fish all day and drink all night. There were many nights Jake didn't make it until closing time. A good time was had by all, at the Werley bar, while the juke box wailed out 'Where the Boys Are', 'Traveling Man' or 'Folsom Prison Blues', and everyone was doing the twist.

Unfortunately, halfway from the guilt I felt about the kids, and partly because it's difficult to serve a houseful of drunks when you're stone-cold sober, my drinking was getting way out of hand. Most nights I'd just throw up my hands and let the good times roll.

*   *   *   *   *   *

In late nineteen-sixty my Dad died peacefully in his sleep, from a stroke, at Grandma's Bray's house. I did see him again, at his funeral. Within the same year my stepfather, Warren, died after a long battle with emphysema. Grandma Bray also passed away. Bad things seem to happen in threes.

Jake never stopped partying. After closing time he'd find a party somewhere, then sleep until noon the next day, and start all over. At first I only suspected he was cheating, then one night Cyle woke with an earache. I picked him up out of bed and headed downstairs.

"Come on, Sweetie, we'll find something to make it feel better." I tried to sooth him. I gave him a child's aspirin and rocked him with the heating pad on his ear. He was starting to doze off when a car pulled in. With the light from the headlights I could see the clock. It was three in the morning. Who would pull in here at this hour? The lights went out. It was Jake with some woman. They were necking, like there was no tomorrow. My face flushed with anger and my pulse was pounding in my temples. I rushed Cyle back to bed. As I came down the stairs, Jake was walking though the door. I met him head on.

"No more, Jake. I'm taking the kids and we're leaving. You can party with your other women all you want, but I don't have stay around to watch it. I'll be talking to an attorney tomorrow, so you can be expecting papers shortly."

"You can walk out just like that?" He said.

"Jake, you walked out on the kids and me a long time ago."

The next morning he pleaded for me to stay. He even left the bar closed for one night and spent time with his family. I would have done anything, rather than break up our family. He stayed sober for two days. That night after locking up, he left in the same car, with the same gal, that had brought him home two night prior.

Sarah's children, Arron, Laurie, and Cyle Cullen

I loaded the kids in the car with enough clothes for our immediate needs and watched our peaceful valley disappear in the rear view mirror.

Chapter Nine

"Hello." Uncle Harlow said, as he answered the phone.

"Uncle Harlow? It's Sarah. How is everyone in your family?"

"Everyone here is fine." He said with surprise. "I haven't talked to any of you since your dad's funeral. I hope your call isn't any more bad news."

"No, it's nothing like that. What's going to happen with Grandma's house?" I asked. "I drove by and I see it's still empty."

"We've been thinking of listing it with a realtor. None of us has had the time to get away. "Why, are you interested?" He asked.

"Yes, my marriage just broke up and I need a place for the kids and me." I replied. "The only problem, I don't have much money to work with."

"Don't worry about that now. I think we can work something out on a land contract. I'll give Bernie a call and get back to you later. Give me your number." He said. "I think Mom would like you to be in the house. She always felt so bad about the way Walter treated your Mom and you kids. Sorry to hear your marriage broke up. Keep your chin up, Sarah."

I gave him Mom's number, "Thanks, Uncle Harlow. I'll be waiting for your call. Beings I'm staying at Mom's, it's not really a big emergency."

At five he called back to Mom's and confirmed I could have the house and they would drive up on the week end to sign the papers. He told me where to get the key and that I should feel free to move in any time.

Jake was moving to Madison. He didn't want any of the furniture, so I would have a house full. The bar had been sold to a couple who jumped at the chance as soon as they heard we were leaving. They had moved our things into one room, and they were anxious for us to get them out of their way. Two of Warren's ex truck drivers offered to move me to Lancaster. Mom still had some pull with them.

So there I sat, alone with my children, in Grandma's house. Luckily for me, my uncles had installed plumbing for her after the war. Uncle Harlow's words haunted me. Little did he know, all I could afford to do, was keep my chin up.

*   *   *   *   *   *

Arron was the only one of the kids that were old enough to go to school. Waitress wages weren't enough to pay the bills and a sitter, so I couldn't work. The money we got from the sale of the bar would be gone in no time, and Jake thought child support payments were a joke.

I met some new friends, the Kabbers,' through Arron. One of their boys was in his class, and he was invited to come over to play. Come to find out the boy's folks, and their folks before them, had always been good friends with the Bray family. We had a lot in common, mainly drinking. Old family tradition. Most evenings the kids would play and the grown ups would drink. We mixed Rum with everything. Rum and Coke, Rum and Lemonade, Rum and whatever was handy.

It was a miserable winter. I couldn't do anything outside, couldn't work, didn't have the money to do anything creative, drinking with the Kabbers was getting old, and cabin fever was taking over.

"Ring…" The phone sounded off.

"Hello." I answered, half expecting it to be Mrs. Kabber.

"Hi, it's just me." I recognized Jake's voice.

"Yes. What can I do for you, Jake?" I asked bitterly.

"You can let me come and see the kids this week end." He said. "I promise not to give you any trouble. I miss all of you."

"I guess it wouldn't hurt anything." I mellowed a little. "They miss you, too. This isn't fair to them, Jake. What time would you be coming down?"

"Tomorrow night when I'm done with work for the week, around six o'clock." He replied.

"It will be okay," I agreed. "The kids will be excited. You'd better not disappoint them, Jake."

"See you about six then. Bye, Sarah." And he hung up.

"Kids," I called to my noisy gang. "Your dad will be down tomorrow night to see you."

They all started jumping around, squealing, and everyone talking at once. I wish I felt so happy about his visit. If I had even one good thing going for me, I wouldn't feel so lousy.

"Quiet down, kids, he's not here yet." I had to shout to be heard at all.

Cyle said, "Mommy, can you fix one of those roasted beefs that Daddy likes so much?"

I didn't even know if I could afford one, but I said, "It's nice that you remembered what he likes."

"But I like it too, Mom," he said.

"You kids get to bed and I might even see my way clear to make some oatmeal cookies." I bribed.

"Goodie." Cyle said. "Come on Arron and Laurie, let's go to bed." In no time at all, I didn't hear a peep.

The cookies were done and cooling on a rack when there was a knock on the door. I quickly checked both doors. They were locked securely, and the curtains were closed so no one could see in.

"Who's there?" I said cautiously.

"It's me, Sarah. I didn't mean to scare you." It was Jake.

I opened the door, "What in the world are you doing here tonight?" I asked. "You said tomorrow."

He stepped in. "I couldn't wait. When you said I could come, I called in sick. The sound of your voice made me think about what a mess I've made of my life."

"Well, yours isn't the only one you know. Those kids need their dad. Today was the first time you've called in months."

"Can we talk?" He asked sheepishly.

"I guess." I said. "You're not going to believe this, Jake. I just finished making oatmeal cookies. They're not as good as the ones from the wood range, but not bad. Come on in, I'll make some coffee."

"Are you sure?" He asked.

"Look, Jake," I said, "I'm not afraid of you. Your cheating was our downfall, not your meanness."

"I know." He shuffled his feet uneasily. "I've really messed things up. The kids must be sleeping. Can I peek in at them?"

"Sure, go ahead," I said, with a wave of my hand. "They've been sleeping since you called. You won't wake them."

He disappeared into the bedroom and stayed there until the coffee quit perking. It would have been nice if he had thought about them instead of those other women? We can't turn the clock back, but he sure did break a lot of hearts with his chasing.

"Coffee and cookies sure smell good." He said as he emerged from the bedroom. "You always did have a way in the kitchen. The kids must be eating good. They've really grown."

"Well, come on," I motioned, "the coffee's ready."

He sat down and started gobbling cookies so fast … I finally asked. "You want something else to eat? You must be hungry." I was out of habit of thinking of his welfare. He must not have eaten supper.

"No, these are fine." He managed between cookies. "Kind of seems like old times, Sarah. They weren't all bad. Guess Werley was just too much for us to handle."

"I guess." I said, but I was thinking otherwise. The thought of all those nights he didn't come home were still too fresh in my mind. Any reply could have turned into a fight so I bit my tongue.

He said, "We did have a happy life before Werley."

"Some of it was happy, Jake, but it sure wasn't easy." I said. "You never gave too much thought to me. Did you even realize how much water I had to carry to do laundry for five people, in and out of the house? There were lots of things you never thought about when you were off fishing and hunting, or out drinking with your buddies."

"Why didn't you ever say anything?" He asked.

"I shouldn't have had to." I snapped. "I loved you and the kids. You were happy when you were doing what you enjoyed, and as long as the kids had enough food and a warm place to sleep, they were happy. You could have made my life easier, like living in a decent house with indoor plumbing. Ringer washers have been out of style for years. A good used automatic washer wouldn't have cost as much as one of your guns, but a washer wouldn't be any fun. Right?"

The look on his face was doing me more good than he would ever know. His skinny wife was actually speaking up for herself. After years of doing the things for him that he didn't like doing, I was standing up to him and getting it off my chest. Our divorce would be final shortly, so I hade nothing to lose by telling him what I thought. It might be my only chance. Until right now I didn't even realize, I was harboring all this anger. Wow, that felt good.

"I guess I had that shot coming, and you let me have it with both barrels," he smirked.

"I guess?" Now the elation disappeared and his 'gun pun' was making me see red. He was pushing all the right buttons. "You know that this isn't my idea of a good time." I said smartly. "Why don't I get you some blankets? You can sleep on the couch."

Jake made himself comfortable and slept through the night until the kids jumped on him.

"Daddy, Daddy, wake up. You're here already." Arron squealed.

"Well, say now. I guess I am." Jake laughed.

They wrestled around while I fixed breakfast. When they finished eating, Cyle piped up...

"Mommy said she would make a roasted beef, Daddy. Can we go to the store for it?"

"How about I go to the store while you kids get ready to go for a ride. I'll take you to visit Uncle Dale and Aunt Marie and the boys." He said. "Mommy can have the day to herself."

I was relieved he didn't ask me to go along. He came back shortly with a large roast I couldn't have afforded and slipped forty dollars into my hand.

"In case you need anything else." He whispered.

They all got in the car and left. Forty dollars seemed like a fortune to me, but it didn't seem like much when I thought about all the child support he hadn't paid. The roast was in the oven, so I sat down with paper and pencil and spent the day drawing. It was the first time I'd been away from the kids for ages. As much as I enjoyed the quiet and the time to draw, they were all I could think about.

That evening, after our big roasted beef dinner, Jake kept skirting around something that was obviously on his mind, and the kids kept snickering. He waited until he was ready to head back to Madison before asking his question.

"Would you think about giving us a second chance? Don't answer now. Next weekend? If it's all right." Then he turned and walked to the car. "I'll call." He yelled as he drove off, waving at the kids.

He must have told the kids that we were moving to Madison. They were all excited about moving and I hadn't even had time to digest the idea. I was ready when he called on Thursday.

"Hi, Sarah, it's just me again."

"Yes, I figured it was you. You play dirty, Jake. Telling the kids we were moving was dirty pool. You know they are my weakness. That's not fair!"

"Come on, Sarah." He said. "I played the only card I had. They're with you all the time. I figured they could persuade you if anyone could." There was silence. "Did it work?"

"The jury is still out." I shot back at him. "We'll talk when you come down, but don't think I'm just caving in. Our world is no longer going to revolve around what Daddy wants."

Friday evening, he arrived at six on the dot. He and the kids worked in perfect unison to try talking me out of my doubts. Four weeks and (Thanks to the forty dollars) lots of peanut butter sandwiches later, I relented. My resources were gone and there was no solution to my financial situation in sight. Going on welfare was not an option for me.

"All right." I said. "Just so you know things may never be the same. I learned a hard lesson in Werley. Our marriage was based on trust and, well …You trampled that in the ground."

"I know, but it'll be different this time." He promised.

It was too. He found a nice little house a short distance from Madison. Out in the country, where the kids had lots of room to play and neighbors close enough so they made friends. Jake had always liked to play ball. He started pitching for a hometown league, for a team sponsored by Kathy's. That was a bar a short distance from where we lived. The bar was located in the small community called the 'Beach', where Jane and Brad and their family lived. Brad was the team's catcher. Picnicking at the games every Sunday was a good way for Jane's family and mine to get better acquainted. Things were going smoothly until the end of the second year, when Jake's party going friends at work got to him. He couldn't stand being left out. At first it was an occasional late night, but when the all night parties started and he couldn't remember where he'd been, or who he'd been with, it was time for me to cut my loses and move on. We had celebrated nine anniversaries together. My dream of spending a fiftieth anniversary with the man I loved faded away into obscurity along with my vow to never drink.

*   *   *   *   *   *

The sale of Grandma's house had left me with a little profit, which I had wisely put aside, just in case. Arron, Cyle, Laurie and I moved to a tiny cottage on the 'Beach', that I could afford. The 'Beach' was like a little 'Peyton Place'. It was like a small town on the edge of a big city. Far enough to be away from the hustle if you wanted. Close enough to be part of the bustle if you chose to. There was everything that anyone needed. One store for necessities, one station if you needed gas, one park for the kids to play in, one bar for a drink or a drunk, and one road to take you home. That one road ran a horseshoe around three sides of our home. The road and lake front homes on the East, lake access to the South, more lake front homes to the West. It was a peninsula, of sorts. The strong odor of seaweed was ever present.

The color of the lake when you woke in the morning determined your mood for the day. Sparkling and bright meant a good mood all around, but when the lake was stormy and black, watch out! It had the mysterious effect a full moon has on a werewolf. People changed.

I had met my next door neighbors at the ball games. Mr. Regent, Carl, also played on the ball team. His wife, Margaret, and I had gotten to be quite good friends. The two of them had a small country band that sometimes played at Kathy's on Saturday nights. Janie and Brad were regulars there so occasionally I'd get a sitter and join the fun.

They had a cute, flirtatious, bartender, Don, who didn't mind making my drinks a little on the strong side.

"You don't need to worry, Sarah," he'd grin, "if you have too much, I'll drive you home." Don flirted shamelessly in front of Janie, Brad, or anyone else. He worked for the gas company during the day, and tended bar at night. He wasn't the handsomest guy alive, but he had a boyish charm. His teeth and eyes sparkled when he smiled because he was so tan. He gave me reason for hope anyway. Guys did still notice me.

*   *   *   *   *   *

Janie was shopping when I stopped at the grocery store. She didn't act too anxious to talk to me and avoided looking me in the eye.

"Hi, Jane, what's wrong?" I asked. "Did I do something?"

"No," she said. "I didn't really want to tell you, but Brad and I are letting Jake stay with us until he finds another place."

My pulse was beating in my temples, all of the sudden, so hard it was going to give me a headache. "Did he move all of his sporting equipment in too?" I asked bitterly.

"Yes." She answered. "Does that bother you?"

"Oh, hell no, Jane," I answered. "When we split, he didn't want any of our second hand, broken down, furniture. It wasn't worth moving. All of his money went into guns and fishing equipment. That's all he's ever worried about, and when he left that's what he took."

"Well, don't be mad at us." She said.

"I'm not." I said, and walked away to get my groceries, and to cool down a little. Before I left the store, I turned to her…

"I really don't care, Jane. He's been your brother for nine years now. Your kids love Uncle Jake. My kids love him too. You'll get along just fine. He doesn't have to be faithful to you." I thought about it for a minute and broke out laughing. Janie just stood there looking puzzled. "Come to think of it, he didn't have to be faithful to me either."

*   *   *   *   *   *

My little tikes' were all in school full days now. The school bus from Oregon picked them up early and brought them home late. I could now look for employment. Madison had lots of jobs if you wanted to work.

Right off, Kathy's ask me to tend the bar a few nights a week. Being around people my own age was a welcome change, but I had to know…

"Did Donald put you up to this?" I asked.

"Naw," they denied any conspiracy, "he wouldn't do that."

"Like heck he wouldn't." I said. "He's been trying to get me to go out with him for a long time."

"Why don't you?" they asked.

"I'm not ready to go out with anyone, yet." I explained.

My job at the news agency during the day and tending bar three nights a week wore me out, but I had no choice. Jake had done his homework well. He moved from Madison to the Chicago area. Cook County, Illinois has a reciprocal agreement with Wisconsin, which means they won't go after their residents for child support.

Rachel, an artistic friend of mine from the beach, did photo coloring for two photography studios on State Street in Madison. She called me one evening.

"Sarah, have you ever worked with negatives?" She asked.

"Never even gave it any thought." I answered honestly.

"Hey," she said. "It pays better than bundling newspapers and you can work at home. My boss lady asked me if I knew anyone and I immediately thought of you."

"It sounds like something I might like. Besides Cyle and Arron have been having a lot of ear trouble lately. When that happens, I miss work, which I can't afford to do." I admitted. "Working at home would solve that problem. Please, find out what you can about it."

The next night she called back. "Sarah, the boss says she'll teach you the process. As artistic as you are, it won't take you long to learn. Don't tell her this, but, the other studio I work for, will also send you work once you get started."

"I'd have to work nights at it for a while." I said. "I can't make it without my paycheck."

"That's fine with her." Rachel said. "She'll teach you at her house in the evening."

"Okay, I'll call her. Give me her number." I wrote it down. "Thanks, Rachel, for thinking of me."

Within two weeks I was able to quit at the agency. Finally I'd be home for the kids once in a while. They were growing up way to fast. My tomboy, Puddin, was so pretty with her big blue eyes and long blonde hair. Cyle and Arron, never gave their sister a minute of peace. If they did, she picked on them.

*   *   *   *   *   *

Jake came occasionally to take the kids for a week end of fun. He would call ahead to see if it was all right. I knew how much they missed him in their lives, so I never refused to let them go. He would drive up in his big, shinny, convertible, with the top down, his fancy pair of 'Grey Ghost' hunting dogs in the back seat, and some bleached blonde flossie in the front. After two days of some fancy motel or resort, where he gave them whatever they wanted, they had to return home to the old lady who most of the time had to say 'no'. He gave them a taste of the good life and made me look like an Ogre.

I finally started seeing Donald. He was at the house often and the kids seemed to like him. He played ball every Sunday with Kathy's team so we still followed the team. His mode of transportation was a pick up truck for which he had just purchased a big camper that slept six.

"Let's not work this week end." Don said. "We can take the kids along and try out the new camper"

Before long we were camping almost every week end and our drinking got worse. Once we parked somewhere, we didn't have to worry about driving under the influence. When we had too much to drink, we could crawl in and pass out.

"Where we going this week?" I asked.

"Who knows? We'll just start driving, wherever the road goes is where we'll go." Once in a great while we'd have a destination in mind, but not often.

"Lets go to Werley this time," Don said, "I found a place where I can get the pine trees you have been wanting to plant on your land. It's the opening of trout season, and the boys can go fishing while we plant trees.

When Jake and I had owned the bar, Mom purchased the property acrossed the road, all the way down to the Big Green trout stream, and gave it to me as a birthday gift. I held onto this when we sold the bar. It had a large cement platform that used to be part of the railroad depot. It was the perfect place to park the camper where there was no mud.

We had a few drinks before we reached Fennimore.

"Let's stop and say "Hi" to your Mom before we go down to Werley." Don said. "We won't stay long, we have to set up camp before someone else gets there. The banks will be full of campers this week end."

"Oh look," I remarked. "Jane and Brad are at Mom's."

Their girl's came running out to meet us and all six of the kids took off down the sidewalk so Don and I walked in the kitchen door.

Jane came around the corner from the living room and she was mad. She got right in my face.

"Mom and I were having a good visit. Why did you have to show up?" Jane barked.

I could tell she had one Martini too many. Maybe I had too. I hauled off and slapped her face. Her head hit the side of Mom's refrigerator and she slid down to the floor. Everyone hurried around to get her up and sitting in a chair. She had a large goose egg on the side of her head. Otherwise, she was fine.

"What in the world happened, Sarah?" Mom asked.

"I don't know, Mom." I said. "When she came charging at me for something, I didn't realize I had done, I just seen red. I sure didn't mean to hurt her or upset anyone's plans. We just stopped to say hello on our way camping and if she's okay we're going to leave."

"We'll put some ice on her forehead. I think she'll be all right." Mom assured us, even though she was visibly shaken.

"I'm sorry, Mom," I apologized, "next time I'd better call first." We walked out, called the kids from their fun, and drove off to Werley.

*   *   *   *   *   *

"You draw a lot, Sarah." Don said. "Can you draw house plans?"

"I never tried," I answered, "but I know the basics. My Dad used to work from blueprints, and he explained to me how they work."

"Why don't you come up with a way to enlarge this house?" He suggested. "My house is fine, but the lot is so small there's no way to add on. This place has a large, double lot with lots of room to expand the house and build a garage."

"But, I only rent here." I reminded him.

"I'll bet your landlord would sell." Don replied. "He's an old man."

"Have you forgotten something?" I asked. "We're not even married."

"Oh," he winked at me before he continued, "I was going to ask you if you wanted to drop the kids off at your Mom's this week end and you and I could drive down to Dubuque, Iowa and take care of that little detail."

"That's an original way to propose," I laughed, "but I accept. This time getting the camper loaded will be with a purpose, and it will be the first time I've ever loaded dress clothes."

Don bought several bottles of booze and mix. We found a place out in the boonies, in the river bottoms, by Dubuque, and got completely wasted. Next morning Don stepped out of the camper and jumped right back in, before he cracked up laughing.

"What in the world is so funny?" I asked.

"This must be the partying place. We're not alone." He motioned for me to look outside.

"Oh, my God!" There was a naked man stretched out on his back over the hood of a big black car, holding a guitar, sleeping. Two other people, one guy and one girl, were passed out in the car, dressed just like the guitar player.

"You mixing, or me?" He asked.

"I will." I said. We started drinking again while getting dressed to be married.

When I sobered up the next morning, I could vaguely remember climbing all the stairs of the historic old court house in down town Dubuque, asking the office personnel to be our witnesses, and saying I do. The paper laying on the table of the camper proved I was now Sarah...no, Mrs. Donald K. Victor.

*   *   *   *   *   *

Late in the fall, after the kids were back in school...

"I'm going into partnership with Ray," Don announced as he opened the refrigerator to grab a beer. Ray was a drinking buddy of ours, from Oregon, who had owned a tree trimming business for years.

"What's that going to cost, money and time wise?" I asked.

"Not too much money, but I'll have to purchase a couple of chain saws and some bull ropes and a few small items, for now." He said. "The rest can be added as I need it. Ray has all the big equipment, the cherry picker, trucks and the permits. He mostly needs the help. I'll be working evenings and some Saturdays and Sundays. Ray even mentioned, that you might be interested in helping later on."

"Me, what could I do?" I asked.

"Ray thought if you worked with us for a while and learned the ropes," he explained, "you could go out and bid the jobs for us."

"Is there that much tree cutting to do?" I asked.

"Thanks to the Dutch Elm Beetle there's more than enough." He said. "You know all the beautiful elms in Madison? Well, they're trying to save them with insecticides and other methods, but so far nothing has worked. They not only have to be cut, if they mark them, but the wood has to be burned at designated burning sites to stop the spread of the beetles."

"Are you going to want me to pack you a second lunch, or will you grab something to eat on the run?"

"I'd eat out." He said. "I probably will be late, most nights, so you can get in some extra work time."

"Gee, thanks." I said. I knew where Ray and his crew end up every night after work.

*   *   *   *   *   *

Don had been a Green Beret. A Sargent, no less. He liked to shout orders, and discipline was a must. You know, a place for everything, and everything in place. Some of his rules were downright maddening ..."Only four squares per call." We all knew what he meant, and he seemed to have ways of knowing if any of us had used more. He wasn't beyond walking right in on the boys.

Cyle stomped out of the bathroom one day. "Can't a guy have no parvacy." We all giggled at his mispronouncing the word, but we understood why he was mad.

Don had few inhibitions when it came to sex. With enough booze, there were none. Our love making was on the wild side but what the heck ... we were young.

We bought the house. I drew up the plans and we increased the size of the house, times four. We added a second story and even put in a spiral staircase. By the time we built the garage it was two stories high too, to accommodate the camper and all the new tree cutting equipment.

*   *   *   *   *   *

Marilyn, a girl who worked at one of the two photography studios I worked for, started coming out to our house on a regular bases. The kids loved her and she fell head over heels for a young fellow, Arnie, who not only worked with Don at his day job but also helped with the tree work. He asked her to marry him. Of course, she accepted.

"Will you and Don stand up for us?" She asked.

"Sure, Mar, you guys are like family." I answered. "You want another drink?"

"Of course." She answered, then suggested, "Let's you and I go looking for dresses, Sarah."

"Sounds like something we can do without the guys." I said. "That'll be different. They'll be working with Ray for the next few days anyhow. I've bid on enough trees to keep them busy for some time." Then I asked, "How about we go after you finish work tomorrow? I'll feed the kids early."

"It's a date." She accepted, happily.

We had been to several bridal shops. Mar had tried on so many dresses she should have been exhausted, but she wasn't. She was hyped up on adrenaline.

"One more shop, then we'll stop for the day." She said. "I like the dress we found for you, Sarah."

"I do too," I agreed, "but to tell you the truth, a drink would taste good right now."

"It would at that." She admitted. "Let's get something really good on the way home so the guys can relax too."

Marilyn and Arnie liked to drink almost as much as we did, but she was naive if she thought they wouldn't be relaxed when they came home. She found her wedding dress at the next shop, but it needed minor alterations.

"You need to take this seam in a quarter of an inch and adjust the darts for your big boobs."

"Can you do that for me?" She asked.

"Sure," I volunteered, "Would be no problem at all."

The shop owner overheard me and asked, "Would you be interested in doing alterations for my shop?"

"Only if I can do them at home on my own machine." I answered.

Arnie and Marilyn were married on a rainy day and we all got soaked.

For the next two years I was retouching negatives, not only doing alterations, but actually making wedding attire, helping out with the tree cutting, and raising my family. The kids even went along and helped with the tree work. They fed the chipper, coiled ropes, and picked up the equipment. We hadn't tended the bar in a long time accept occasionally when Kathy's had an emergency. Camping ground to a halt as we were too busy working, and the camper was used to haul around chain saws.

"Let's knock off early tonight and go out on the town, The Regents' are playing at the 'Joker'. We'll eat first and go dancing," Don said. "Arnie and Marilyn were coming along too. Even being pregnant, she still loves to dance."

I thought to myself. Don could sometimes be so insensitive. The kids have been working their little fannies off for him and he seldom gives them a thought. We get a night on the town and they get…nothing.

"I'm running to the store for sodas for the rest of your crew." I said coldly. "I ordered two large pizzas from Madison for them and the sitter. You and I might be workaholic, but they're still kids, and they deserve a little credit."

*   *   *   *   *   *

After several good snowfalls the winter of sixty-nine, Donald introduced us to snowmobiling. With a dog sled type of sleigh to pull behind, the kids could go along with us …sometimes. The trails around Madison went from one bar to another so there was a lot of drinking. Way too much drinking. If I was too busy and didn't go, Don would go alone. His running got increasingly worse for about two years. He was staying out later and later. Sometimes he forgot to come home at all. Giving up on my second marriage was tearing me to pieces, but the bad turned ugly.

"Enough is enough, Don." I confronted him. "I've been down this road before. Tonight you don't even have to worry about coming home. I've had my fill of this game you're playing."

"I haven't been doing anything except drinking with the guys, Sarah." He protested.

"Ya, right." I held up a small jar in which I had saved two little black critters I found in our bed after his last excursion. "And which one of them gave you these?"

Chapter Ten

For a couple of days I'd had no contact with Ilka. Our little world was filled with rain, rain, rain, umbrellas, and more rain. Rain and fast food. What I wouldn't give for a plain, old peanut butter sandwich and a cold glass of milk.

There was a knock on the door. I opened it to find the owner of the motel.

"Hi, Colleen, what are you doing out in the rain?" I asked.

"I come bearing a message from my leader." She laughed. "Ilka says she'll be here at six to take you two out of here for a while. She wants to get you something besides fast food."

"You mean there is something else?" I asked.

"You've cooked long enough," she said, "to know it's not all burgers and fries."

"Bless that Ilka." I sighed, "I don't know what I'd do without her."

"She's right on the top of my list, too." Colleen agreed.

"Thanks for bringing me some good news." I said. "We'll get our noses polished a little, before six, not that it will help this face of mine."

"At least most of the swelling has gone down." She couldn't hide looking at my mutilation.

Ilka got there right on time. The rain had turned into a mist, so we made it to the car without getting drenched.

"Hi, Ilky." Bobby greeted her as he climbed in. "You got a nice car."

"Hi, Sweetie," she said. "Slide on over here next to Ilka, so Mommy's got room."

"Na Doo," I said.

"Na Doo, yourself," she answered. "You should be more than ready for a change of scenery by now. How would you like to go for a swim?"

"Yippee," shouted Bobby as he jumped up and down.

"Whoa there, tiger." I put my arm around him to settle him down. "Where's the pool?" I asked.

"The Lodge opens their pool to the public during the week. I just like to go out and soak in the Jacuzzi," she said, "but I thought you two might enjoy the pool."

"Let's go, let's go." Bobby couldn't contain his excitement.

"We don't have suits, Ilka." I reminded her.

"Don't worry. They have extra suits there." She said. "I just wear shorts and a T shirt. For the whirlpool that's all that's necessary. If we go during the supper hour, there'll be no one in the pool. We can eat later."

"This is a great idea." I said. "The Jacuzzi might whirl away some of my aches and pains."

"It always makes me feel good." She said. "It's amazing how light I am when I'm in the water."

She pulled into the lodge and we found suits at the desk. While we were changing, she showed me the scars from her mastectomy. It made any that Carl had given me seem insignificant.

"Bobby, you can play in the pool. Ilka and I are going to sit in the whirlpool. You be good. I'm watching you." I warned with a fake scowl.

We eased our way into the hot swirling water. The hot steamy air was saturated with the smell of chlorine.

"Oh, my, that feels good." I said. After I sat, my legs just kind of floated with the fast-moving water.

"Now I feel as light as you." Ilka joked. "Isn't this great? Say, you never told me how you came out at your hearing the other day. How did it turn out?"

"It was only to establish temporary support and set some ground rules. The support is barely enough to buy a few groceries." I shrugged my shoulders. "I got a doe last deer season. The judge said an officer would go with me to pick up my venison after I find a place to live. That will help. Carl is to have Bobby every other week end, starting this coming Saturday, and I'm not looking forward to him going. He also told Carl not to take Bobby to bars or be drinking when Bobby's is with him. What a joke. That's the only place Carl ever goes."

"At least he's been warned not too." Ilka said. "Did the judge say anything about your wounds?"

"Oh, yes." I chuckled. "When he was almost finished, the judge said…

"Mr. Regent," I said, trying to mock the judge, "if you ever lay another hand on your wife or child, and I see you back in my court for that, you'll be doing time."

"I'll bet Carl loved that." She giggled.

"Not at all." I said. "He whispered, 'Bitch' to me when we left the courtroom, after he was sure the judge couldn't hear him."

"Sounds like something he'd do." Ilka said.

"Then the strangest thing happened." I told her. "Pidge drove by as I was leaving the courthouse. She had to have seen me, but when I waved, she never waved back." I shrugged my shoulders. "Maybe she didn't see me."

"How are you doing with your memories?" She asked. "Is it helping you to remember you're past? You seem a lot more relaxed."

"So far, so good." I said. "I've cried and laughed my way through a lot of years already. The one thing I've noticed is that one memory leads to another, just like the events happened in life. It's almost like my life was planned out and all I had to do was follow the path."

"You don't think you had any choices?" She asked.

"Oh, I had choices," I said, "but it's like even the choices were part of the plan. Anyhow, Ilka, I'm not going to cry any more about water already over the dam. When I was younger, a lot of my choices were made because of my over active hormones, and wanting someone to drink with. That part of my life should be behind me now."

She acted surprised. "You don't want another man in your life?"

"Hell no!" I said. "If there ever was another one, it would be a one night stand. You know. The way men use women. Turn about is fair play. Don't you think?" I laid my head back and peeked over at Bobby. He was sure enjoying himself. Climb out, jump in. Climb out, jump back in. He looks so cute in the swimming trunks. He may be six now, but I think he'll always have a size two butt. "Have you ever seen crabs?" I asked her.

"Which kind?" She laughed.

"The nasty little black ones."

"When I lived in war torn Germany as a kid, we saw just about everything. Roaches, crabs, bedbugs. Why did you ask about crabs?" She laughed.

"That was my going away present from my second husband. Work your butt off to make ends meet and get crabs for all your trouble." I motioned for Bobby.

"Bobby, come over and try the Jacuzzi."

He climbed out of the pool and ran over. He never walks. He eased himself into the hot water slowly, then right back out again.

"I'd rather swim, Mommy," he said, "but I'm getting hungry."

"I am too." Ilka agreed. "Let's go get us some food. What is everyone hungry for?"

"Blueberry pancakes." Bobby said as he licked his lips.

"The one thing that sounds good to me is a hot roasted beef sandwich, with lots of mashed potatoes and gravy." I answered.

I never heard it called that, but I know where we can get both those things."

"That was another old memory." I said

"I should have known that." She came back.

We went to the Truck plaza and ate our fill of good solid food, then headed back to the motel.

"We sure enjoyed tonight, Ilka. Thanks for taking us." I said.

Bobby, who was standing on the seat between us, reached over and gave her a big wet kiss on the cheek. "Thanks, Ilky."

"You're welcome, Sweetie." She said. "It was nice having company. I usually have to go alone. You seem to be in better spirits now, Sarah. Whatever you're doing seems to be working."

As we got out of the car, we both thanked her again and then unlocked the door to our tiny little room. Bobby was asleep in no time. I wasn't tired so my thoughts drifted back again...

*   *   *   *   *   *

My skin crawls every time I think about sleeping in the same bed with those crabs. Only after days of scrubbing, disinfecting, and using goodly amounts of 'Blue Ointment' on my body was I able to feel clean again. I must have changed bedding and disinfected the mattress a dozen times.

Looking into the light I had to use for retouching negatives had been really bothering my eyes lately. I didn't want to leave anyone in a bind, but the studios were using mostly colored film now, so black and white negatives were on their way out anyhow. It was a good time to get rid of another aggravation, so I dropped the studios. The lord knows I wouldn't be cutting trees with Don, so my work load dropped enormously. Sewing might even be enjoyable without all the other pressure.

Nancy Regent, Laurie's friend and Carl and Margaret's daughter, was standing, looking out of our dining room window, while I sat there sewing.

"Our house sits so much higher than yours." She said. "You know we can look right down into your dining room from the picture window in our living room, in fact from any window on this side of our house."

"You shouldn't do that. That's window peeking, you know." I told her, thinking back to all of the window peeking during World War II.

"At night when your lights are all on, it's hard not to." She persisted.

"Well," I huffed. "I'm going to have to remember to draw my drapes at night."

"That'll spoil all of my fun." She quipped.

"Big deal, you little twerp." I shot back.

I liked Nancy, although I didn't trust her too far if there was money laying around. She had a very pretty face, even with freckles, long brown hair, and azure blue eyes. It's a combination you don't see too often. She played drums and sometimes sat in with her folk's band. She was one of the Regent's five girls. The others were Peggy, Brandy, Brenda and Holly. They ranged in age from Peg, who was a senior in high school to Holly, just a toddler of two. Peg had moved out of her folk's house, and lived with her grandparents, farther up the beach. She couldn't take any more of her folk's constant bickering and drinking. I didn't know Brandy and Brenda too well. They were kind of reserved and didn't hang around when their mom and I were drinking. Little Holly was always under foot.

Margaret and I had gotten to be good friends. Maggie, as I called her, also sewed a lot for her girls so we had that in common. Don had always known that I went over to Maggie's for coffee or vice-versa, but he didn't know how much we drank together that wasn't coffee. The Beehive hairdo was popular, so I usually styled her hair before a gig.

"Hey, Maggie," I said one day. "I have lots of material left over from bridesmaids' dresses. Most of the pieces are large enough to make dresses for the girls for church or communion or whatever. You're welcome to it. After sewing for weddings as long as I have, it gets to be nothing but litter."

"Sure," she replied, while mixing us a highball. "I've seen most of the dresses and the material is gorgeous, but don't you want it for Laurie?"

I started laughing. "I can hardly get her into a skirt for school. She'd never get into a fancy dress. Her brothers tease her when she dresses like a girl."

"She is kind of a tomboy, isn't she?" Maggie replied.

"Like mother, like daughter." I said.

Ratting her hair took time. She wanted it as high as possible. Taking the last swallow of my drink, I savored the taste and listened to the ice tinkling in my empty glass, wondering if she would take the hint and offer to refresh it.

"You don't dress up very often, Sarah." She said. "How come? You're a pretty woman."

"I'm a busy woman." I said. "When I sewed all day and then went out cutting trees, there wasn't much energy left to dress up and go out. We usually just found a place we could stop and drink in our work clothes." I patted her hair softly. "Is that the way you like it? It looks good to me. A little hair spray, and you'll be done."

She held the hand mirror up where she could admire herself. "Looks great, Sarah. But it always does. You know just how I like it. Now that Don's gone, why don't you get dolled up and go out with Carl and me some night?" She wasn't going to let it rest.

"Please!" I pleaded. "For right now I just like hanging around the house in my beaters. A couple of the married men from the beach have already been giving me goggle eyes. And, don't ask, I'm not telling you who they are." I held both hands out with palms toward her to ward off any more questions. "They may think I'm the merry divorcee, but getting involved with a married man isn't what I need right now." I rolled my eyes. "And, yes I'll have another."

* * * * * *

Arron was driving now. I'd bought him his first car and the boys were gone more than they were home. I knew the kids and I weren't as close as we had been. I guessed it was just a natural part of their growing up, and didn't realize how wide the rift was getting. Nor did I realize how my drinking was alienating them.

"Mom, phone call!" Arron called to me.

You could have knocked me over. It was the manager of one of the major department stores in Madison. He wanted me to come in and talk to him about

103

making custom slip covers for the store. It seems like my boss lady from the bridal shop had been talking me up to some friends. I went the following day and came home with an offer of a contract. If I proved I could handle it, and I did. It was lucrative enough for me to order a brand new, sixty-nine, cherry red, one ton, Chevrolet Chassis. Then I had a flat bed installed and added side racks, a canvas top, and side curtains for bad weather days. Laurie helped me move the furniture. It gave her some hard earned money to play with, and the two of us worked well together.

My patience was running short for temperamental brides. Every Two-Ton-Tessie was sure I could get her into a size ten. I gave up the ladies in favor of furniture. Couches and chairs don't give you any lip.

During a break, with a cup of joe and a smoke, the phone rang.

"Sarah's Sewing Service," I answered.

"Waa…Oh, Hi, Sarah, it's Carl. I never heard you answer your phone before. You sound very business like."

"It is a business." I said. "What's up?"

He hesitated for a minute, then said, "Could you meet me after work for a drink?"

Now it was my turn to falter. "Um …What time is after work? I don't have regular hours."

"Could you make it at three-thirty, at the 'Hide Out', on the beltline?"

"Sure, I guess." I was leery. "Is anything wrong?"

"There's not too much right lately." He said.

I'd never heard him talk on the phone. His voice was soft and sexy. I was starting to wonder about his call now. Was he like all the other married men? Margaret and I hadn't seen each other for some time except glimpsing each other acrossed the road. When I took on this new job, I decided to cool it on drinking.

"I guess I can, Carl." I answered him finally, still a little puzzled.

Hanging up the phone, I returned to work, and tried to think of something to make the kids for supper.

After an hour my work on the latest piece was completed, so I jumped in the shower. Maybe I should call and leave a message for Carl that I couldn't make it, after all. Instead I got busy and made a hamburger casserole, the kids could warm up when they got home. Should I go, or not? Maybe he just needs a friend to talk too. Maybe he has something completely different on his mind. Maybe he has exactly what I think he does on his mind. What to do? What to do? I'll never know if I don't go. I put the casserole away, ran a comb through my hair, grabbed my purse, and walked out the door.

*   *   *   *   *   *

Carl waved to me from the back end of the bar, as I walked through the entrance. The stench of stale beer filled my senses. Has it been that long since I noticed how bad most bars smell? It has been a while since I've been in one. How soon we forget.

"Hi, Sarah, glad you could make it." Carl said as he motioned me to sit on the next stool.

"That's the nice thing about being my own boss." I said. "I can set my own hours, as long as I get my work done on time."

"I always admired you for that. I've watched you go through two divorces, and you always seem to come out on top." Then he added. "You haven't been around our place much lately."

"To tell you the truth, I haven't been out of the house much except to deliver or pick up furniture. The drinking was taking time from my work and the kids."

"Sometimes I watch you working at night from my recliner. Margaret thinks I'm sleeping. It's easier than fighting with her, and it's much more pleasant watching you."

The drapes. I'd forgotten, but I didn't have anything to hide. All I did was work.

"Why are you telling me this?" I asked. That was a stupid question. From Carl's demeanor, his intentions were coming crossed loud and clear, and it was making me a little uncomfortable.

The bartender nodded in my direction.

"I'll have a Manhattan, brandy Manhattan." I said.

Carl said, "Let me get that."

He laid down a bill and put his hand over mine on the bar. My body was quivering from my toenails to earlobes. Small pangs of guilt kept creeping in, but this was exciting. After all the times my spouses had cheated on me, maybe now I can find out their motivation.

His hand felt warm and his touch sent wild vibrations running through me.

"I've wanted to know you better, but you were always so tight with Margaret. Since her drinking has gotten worse, you don't even come over."

"We both drank way too much. I didn't realize it was such a problem for her." That was a lie. I knew she had really gone off the deep end, but I was fishing for more information.

"She always drank more after you left." He said. "Last week she fell off the stage when we played at the 'Joker'."

"Did she get hurt?" I asked

"Well, she broke her glasses and skinned her nose. She landed straddling a chair. If she hadn't had so much to drink, it would have hurt her pride more than anything." He laughed. "The crowd got mooned. They received more entertainment than they paid for."

"You didn't answer my question earlier." I repeated the question. "Why are you telling me all of this?"

"Margaret will be getting papers, if not today, then tomorrow." He said. "You and Don are having problems too, huh. At least I've heard rumors."

He was playing dumb. He had to know Don was gone, with Nancy being at our house all the time and Maggie knowing all the beach gossip. "They aren't just rumors, and its past tense. Don left two months ago." Then I asked, "are you leaving the beach?"

"I have no doubt they'll let her have the house, with four girls still at home." He said. "How about you, are you leaving or staying?"

"I'm sure not staying." I said abruptly. "I made an offer on a house, south of Oregon. The answer will be coming next week. The kids need to stay in the same school district. They're all so close to graduating."

"Right, they've all been through enough without having to change schools." He agreed. "Are you real upset about the divorce?"

"Not anymore. When Don first started chasing, I was devastated." I said. "It seems like one-sided love is my lot in life."

He made a circular motion to the bartender to refill our drinks.

As the night and the drinks progressed the cozier we got. It was good to have someone paying attention to me for a change. Although he had ulterior motives, I didn't care. My own motives weren't so innocent any more either.

The balding, red faced bartender knew we were cheaters. It comes with the territory. He kept our drinks full and left us alone otherwise.

Carl asked, "Do you have to be home at any certain time?"

"No, I left supper for the kids." I answered. "None of mine are babies any more."

"You want to go some place?" He asked. "We can get a bite to eat. Maybe even find a place to dance."

"Sounds good." I said. "I want to call home first, though."

"Leave your truck here?" He asked, when I returned from the phone.

"Not here," I answered, "everyone knows my truck. I'll leave it at the truck oasis down the road."

"I'll follow you there," he said, then drained his glass.

Finishing my drink, I left the bar, knowing he would wait a few minutes and follow. My head felt light, not tipsy. This was an unfamiliar role for me. I knew what Carl had on his mind and I didn't care. He was an attractive, sexy, man. After my experience with Ron Reagan and two dandy husbands, maybe it's my turn to cheat. It made me tingle all over with anticipation. I was getting excited for the first time in a long time.

I couldn't say I hadn't noticed Carl before, but loyalty, for me, was a part of friendship, so my mind didn't stray to my friend's husband. Tonight their marriage was as good as over.

"Where to?" I asked as I closed the car door.

"Let's just ride around and talk until we find somewhere inviting." He suggested.

We drove around the outskirts of Madison and ended up in Sun Prairie. The steak house was dark inside with only candles for light, and soft romantic music filled the air. We found a booth in a back corner. I slide in first and Carl beside me. The feel of his body so close was sending shock waves through mine. I could smell his aftershave. It had been months since the sweet overpowering smell of a man had broken down my inhibitions.

He slid his arm around my waist and nuzzled my neck while whispering naughty things in my ear.

We sipped Manhattans throughout ordering and eating our meal. The melt in your mouth fillet we shared took second place to the magic going on between us. Then he stood, still holding my hand, letting me know without words that I was to follow him…to the dance floor. He was a smooth dancer. We danced close, two bodies moving as one. His touch was setting me on fire. I was beyond caring where the touch was. It wasn't the drinks that were making my head spin with intoxication. When the dance ended, we started for the table.

"Excuse me for a minute." I said, and then headed for the ladies room.

Maybe some cool water on my face might erase any sign of the heat running through my body. I had forgotten this part. How good it feels to be desired, and to return the feelings. The club also had motel accommodations. When I returned to our table, Carl slipped the key to room number four into my hand. He had also gotten a bottle of champagne, not that we needed it.

My feet didn't touch the floor as we walked to the room. He was treating me like a queen, and I was enjoying every second of it. Any guilt I might have felt had taken flight like a feather in a hurricane. The room also had soft candle light, and was warm enough to be comfy without the restriction of clothing. Not misinterpreting the silent message between us, we were ready.

Chapter Eleven

For the next two months Carl and I saw each other every chance we had, secretly at first. The kids all suspected something was going on. I was gone more than usual. Margaret got her papers the day after our first night together. It was difficult for me to act surprised when I heard the news. Carl moved to a small efficiency apartment, only three miles from the house I was buying. He laughed when I first took him to see the house.

"I know this house well. My folks lived here when all five of us kids were still at home. That window was our escape route when us boys were sent upstairs for punishment." He pointed to the window above the back door. My darling sister got away with murder, while my three brothers and I took the blame." He sounded bitter. "There was an outhouse back then. Mom would lock Dad in it when he came home with a snoot full. I have many memories of this house. In fact, most of your neighbors are relatives of mine."

"Maybe you can talk to them." I said. "I have to find out where the dump is. I think I'll need it."

"When do you get possession?" He asked.

"Not until January first," I said, "but they'll be all moved out by the end of November. I can start cleaning then. The old garage on the back of the house is full of old freezers, rotten lumber and bag after bag of trash. No telling what's living in there. I'll need to set out traps and some poison."

"Will I be allowed to help you?" He asked.

"The kids won't be down here until I move in." I explained. "I guess we can get away with it."

"Good," he said, "because it looks like your going to need help."

When the time came, we backed my truck up to a window and started shoveling. Old broken linoleum got ripped up and thrown. Anything we could pull loose got thrown away.

Two days after Christmas, I signed the papers. The house needed so much more to be done yet, but it was clean enough to live in. I'd get more accomplished if I was there full time. The kids and I moved our furniture and left what belonged to Don. The last thing we moved from Don's house was the Christmas tree. We sat it out by the road, decorations and all, locked the doors, and drove away.

* * * * * *

Carl came out often after we moved, not only to help me with the repairs, but just to spend time with me and the kids. He took Cyle target practicing, rabbit hunting and fishing. We also went out to eat quite often. My children were getting used to him being around, but told me frequently, they didn't like him, and never had. I couldn't understand. He did so much with them. I quizzed them as to why they felt that way.

"Mom, you just don't know what kind of creep Carl really is. You must not. You and him are always so lovey, dovey." Laurie said. "I've seen the way he treated his own kids."

"I don't like you calling him a creep." I said. "I'm sorry that's the way you feel. He's been good to all of you, and to me."

Arron said, "Don't worry about me, Mom. I'll be graduating in June and I'll be outta here. Bart and I are getting an apartment." Bart had been his best friend since second grade.

I hoped he was getting an apartment because he wanted to, not because of Carl being around.

"Sure, that's fine for you," Cyle shrugged, "I still have to stay here another year."

He wanted to leave too? I thought. Something's rotten in Denmark.

"Wait a minute kids." I asked. "Is this because of Carl, or me, or has your Dad been putting in his two-cents worth?"

"Sure, Dad's told us what he thinks of Carl." Laurie said, wrinkling her nose and pinching it with her thumb and forefinger. "You know, Mom, Dad did play ball with Carl, and Don. You know he's going to voice his opinion."

I'd even forgotten they all played ball together when we first came to the area. The thought made me shutter and I thought to myself, "Little Peyton Place."

*   *   *   *   *   *

During the last year on the 'Beach', when the tree equipment was still around, I had gotten Laurie a Palomino horse. I made a deal with the horse man. Laurie and I would clean out several trees from his house yard in trade for the horse. The work took the two of us the better part of a week. We had a pasture lined up to put her in. As part of the deal the mare was to be bred when we got her. Boy, was she. Nugget, as Laurie named her, got bigger than any other horse I'd ever seen.

During a thunderstorm, in the fall, she dropped twin fouls. We had to go and bury them. Two days later the pasture owner called. They had found a third foul. She had only been rough broke anyhow and after this she turned wild. We knew moving her would be impossible. We'd never get her into a truck. The boys decided to walk her the eight miles, on back roads. We took refreshments for both boys and horse, once an hour. The stable and a small corral were ready for her. Possibly the close confinement and being around people would settle her down.

Carl's cousin, who farmed a half a mile north on highway ten, said we could clean the loose hay out of his barn before he refilled it. We loaded two truckloads and made a huge haystack in the corner of her corral.

Arron's present girlfriend had been around horses and was willing to work with Nugget. They walked her patiently in circles around the acre and a half that was my back yard. She eventually even allowed them to dress her in bridle and saddle. Letting anyone on her back was another story. I tried, only to be thrown off. It knocked the wind out of me and hurt my back. I was reluctant to let anyone else be hurt. From that day on she seldom left her haystack. Her hide glistened like gold as she ate, drank, and did what mother nature told her to do. She had won, and she knew it. I just walked on by.

* * * * * *

Over on highway ten, the next place up the hill from Carl's Aunt Flossie, was a country bar. Elly's Place was a favorite watering hole for most of the farmers. Some nights they had a two-piece band play music. On those nights, people from town would drive out and the joint really percolated. We often walked up for a nightcap.

One night as we were relaxing at Elly's, I said, "Carl, I think I'll tell the big store what they can do with their slipcovers." I took a long drink, "Today one of the customers showed me their bill from the store. You wouldn't believe what they charge people for my work. Customers go to the store and pick out material, the store orders it and send me a work order, when the material is shipped to me, I pick up the furniture and when the job is done, I deliver it. The store never sees it. Then they charge the customer three times what I get paid for my work, and the material and delivery. I do all the work and delivery, then they get paid triple for it."

"That's crazy." He agreed. "When is your contract up with them?"

"In two weeks." I smirked. "How's that for a coincidence?"

"Do you have enough to do without their work?" He asked.

"Heck yes." I said. "Since I started upholstering, I've been turning work down. Believe me. It won't be a problem."

"You'll be happier being your own boss anyway, Sarah." He replied. "You always have liked doing things your own way."

He was right. I had always appreciated being in control of what I did. I called the company and told them not to take any more orders for me to fill. I would finish what was already ordered. At the end of the two weeks, I went to the store with my final invoices and quit in person. When I confronted the boss with what, I had uncovered, he quit talking. I left the store with a clean conscience.

*   *   *   *   *   *

My divorce became final and Carl moved right in. Arron and Carl's second daughter, Brandy graduated in the same class. Arron had moved into a small house with Brad and was busy working so I seldom saw him. I guess he wanted it that way. We went to the graduation ceremony, but neither of the graduates came around to talk to us.

Carl's girls wouldn't visit. Peg graduated two years ago, was married and had a little girl, with a second baby on the way. Nancy had quit school and moved into Madison with Brandy. Only Brenda and Holly were at home with their mother. Brenda had run away twice and Carl had assisted in finding her, which only increased her hostility toward him.

Margaret would stay out drinking until bar time, then she'd go home and drink some more and dial our number. When we answered, she'd hang up. On her worst night she called us seventy times, ending just in time for breakfast. We hooked up a tape recorder and tried goading her into saying something. Finally I asked her how her psychiatrist was. She started swearing and cursing at me, but we had her on tape. Now the sheriff's office was willing to call and warn her that she could be arrested if she continued. It did continue, but we chose not to press charges for the girl's sake.

Cyle still had to go to school, but he took a job on a big farm close by for room, board and wages. He stood six-foot, three-inches, in his stocking feet and weighed one-hundred-eighty pounds. He was a good worker and the people loved him. I missed both my boys.

Carl and I tore down the old garage from the back of the house, and at the same time were tearing down a large building in Madison for the material. We planned on adding a large family room and laundry. Good, bad, or indifferent, Carl was part of my life.

"Mom, I can't live here anymore with you and Carl and your drinking," Laurie announced. "You're not going to talk me out of it." She insisted. "Just make arrangements with the school and I'll talk to Dad. I'm moving down with him and his new family."

I felt deflated. The last of my kids wanted to leave. Carl's girls wouldn't visit. Just why in hell are we building a family room

Chapter Twelve

After two days of long distance phone calls and Laurie's bratty behavior...
"The school says they'll switch your records down to Illinois," I said, "just so long as you understand that you can't hop back and forth. If they go to all this trouble, you have to stay down there a whole semester."

"I'm going for good, Mom," she snapped back.

"If that's your decision, I'll let them know. When is your Dad coming for you?" I asked.

"Friday." She said. "You can tell the school. I'll start in Illinois next Monday."

Two weeks later she called me from a pay phone collect to let me know when the semester would be over and where I should pick her up. I had written to her, at least once a day and she had written to me. Our letters stopped at the stepmother. Now she mailed her letters from school and called when she could. My calls and letters met a dead-end.

*   *   *   *   *   *

Carl's widowed Aunt Flossie, who had more than a little problem with the bottle, lived next door to us on the highway. At first she enjoyed having the horse to pet, but decided Nugget's habit of eating her grass over the fence was unforgivable. Good old Flossie hit the horse with a stick and blinded her in one eye. Then called the zoning office and reported that we didn't have enough land for an animal of Nugget's size. She was right, of course. They sent me a very official document in the mail stating; "Get rid of the horse or pay a fine of two-hundred-dollars per day."

With Nugget being so jumpy, and with only one eye, I couldn't find a buyer. I had no choice but to sell her to the fox farm. She was too dangerous to have around. But I still cried when they loaded her.

Even though my heart wasn't really in all the hard work, I was getting anxious to finish our new room. It helped, just knowing Laurie would soon be home.

When Carl walked in the door I said, "Peggy called today, Carl, she's coming down, in fact she'll be here any minute. She wanted to wait til you were home from work."

"Wonder what's up?" He said.

"I couldn't tell you." I replied. "She didn't sound mad or like there was anything wrong. Just said she wanted to talk to us. I made some cookies and the coffee's done. You want some?"

"You might as well wait a minute." He said. "She just pulled in." He was watching out of the window where I joined him.

Peg was grabbing all the paraphernalia needed when you have a small one from her car. From where I was watching I could see she was already putting on quite a few pounds with her second pregnancy. She and Rick hadn't wasted any time after getting married. Carl hadn't seen Missy since she was a baby.

They reached the door and Carl picked up Missy.

"Waa..." She screamed.

"Sorry, Dad, she is a little shy of strangers, and you are a stranger to her." Peg said.

"Don't worry about it, Peg." He handed Missy to her Mom and she quieted right down.

When everyone was comfortable, Peg said, "My kids are going to need some grandparents, Dad. Rick's parents live way up North and I can't count on Mom at all. I know Sarah about as well as I know Mom anyhow. Do you think we could at least act like family?"

I put coffee in front of Peg and a plate of cookies to maybe tempt Missy. She had been watching my every move.

"Peg," Carl said, "I've just been waiting for you girls to make the first move. I didn't want to push any of you, but you are my family and you're welcome in my life anytime."

"Thanks Dad," she smiled, "and you too, Sarah. By the way, I love your new room."

After the pressure was gone, Carl got out his guitar, played some kids tunes, and let Missy touch the guitar, carefully. She was forgetting to be shy. Peg and I talked small talk and baby talk, avoiding any mention of Margaret. They stayed for an hour and left with a promise to do it often.

"Did that make you feel any better?" I asked Carl.

"Well that's one out of five." He said. "At least it's a start. Maybe someday all of my girls will talk to me again."

Carl and I were tape-coating the drywall in our new room. The room was all done except for the finishing touches. We even installed a free standing fireplace.

"Christmas vacation will be dull this year, Carl. Last year we were cleaning this place to move in, trying to avoid the kids. I didn't know how important they were to me, til they all left. Even getting meals ready doesn't mean anything, anymore."

"Cheer up, honey, I'm still here." He said.

My mind was flashing all the reasons my kids had left, mainly ...Carl.

"Cyle is bringing a Marine recruiter down this evening." I said. "It seems he's decided to enlist. He loves all that discipline they have in the corps."

"Why's he bringing him here?" Carl asked, while refilling his coffee cup.

"I am still his mother." I bristled. "He won't be eighteen until February, so he needs my signature."

He said, "Good time for me to go to Elly's."

I thought to myself, grow up, Carl. As if you need a reason to drink.

"Are we going to be able to finish the painting before Saturday?" I asked.

"Why?" He asked, "I suppose you want it done before Laurie gets home."

"It would be nice." I said. "I'm gonna have to leave early Saturday. Laurie's map will make it easier for me to find her. I've never been to her Dad's before."

"We can probably finish tonight if the recruiter doesn't stay too late." He said. "Are you sure you don't want me to go along to Illinois?"

"No way." I answered abruptly. "Laurie and I have a lot of catching up to do. She won't talk if you're along." Then I rubbed the top of my arm and said, "Man, this sanding is giving me a sore shoulder. A day of sitting in the car, driving, will feel good."

By the time Cyle and the recruiter left, Cyle was all <u>signed,</u> and <u>sealed</u> into the Marines. The <u>delivered</u> was going to have to wait til after graduation. When he walked out the door Cyle gave me a kiss and whispered...

"Before I leave, Mom, I'll let you cut my long hair off. I know you've wanted to. They're going to shave my head anyway."

Actually I'd gotten used to it. All the boys wore shoulder length hair, bright polyester shirts and platform shoes, (Which Cyle didn't need) but it made me feel good that he had thought about me. It had been good to have him home, even for a short visit.

We wrapped up the sanding and put away all of the dry wall tools. Painting was all that was left. Carl would have to do the high ceilings. I could handle varnishing the exposed beams and woodwork. We both grabbed a paintbrush, rag and paint and climbed separate ladders. I was grateful he hadn't stayed too long at Elly's. We may be able to finish tonight.

* * * * * *

"There's the phone, Sarah," Carl said, "can you get it?"

"Sure, I'm almost done anyway." I sat down the paint can...

"Hello." I said.

"May I speak to Mr. Carl Regent?"

"Hang on. I'll get him." I replied.

Carl took the phone, placed his hand over the mouthpiece, and asked in a low voice,

"Who is it?"

"I don't know. Some woman." I answered, "Only one way to find out."

"Hello, Carl Regent here."

Carl ran his fingers through his hair nervously. I knew he only did this, when he had a problem.

"Can I call you back in a few minutes? I need to talk to my landlady."

"Give me your number. I'll get right back to you." He jotted down the number, quickly, on an envelope lying by the phone.

"Who was that?" I asked.

"Social Service. They took the girls away from Margaret." His hand ran back through his hair again. "They need to know if I have a place to keep them. She said if not, juvenile authorities will get involved and they may end up in foster homes."

"We've got enough room for two girls, Carl." I said. "My kids are almost all gone."

"Are you sure this is all right with you?" He asked. "You don't have to do this."

"I know I don't have too." I said "Of coarse, it's fine."

He called them back, made the arrangements, and took off for Madison to get the girls. I finished my varnishing, cleaned up the brushes and put things away. Then I headed for Cyle's room with fresh linen. I wasn't sure how they would like bunking together, but it would have to do.

While I waited, doubts flashed through my mind. Holly was more or less a stranger and Brenda had shown only animosity toward me. What am I letting myself in for?

When the girls walked through the door, no mother would have felt any different from what I did. My heart went out to them. They looked so small and helpless. We didn't have to worry about getting them unpacked. All they had were the clothes on their backs. I found clean underwear in Laurie's room and Carl gave them each one of his T shirts to use for a nightie. I tossed their clothes into the washer. They weren't much, but they'd have to do until Carl could get them something different.

I fixed the girls something to eat, they showered, and then we sat down to talk.

Carl said, "The neighbors called in with complaints that the girls were dirty, undernourished and were unsupervised."

"Mom wasn't home very often." Brenda said. "And when she was home, she and her boyfriends were always drinking."

Little six-year-old Holly added, "Some of those men weren't very nice."

"A good thing it's Saturday, tomorrow, girls." Carl said, trying to change the subject. "I'll take you in shopping. Sarah has to go get Laurie, so it will be just we three. How do you like that idea?"

The girls gave their dad a hug, and Brenda asked, "Are we going to live here, Dad?"

"For now, anyhow." He looked over at me with a puzzled expression. "We'll have to see."

He took them upstairs and got them settled for the night. When he came back down, he filled me in on their living conditions at Margaret's. "I can't believe we have been living so comfortably while my little girls were living in squaller. Their mother did as she pleased, and the girls had to fend for themselves. There wasn't much food in the house and the mice had taken over. The social worker said the living conditions were deplorable."

"Well, you can bet they're not sleeping right now" I said. "I know, from experience, what it's like to be yanked from one home to another in the middle of the night. That shouldn't happen to a dog."

* * * * * *

I left before daylight next morning. By the time the sun was out, I had already bypassed Chicago. Jake lived in a suburb, but the map Laurie made me showed the way very well. I stopped for directions only once, a block from the house. I needed coffee anyway. Laurie must have been watching for me. When I pulled up to the house she ran out with her bags, jumped in and said,

"Let's go, Mom, I've had enough of this." She looked so good to me and we were both ready to head for home.

She told me all about school in Illinois, her friends and about her relationship with her stepmother and her many stepbrothers and sisters. It seems Jake married into a big family. I told her all about the girls coming the night before and about Cyle enlisting. I hadn't seen too much of Arron lately so she'd have to check on him for herself. We were so busy talking that we were home before we knew it. God, it's nice to have my Puddin home.

* * * * * *

Clothes were spewed all over when we walked in the house, and Nancy was there. She hadn't been to my house since her folks had split, and never to this house.

"Hi, Nancy." I blinked. "This is a surprise."

Laurie was trying to figure out what was going on, but she said, "Hi, Nanc."

Nancy was pouting, and wouldn't answer. I'd be damned if I was going to ask why. I knew her too well.

"Sorry." Carl apologized. "Girls, get these things picked up and put away."

"Don't Laurie and I get a fashion show?" I asked.

"You really want one, Sarah?" Holly was bubbling. "I never had so many new clothes."

"Sure she does. And so do I." Laurie said. She knew how the girls were feeling, kind of at loose ends. "I'll help you put things away after you model it for us. How's that?"

After they flaunted their goods, the girls all disappeared upstairs. Nancy even gave up being mad.

"Don't pay any attention to Nancy." Carl said. "Brenda called her this morning and told her we were going shopping. She wheedled her way in on the shopping trip and was bound and determined I would buy her clothes too."

"And, did you?" I asked. I already knew the answer, from Nancy's mood.

"No, I didn't. She's the one that quit school and can't hold on to a job."

"Good." I said. "I'm proud of you." I cleared my throat. "I can't believe she didn't con you."

"Oh, she tried. She even promised to go back to school. I'm onto her, so now she's mad."

"Laurie is glad to be home." I said. "She even seems pleased that your girls are here."

"We didn't go to town until almost noon." He said. "When the girls went outside this morning, they found out each of them has a friend close by. Lisa from next door is in Holly's class. The people who own Elly's Place, have a daughter, Belinda. She is in Brenda's class.

I breathed a sigh of relief. "Anything that will make this move a little easier." I laid my head back and relaxed. The shiny, freshly varnished, beams reflected the flames in the fireplace. The smell of paint and varnish made this century old house smell brand new. Our new family room was finished just in time for our new family.

School started and time flew by. Spring was peeking her long awaited head out of every branch. We were all anticipating Cyle's graduation. His excitement for the corps had dwindled since he started seeing a young Miss from Monona. She was the first girl he had really cared for and the feelings seemed to be mutual. Cyle feared if he left, he might lose her. Is love ever easy?

Silence! Can you hear the silence? When the hassle and hurry-scurry of everyone getting off to work and school in the morning was finally over, I sat and drank my coffee in the silence…Not for long, though. I knew my work awaited me in the basement. With a full cup in my hand, I descended to my shop, turned on country music, plugged in the air compressor, and the silence disappeared.

*   *   *   *   *   *

"Dad, can I get a dog?" Brenda asked as she sat by the fire brushing her beautiful long hair.

Carl looked up from his guitar, quit playing and said, "Where the heck did that come from?"

"Well, Arron's dog is in the pen out back," she said, "Billy (Belinda) has two Dobermans that guard their living quarters, Sarah has Mousey, and Holly has Patches. I need a pet of my own."

"I don't think we need any more pets around here." Carl barked back at her.

Mousey wasn't really my cat. She had belonged to the family that lived here before us. They gave her to Lisa, the girl next door, but she kept coming back to our house. She had a litter every time she came in season. We had allowed Holly to keep one of Mousey's kittens. The kitten was three colors in big patches, thus the name. The kitten and Holly were company for each other.

I was standing at the stove, in the kitchen, where Brenda couldn't see me. I shook my head, in agreement, when I caught Carl's eye. He looked puzzled, so he came to the kitchen for coffee.

"You know," I whispered, "a pet might help her get over being so moody and obstinate all the time. Think about it."

"Okay," he said, loud enough for Brenda to hear, "we'll go to the pound Friday after work. You and the girls can meet me in town. The pound is open until five. We'll see what they have."

Brenda lit up, "I'll take care of my dog and help Sarah with the house work. I give my word."

I'd like to have a nickle, for every time I've heard that promise, I thought.

Carl was back tuning his guitar, so any further conversation was falling on deaf ears.

"You'll have to, if I'm going to have a dog in my house, Brenda," I said, as I refilled Carl's cup and sat down to have one myself.

"The fireplace really makes it cozy out here." I said. "I never had one before. I could sit and stare into the fire for hours."

"Me too," said Holly, who was sitting with crossed legs in front of the fireplace doing homework.

"You'd better move back a little, Holly," I said, "your starting to look like a marshmallow."

She grumbled, but slid back, disturbing the papers she had spread all over the floor.

"You girls wrap things up before supper." I said. "Brandy and Ike are coming down tonight for a ho-down with your Dad."

"Really? What time?" Holly squealed. "I haven't seen Brandy for ages."

"Ask your Dad." I said. "He talked to Brandy today."

"Well, Dad." Holly asked.

Carl's eyes had that far away look, which he always gets, when he tunes out everything but the music. "Huh, what?"

118

"What time are Brandy and Ike coming?" Holly repeated again.

"Oh, sorry." He said. "They'll be here about seven. They're bringing fresh donuts for a treat. I forgot to tell you, Sarah."

"That's terrific." I said. "I haven't had much time to bake lately."

"Yes, I've noticed." He said sarcastically.

I don't know if he expected me to feel guilty. I was just getting used to some free time after the boys left. His girls were extra work and my upholstery business had expanded so free time was at a premium.

Carl said, "Why don't you call up and order a pizza from the bar? I'll go pick it up when it's ready. Find out how long."

"Does everyone want mushrooms?" I asked. No answer, so I called for a large pizza with mushrooms.

"It'll be ready in thirty minutes." I told Carl.

He jumped up, put his guitar aside, and said, "I'll go now. It'll give me a chance to have a couple to relax with." He went flying out the back door.

An hour later, the girls walked up to pick up a cold pizza. Carl came home tipsy about five minutes before the company arrived.

They brought wine with them also. The two of them were perfect examples of hippy flower children. They were both good musicians. She wore her hair long and straight, had sad, doleful eyes with gobs of thick eyeliner. Their clothes came straight from the rag bag. Everything about them, including their music, was a protest. Ike was pencil slim and his jeans needed a prayer to hold them up. Nothing else seemed too. Sometimes they slipped so embarrassingly low that I had to leave the room, and I wished the girls would too.

When they finally warmed up and got going, they played a few westerns, like Rawhide and Five-Hundred-Miles. The girls and I filled in the background with sounds of wailing coyotes. We taped it so we could play it back for laughs.

Carl was already in good shape but he topped it off with a couple glasses of wine. We finally had coffee and donuts and the company left. Laurie came home from her job at the drive-in. She and the younger girls went to bed. Carl still wasn't ready to call it a night.

"Let's walk up for a nightcap." He said, though he really didn't need one. Tonight for a change I really didn't want one. When I had one of these exceptional times, no amount of booze seemed to affect me.

Coming home from Elly's he staggered from one side of the yard to the other, ran into bushes, and fell a couple of times.

"The kids all had a good time tonight, how about you?" I asked.

"Sure, I was with my family. All the girls have come back." He was slurring his words.

"To bad Arron and Cyle couldn't have been here." I said.

"Damn," he screamed, "can't you forget your boys for one night?"

"I wouldn't be much of a mother if I did." I shot back at him.

"You never miss a chance to rub my nose in the fact that I don't have a son." He was screaming, at the top of his lungs. He'd have all the neighbors awake at this rate. He grabbed my arm, swung me around and threw me at the house. When I hit the wind left me, and I had to hold on or I'd have gone to the ground. He staggered into the house. What in the world just happened? Carl had never laid a hand on me before. He was like an animal and just as strong. My puny body never stood a chance. It must have been the booze.

When I finally got my breath back, I went in and fed the fire, trying to dispel the chill and aches in my body. Carl was passed out on the bed, fully clothed. The solitude was soothing, but I turned on the radio very low. Country music allowed me to drift to another time and place. I assembled everything needed, just like Grandma did, and made several batches of cookies. I was too upset to sleep, and his suggestion, that I hadn't been fulfilling my obligation had slowly and without warning taken seed deep inside.

*   *   *   *   *   *

Brenda got her dog on Friday. He was a young, Bezengi, the barkless dog. He was small enough to scoot under all the tables in the family room, had short pointed ears and his tail curled tightly over his back. His slanted eyes, the way he washed his face, and the sounds he made, resembled more the felines in our home than any dog.

Laurie came bounding in the house after work. The dog met her and backed her to the door. She was a stranger, he was taking the role of watchdog seriously, and he never forgot. Brenda had to keep him confined in her room whenever Laurie was at home. Eventually he got it through his head that Laurie was family.

"You two want to go swimming at the high school?" Laurie asked the girls.

"Can we, Dad?" Holly squealed.

"Sure, just be home in time for supper," Carl answered. "You'd better drive careful, Laurie," he called as they ran out the door.

"Of course, I always do." Laurie flipped over her shoulder as she took the front steps all in one stride.

They piled into Laurie's little, yellow Bug. She loved her car and I knew she was a good driver. Her relentless brothers teasing had molded her into an independent, no nonsense, pert, little snippet with built in defense mechanisms.

"Your daughter has a smart mouth, you know." Carl complained.

"She's just Laurie." I said a little on the defensive side.

"She needs someone to put her in her place." He growled.

"Nobody will touch her while I still have breath in my body." My hackles were up and Carl knew it. He backed off, but I wondered what he might do if he were as drunk as he had been the other night.

* * * * * *

"Thank you, Mom." Cyle said as he admired himself in the floor length mirror. "I knew you'd be able to get the wrinkles out."

"I'm just glad you felt you could come home to get ready. I want you to know you're always welcome in my house. Just because…

"Let's not talk about him tonight, Mom. This is my graduation and I wanted you to be part of it." He looked so handsome in his cap and gown. His hair shined, and he stood so tall. He had grown into a man since he left home.

"It's a good thing the gown doesn't have to be a certain length." I said as I admired my son. "I'm so proud of everything you've done for yourself, Cyle. Some day I hope you'll understand the way I feel."

"I do, Mom." He said. "I don't understand your choice, but I know the feeling. I plan to give Julie a ring before I leave for boot camp."

All the sudden, when he said that, I remembered my Mom saying, "whichever of the boys gets married first can have my wedding rings."

"Cyle, I may have a great big surprise for you." I said. "Let's give your Grandma a call. You can tell her what you just told me."

* * * * * *

Brenda and Holly didn't want to go to the ceremony. Beings Brenda was twelve now we decided the girls would be all right alone while we were gone. It had been a beautiful day, but before we left the sky turned dark, and it looked a storm was brewing.

"Let's not go into the gymnasium, Sarah. We can see the program from out here in the entry way, and we can keep an eye on the weather." Carl said as he watched out the window.

"That suits me fine." I replied. "It's too hot in there, anyhow."

Just before the last speaker they announced there were tornado warnings out. Mother Nature cut loose, and it sounded like the roof was going off of the school. I finally got Laurie's attention. Regardless of the drenching and almost getting blown away, everyone reached their cars safely. We all headed for home, soaking wet.

When we arrived home there was no one anywhere to be seen. No kids, no cats, no dogs. The big maples looked like they were ready to snap. The house rattled so badly, I thought we were headed for Oz. We started to panic. When I checked the workshop in the basement, I could faintly hear Holly talking.

"They're down here." I shouted to Carl and Laurie.

Both girls, the cats, and two dogs, were in the root cellar listening to a portable radio. So we joined them. Back in the forty's or fifty's someone had built this room as a bomb shelter and it was virtually soundproof. It was by far the best place to be in this storm.

"I guess we didn't have to worry about you girls," Carl said, smiling with pride.

Laurie found a box to sit on and said, "It's a good thing Nugget wasn't still here, they would have had trouble getting her down the stairs, but, Mom," she added, "they forgot your goldfish."

We all laughed and it relaxed some of the tension. We made ourselves as comfortable as we could. Then it dawned on me. That was the first time Laurie had mentioned Nugget since she had returned home from her fathers, but this wasn't the time or place to talk to her about it.

*   *   *   *   *   *

Nancy came to the house one night with a man in tow, and you can believe me, I only call him a man because he was my age, not hers. They announced they were getting married and why. I had noticed she was gaining weight but never imagined she was pregnant. She was due before Peg. No amount of talking could dissuade them. It upset me more than Carl. This man was more than twice her age. I have to admit he was a good-looking fellow, but I had a feeling the beauty was only skin deep. If she had stayed in school, she would only be a junior. What was happening to our kids? One more year and Laurie will graduate, then I won't even be needed anymore. Oh sure, there's Carl's girls. But they don't listen to anything I say. I'm just here to clean up after them and cook their meals, and I'm not even sure that Carl will stick around, or if I want him too. I could end up in a year, all alone, with just my work.

One evening after work Carl suggested the two of us go into town grocery shopping. On the way home he handed me a ring box. I opened it to find an Autumn Haze Star Sapphire, set in white gold. It was beautiful

"What's this for?" I asked.

He answered my question with another question. "Don't you think it's time we make it legal?"

"You know I love you, Carl, but we've been living together for two years and you've never even mentioned marriage. Why now?" I asked.

"Social Service has been keeping tabs, you know." He said as he squinted from the bright sun and reached for his sunglasses. "They took the girls from

Margaret and gave them to us, even though we weren't married. It's not the most ideal situation."

That wasn't exactly the romantic answer I thought might be forthcoming. Now I felt like a way to appease City Hall, and to insure him and the girls a place to live. Then the thought of being all alone flashed through my head again.

"Yes." I said.

Carl said, "What does that mean?"

"Yes, I'll marry you. It was a proposal, wasn't it?" I was almost ready to laugh. This was starting to sound like 'Abbot and Costello' doing their 'who's on first' routine.

"Boy, this sure got screwed up. I'm sorry I didn't get down on my knee, but I'm driving the car you know."

That night we walked up the hill to Elly's when all was quiet on the home front. It didn't stay quiet long, and I can't tell you a lot of the details, because I got wasted. Either on the way home or after arriving there, Carl beat me until my face was all bloody. I escaped and found myself staggering toward town, drunk, hiding in the bushes at every set of car lights, for fear it was Carl. I reached Oregon all bloody, muddy, and scratched up, and found a pay phone to called Arron.

When he got to where I was he said, "Mom, what in the world are you letting this happen for? You don't need Carl in your life. Get in the car," he ordered, "We're going back to your house."

"I don't want to go there." I screamed.

I couldn't stop him, so we headed back home. When we arrived, he called Carl outside, and the two of them got into a fist fight. I panicked. I was afraid someone was going to get killed. I ran into the house and made a phone call. Then I ran back outside.

"Stop it, Arron." I managed between sobs. "Carl, cut it out. I called the police."

Arron started swearing, and I wasn't sure at whom. He let go of Carl and left before the cops showed up. He would never forgive me, I knew. He was in training, himself, to join the police force.

Our wedding day was coming soon and I was sick at heart most of the time. I didn't want to spend the rest of my life alone and I loved Carl, but could I live in constant fear of his rage simply because we had a few drinks? The bridge between Arron and I had crumbled and I had no faith at all in my own decisions.

*　*　*　*　*　*

Carl and I were married in a small church in Oregon. Only the family and a few friends were present. Arron wasn't. Cyle beamed as Julie displayed her ring, while Mom smiled with pleasure at being able to help make them happy. The minister was detained at another church so Brandy played the church organ to entertain everyone. I was terribly nervous but it gave me a chance to talk to Cyle and Julie.

"Will I get to see you before you leave?"

"I'm coming out Tuesday morning for my haircut, if it's okay, then Julie will take me to the airport."

"I forgot about that haircut. How do you like the rings, Julie?"

"I love them," she said, "and your Mom is a dear lady, Sarah."

"I always knew that. I know she's pleased that you have them. When did you go down to Fennimore?"

"We drove down last night." Cyle answered. "I called her first, in the afternoon and you know Grandma, we had to be there for supper."

"That sounds like Mom. Are you coming out to the house for the reception?" I asked.

"Sure are." He said. "Too bad Arron didn't come to the wedding."

"I don't blame him. I don't think he'll ever forgive me for that awful night."

"He won't stay mad forever, Mom." He said. "By the way, you look great today. I love the way they piled your hair in curls with the little flower buds. I'm used to seeing you with a ponytail."

"Well, touch it." I said. "I think they used two full cans of hair spray. It feels like a block of wood on my head. It's not very comfortable." Then I asked, "Could one of you let Brandy know that the minister just arrived?"

We said our vows and signed the papers. (To make it legal.) When we opened the church doors there was a downpour. Ordinarily, rain doesn't bother me, but my hairdo turned to glue.

Everyone pitched in and sat out the lunch I had prepared while I sat on the floor and let Carl pick flower buds out of a gooey mess. I had to shampoo in the middle of our reception.

Cyle left for the San Diego Marine Base. We cooled it on going to Elly's for a while and planted a big garden where the corral had been. Nugget definitely did an excellent job of fertilizing. In the fall I canned everything I could. The root cellar was full to the brim. Nancy had her baby, and her 'man' was long gone. Laurie was on the honor roll her senior year even with her job, and the other girls seem happy in their new home.

*　*　*　*　*　*

We had a successful deer hunt and I just finished putting the tools away from butchering our venison when the phone rang. I had talked to Carl at lunch time so I knew it wasn't him.

"Sarah's Sewing Service." I answered.

"Hello, is this Mrs. Regent?" The man asked.

"Yes it is." I said. "What can I do for you?"

"I hate to have to bother you, but we need the license number for the trailer." He said.

"The trailer?" I asked. What in the world is he talking about, I wondered.

"The fourteen-by-seventy mobile home," he explained, "purchased at Barry's Trailer Sales. Everything is fine. We just need this number on the papers."

"I'll have to have Mr. Regent call you back." I told him, still not knowing any more than I did before. "I don't have the papers here."

"That will be fine." He said. "Just have him call the Credit Union."

I poured myself a strong drink and sat, hoping the heartbeat in my temples and behind my eyes would go away. My blood pressure must be soaring. What secret life has he got? He is so sneaky. Lately I've picked up on the girls doing the same kind of sneaky things. I had a couple more drinks before he pulled in the drive.

He walked in, took one look at me, and said, "Got an early start today, huh?"

"You bet," I said, "and I had a reason. But first you're supposed to call the Credit Union with a license number for your trailer." I accentuated the your. This was no doing of mine.

He couldn't say anything. I had caught him with his hand in the proverbial cookie jar. He picked up the phone, pulled some papers from his billfold, and when he reached them, gave them what they needed.

After he hung up, I asked, "When did you plan to tell me about this trailer, or didn't you ever?"

"I didn't think you needed to know."

"Carl, damn it, I'm jointly responsible for your debts too. Don't you think you need to fill me in?"

"I'm going to mix myself a drink first. You want another one?"

"Yes, and make mine a double."

I went out to the family room and started a fire in the fireplace. It seems like a fire has a way of soothing my nerves. Carl came out with the drinks and handed me one.

"Here's your double. There's a nip in the air today, Hon, and the fire feels good." He said it like there was nothing wrong at all.

"There's more than a nip in the air in here." I said. "Are you going to tell me what's going on?"

"Oh, all right." He huffed. "First, Brandy and Nancy lost their apartment last month. Neither of them has a job nor any money. Nancy can't live in the streets with the baby and Brandy is in school full time you know. They called me at work to see if I could help them." He took a healthy swallow of his drink and then continued. "I found the trailer, bought it, and had it moved to French's Trailer Park between Oregon and Madison. It cost nine-thousand dollars." He said that so nonchalantly, like he could pull nine thousand out of his ear.

"So now your making payments on a trailer and paying lot rent?" I was angry.

"Yes," he said boldly, "and I give them money for groceries, heat, and lights."

"My God, Carl, your supporting a whole other household, and I don't need to know?"

"Not really. It also came to mind," he continued, "if things don't work out between you and me, the girls and I will have a place to live."

"You know," I bristled, "that's the best idea I've heard today. Do you want me to help you pack?"

I walked to the kitchen, mixed another drink, and went down to my workshop, where I felt at home. I listened as Carl walked around upstairs, taking things to the car. The girls came in from school, and they talked for a few minutes. I heard the door slam, and my house was completely quiet.

There wasn't a trace of them left. After all this time, everything they owned fit into his car. It was really kind of sad. I had already cried enough when Carl was here, and I wasn't planning on wasting any more time doing that.

Chapter Thirteen

"You can't just spend all of your time alone here, Mom." Laurie said after a few days. "Why don't you get out of here and do something fun?"

"Don't worry about me, Puddin, the piece and quiet are nice. Besides that, I don't have to worry about getting belted in the mouth for whatever reason he thinks of after a few drinks."

"If you decide you want to get out we could go to the thrift shops or antiquing, or maybe even an auction."

"It's tempting, Puddin," I said. "But I have some things to do now that I don't have to stumble over all the people."

The repair work to the upstairs had been done in a hurry and not like I had originally intended. I tore out a couple of walls, built a new one, dry walled, painted, paneled, and carpeted.

Peg came out to the house quite often. She was getting big and was very uncomfortable. She knew I would wrestle with Missy and give her a needed break.

"You know Dad misses you." She said. "The trailer is too small with the five of them living there, six with the baby."

"I suppose it is." I said. "That's not my problem, Peg." I wasn't about to give any indication as to how much I missed her father. Deceit, lying, stealing and being sneaky were things I could never tolerate, and this family seemed to thrive on them.

"Dad also has to do most of the cooking." She said. "The girls only know how to open cans."

"Oh, they'll get by." I said. "Laurie and I do."

One afternoon she called and pleaded, "Sarah can you please take me to the hospital?"

"Is it time?" I asked.

"Yes," she said, "and Rick can't get back to Madison in time. He's making a delivery out of town today."

"I'll be right out." I said. "What about Missy? Have you got someone to watch her?"

"All taken care of." She replied.

"See you in about ten minutes." I said and hung up the phone.

I splashed cool water on my face, changed clothes and took off. They lived in her Grandparents house on the Beach, so they were only eight miles away. When I arrived, Peg was ready, suitcase and all.

"Are you in labor?" I asked.

"I think so. The pains aren't really hard yet, but I can tell something's happening. We can stop at the doctors office. It's right on the way anyhow." She said.

"Who's watching Missy?" I asked.

"Rick's sister is staying with us for a couple of weeks. She's good with children. Missy won't even miss me." Peg pouted.

The doctor confirmed, she was indeed in labor, but there wasn't any hurry.

"Can we stop for a Jamoca shake, Sarah?" She pleaded. "I crave them all the time."

"If that's what you want," I chuckled.

The drive-in where Laurie worked was only two blocks from the clinic. Brandy had dropped out of college and started working there a week ago. When we walked in, Brandy came to take our order.

"We're on our way to the hospital," Peg bragged to her sister."I was so hungry for a Jamoca shake, we had to stop and have one. Give Sarah whatever she wants too."

"Jamoca's fine." I said, rolling my eyes at Brandy.

"Peg, you're the only one I know who would stop to itch a craving while your in labor." Brandy said, before scooting off to get the shakes and pass the word around. All of the hired help kept an eye on us, as if the baby might pop right out in the restaurant.

I said, "We should be going, Peg. Thanks for the treat."

"By, everybody." She waved to the help. Peggy was loving the attention.

As we started toward the hospital I told her, "I'll stay with you until Rick gets here. If your Dad or Mom comes, I'm making a quick exit."

"I should have told Brandy not to say anything to Mom until the baby gets here." Peg said. "I sure don't want her at the hospital, drunk." She winced in pain and held her hands against her abdomen. I waited until she relaxed...

"You made it through that one." I said. "We'll be there soon. We're only two blocks away."

Whenever Peg was around, I had the urge to talk to her about her Mom. There were some guilty feelings. I felt sometimes like I had betrayed a friend. This wasn't the time or place, but...

"I feel sorry for your Mom, Peg, she had so much and now..."

"You know, Sarah," she interupted, "I used to blame you. When things fell apart, I needed someone to blame and you were it. I know now it wasn't your fault."

"Maybe I was to blame, at least partly." I said. "Your Mom and I used to drink way too much, together." Then I added. "Marrying your Dad didn't help either."

"But you don't drink the way she does." Peg said.

I wasn't sure about that. Sure, going to bars alone wasn't my style, but there was never a lack of something to drink at the house.

Peggy gave out a moan, just as I pulled into the emergency entrance. While attendants were putting her in a wheel chair, I saw Carl pull into the parking ramp.

"Your father's here, Peg, so I'll be leaving. Brandy must have called him at work. Give me a call and let me know how your doing." I said. "The situation being the way it is, doesn't make me feel any less like a grandmother."

*   *   *   *   *   *

Carl called early the next morning. "Hello, Grandma."

"What was it?" I asked him.

"A big boy, eight pounds, four ounces." He said. "Peg said to tell you, the Jamoca shake added the four ounces."

"She had everyone in the restaurant's attention." I laughed.

"She told the nurses and me all about it." Carl said. "Had us all in stitches."

"How is Peggy?" I asked. "That's a big baby for her."

"She's fine," he answered, "and Rick couldn't be prouder of his boy."

There was a long, awkward silence. Idle chitchat didn't feel comfortable between us any more. A new grandchild being born had not broken down any fences that Carl had constructed between us. Now that he had let me know how Peg and the baby were, I just wanted to get off the phone. I couldn't think of anything to say right now, at least nothing I wanted to say over the phone.

"Do you mind if I call you once in a while?" He asked, breaking the silence.

"Yes, I do mind." I said curtly. "I'm swamped with work right now and I'd just like to keep at it. In case you've forgotten, we have many more bills to pay now."

"You were busy before and I always called." He argued. "Why not now? And as far as the extra bills go, you don't have to worry about them. I will."

"Six of one, half a dozen of the other." I said. "There has been a lot happened since then. I've had time to think. I'm not going to be your punching bag, or anyone else's. I'm still healing from our last bout, and right now, I'm enjoying not having to argue with anyone. Not you or the girls."

"Don't you ever get lonesome for me?"

"Of course I do. What's that got to do with the price of beans." I said. "You let someone use your body for a punching bag, then tell me how often you want to go back for more."

"Okay, Sarah, I give up. If you ever change your mind, our number is the Oregon exchange, then twenty-eight, twenty-eight. I do love you, Sarah." And he hung up.

Damn you, Carl. You couldn't say you were sorry or that things would be different, the two things I'd like to hear. Maybe after a month or two of living in that dumpy trailer with wall to wall people, you might appreciate a home.

Three weeks later he called during his lunch hour. "Sarah, Honey, can't we go out to eat sometime?" He pleaded.

"Okay, Carl, I'll agree, but only under certain circumstances. Only during the day, with all of the girls along, and only if there is no drinking." I gave my demands.

"How about Saturday?" He asked.

"No." I said. "This Saturday I have plans."

"Well," he sighed, "can I call tomorrow?"

"I suppose," was all I said, then hung up the phone. Even if I hadn't had plans, I would have found something to do. I wasn't ready to jump through hoops just because he said to. But I did have plans for Saturday. I was going to look at some Malamute puppies. Brenda had to get rid of Benji when he nipped someone at the trailer park. They had to pay a fine too.

The owner of the dogs came out when I pulled in his drive, next to the dog kennel. The bitch was laying down and the puppies looked like maggots crawling all over her. She had twelve of them. When he opened the pen, there was mayhem. The mother wanted some people attention and the pups covered the ground around her, wiggling and squirming, like a moving swarm. They were pretty much all identical, black with some white on their under bellies. One decided to sit on the toe of my western boots. If I moved, she did too...

"Have you selected one?" he asked.

"No," I said, "but one seems to have chosen me." I picked up the fat, little, black puppy from my boot. She had a small white blaze on her chest and another between her back legs. It looked like she had on a bikini. I had to laugh when I noticed that.

"Her name will be Mega," I told the man, "which I understand means a friend who is a girl." I wasn't sure if that was correct, I didn't know any Spanish, but it sounded good to me. I needed a friend who would be loyal to me, and the males in my life just weren't cutting it.

The days didn't seem so long with Mega laying around my shop. She was content to just watch me work. Evenings we romped around in the back yard. She never did make messes in the house. I couldn't have found a better friend.

Finally I agreed to a picnic with Carl and the girls. Carl would pick up chicken and some soda, and I would meet them at Vilas Zoo. Mega went along. She loved the attention and the animals, but hated that leash. By the time everyone had shared their lunch with the pooch, she was well on her way to understanding 'Sit' and 'Speak'. The girls wore themselves and the pup out running around. They even took her wading in Lake Wingra. We were finished and it was still early…

"Do you want to follow me home for coffee and a visit?" I asked. "I think Laurie's home."

When we arrived, Laurie had just brewed coffee. She looked at me like I was crazy. Maybe I was.

Brenda asked, "Sarah, can we go up and see the work you did?"

"Sure, go ahead. How did you know I did anything?" I asked.

"Peg told us." She said.

Brenda came down all excited. "Our room is really nice now, Dad. You ought to see it."

For the first time, I was offended by her saying 'our room'. This is my house. I bought it myself and made all the payments. Carl bought groceries and paid the heating and phone bills when they had been here, but why shouldn't he? They lived here too. I did all the cooking, cleaning, and laundry. The only way to get the girls off their behinds was to call them to supper or the phone.

After that day Carl courted me, and couldn't have been sweeter. Months later, just before Christmas, they moved back into the house. The girls made all kinds of promises, which I let go in one ear and out the other, for all they were worth.

It was comforting to have Carl back in my arms, but I couldn't delude myself, that things would ever be the same. Each time I traveled the road to Madison and past the trailer park, the feeling of deceit returned. The girls liked the room but not the chores. It was a constant battle to get them to do anything, even move from the television so I could clean. Being asked to do the dishes brought an immediate and expected reaction.

"I wish we had stayed at the trailer," from either of them. It depended on who didn't want to get off their lazy behind.

Well, the feeling was mutual. At least for the girls, not one iota had changed.

Two packages came in the mail for Carl. When I asked about them, Carl said…

"Your slow time for upholstery is coming and I thought we could use the time to build some black powder guns. Dane County is talking about a special season for them."

"That sounds like fun." I agreed. "That's with a cap and ball, right?"

"Yes." He said. "These are kits. It's a lot of work, but you always like that kind of thing. You can be as creative as you want to." Carl knew how much I enjoyed deer hunting. Arron and Cyle and I had always gone together. Building our own guns sounded like a challenge.

That winter we also ran trap line. He left for work at five a.m. I'd get up with him and pack his lunch, get all bundled up, strap on the twenty-two pistol, and head for the woods. I couldn't leave until I called the girls or they'd miss the bus. It was at least noon before all the muskrats were skinned and I could clean up to work in my shop. Mega loved these trips to the woods. Then one of the neighbor dogs caught her in her first heat. She got way to fat for all that running. She still wanted to be with me in the stable while I skinned the animals so Carl built her a box under the workbench. That's where she gave birth to eight puppies. The first one was Buckskin color and twice as big, the rest were black and tan. Mega liked to romp in the yard while someone was in the stable to watch her family. One day when I only had enough time to run the line, I was in the kitchen getting supper while Carl was skinning the day's catch. I heard brakes squeal. Carl came to the house and I knew before he opened his mouth that Mega was dead.

"You sit down and eat with the girls," I said. "I'll go do what has to be done."

"I can do it, Sarah." Carl said

"So can I. She's my dog." I insisted. "You keep the girls occupied." I put on the twenty-two pistol and walked out.

Mega and her seven black pups were buried together in a hole moistened with my tears. Saying good bye to my friend was very hard to do. The pups were only a week and half old now. We never could have raised them all. When the hole was filled in, I cradled one fat little buckskin puppy in my arms and walked to the house. We made 'Buck' a box in the corner behind the fire place. We all laughed when I put my new friend in his box, because Nuffers, our young, black, tomcat climbed in with him and laid down. It was as though these animals had a language of their own, and right now Buck needed a friend.

Nuffers and Buck, best of buds

Hand feeding Buck was a real experience, and a pain. I do mean actual pain. I'd put a towel acrossed my lap, and hold the baby bottle. He was a voracious eater and he'd rake my forearms with needle sharp claws. He grew so fast, it was no time before he had his muzzle buried in the food dish. Nuffers and Buck were an inseparable pair. They even ate together. My arms eventually healed.

*　*　*　*　*　*

Spring break was three weeks off. Laurie had planned her classes in high school so that her senior year was a snap. With fewer classes she was able to

133

work almost a full eight hours at her job. I had promised her a vacation for graduation and she'd been saving for it. Somehow our vacation together had turned into a family thing.

"Carl, can you give me a ride into Oregon when you get home from work?" I asked when he called during his lunch break.

"It's not much fun, not having your own wheels, is it?" He asked

"You got that right. But I won't be without them long. I decided to get that long wheel-based van I saw in Oregon. It will work as well as the truck for hauling furniture." I waited for his reply. He usually had two-cents worth, to put in. It was as though he thought I wasn't capable of spending my own money.

"I think that's a good choice." Surprise, Surprise.

"Then you'll take me?" I asked again.

"I can't, I promised the girls I'd pick them up at school and take them shopping for vacation clothes."

"Fine," I said. "I'm sure beings I'm buying a brand-new vehicle from them, they'll come and pick me up. Don't you worry your head about me. I'll see you later."

Two days ago, Tag's plumbing shop in Fennimore had picked up my truck. Turned out to be just what they needed to mount a drill rig on. That big truck was hard to handle when it was empty. It wanted to bounce all over the road. Just the same I hated being without transportation. Carl had a way of making me feel like any ride I needed was an imposition.

"Hi, Honey, I'm home." Laurie laughed. "I had to pop home. I forgot my time card."

"Glad to see you, Puddin. Can I catch a ride into town with you?" I asked.

"You just need a ride one way?" She looked puzzled.

"Yep, I'm picking up my new van." I grabbed my purse and the two of us took off in her 'bug'.

"We can take the van on our vacation, Laurie. I was thinking about the five of us in Carl's little car all the way to Florida. Just the thought gives me the chills."

"I never thought about it either, Mom, but you're right. After two weeks we'd hate each other, if we even survived."

We all had new bathing suits, shorts, halters, sunglasses, and other fun stuff. Bags were packed, and sleeping bags aired out. The girls had just this last day of school and we would leave early tomorrow morning.

Laurie came home from work at nine.

"Mom, I have to be back in ten days. They have me on the schedule. If I'm not back, I'll lose my job."

"Well," I said, "ten days isn't bad. We'll have to be satisfied with that. With your promotion coming up, you can't afford to lose your job now."

Carl shot me a dirty look and stomped out the back door headed for Elly's. I finished my last minute packing and closing the house down. I threw everything out of the fridge that would certainly be rotten in ten days. Then I walked to the bar for a night cap. I needed to talk to Belinda anyhow. She would be feeding our animals while we were gone. We didn't stay long at the bar, as Carl wasn't talking to me. I slept restlessly at first, but must have gotten into a deep sleep at one point. When I awoke, Carl wasn't in bed. In fact he wasn't in the house at all. He, Brenda, and Holly were all packed into his car. As he backed out of the drive, he yelled back at me...

"Hope you and your little Darling have a fun, ten day, trip," then they drove away.

I ran up to Laurie's room and shook her."Didn't you hear anything, Laurie?"

"Waa... What was I supposed to hear?" She mumbled, only half awake.

"Everyone else is gone." I said. "They left for Florida in Carl's car. I didn't hear them either, but they waved at me when they left." We both started laughing. This was crazy.

We were kind of in shock, but this stupidity wasn't going to spoil Laurie's trip

"I'd rather it be just you and I anyhow, Mom." Laurie said.

We took two of the snap-out bench seats from the van, which gave us enough room to roll out our sleeping bags. We couldn't have done that before. Now we had our bed in the back. After loading our bags, I locked the house and we were off.

"Let's not take a chance on running into them, Puddin, let's head for Texas." I said.

"Good thinking." She answered. "I have to stop in Evansville and cash my paycheck. I need some more spending money."

After that was done we headed straight South on highway fifty-one. The first night we just pulled the curtains and slept in the van at a truck-stop close to Nashville, Tennessee. The big rigs pulling in and out woke me early. I was down the road another two-hundred miles before I heard a peep out of Laurie.

"I'm hungry. Let's eat." She mumbled from the back of the van.

"I was about ready to wake you anyhow." I said. "You're missing all the sights."

"Where are we?" She asked.

"Somewhere in Mississippi." I said. "You gonna try some grits for breakfast?"

"Oh, yak." She grimaced. "You're always talking about grits. You eat them, Mom. I'll stick with hash browns. Hope it's not too long. I'm starving."

"I'll stop as soon as I find a café. A couple more hours of driving and we won't be too far from New Orleans." I said. "We turn off before we get there,

135

though. If we go West through Louisiana, we should be able to make Galveston before bedtime."

"Are we sleeping in the van tonight?" She asked.

"We'll see. Maybe we'll get a motel room so we can shower tonight. After we eat, you may have to drive for a while." I said. "Think you can handle this big rig?"

"I"ll try. Hurry up and find a place to stop." She pleaded. "I have to make a pit stop, very badly, Mom."

We ate, then I showed her in the Atlas, which road to look for to take us toward Texas. Laurie drove while I slept. When she pulled to a complete stop, it woke me.

"Let's go in this truck stop and have some coffee to wake you up, Mom. I hate to say it, but you'd better drive again. These drainage ditches along the roads make me nervous."

"That's fine." I fibbed. "I just needed to shut my eyes for a while. Let's eat lunch. Then we'll be good for a few more miles." I stretched and yawned. Oh, for six more hours of sleep.

All of the billboards for miles had been advertizing Galveston. There were tourist attractions everywhere. Maybe now I'd find out what Glen Campbell had been singing about.

"We should be able to go to the beach in Galveston tomorrow." I told Laurie. "Get a little Texas sun on our pale, Wisconsin bodies."

"Why don't you pull over and buy a six-pack of Texas beer, Mom?"

"I don't even like beer." I wrinkled my nose.

Laurie giggled, "But I do."

We put the beer in the cooler to chill, and then went down the road til we ran into a roadblock. A drawbridge was stuck in the open position, right at quitting time for the refineries. Lots of the young fellows were out of their cars, milling around. Laurie made friends with one carload of them and invited them to come to the van for a beer. It was almost dark before they got the bridge locked down.

"If you girls want, we can show you the way to a nice motel," the driver among the guys offered.

"Sure would help." I said. "Driving at night in a strange city is hard." They led the way, right into the driveway.

"Thanks for the beer." They all waved as they pulled back out.

We showered, ate supper and got a good night sleep. The next morning we drove around until we found a fish market where I purchased five pounds of fresh shrimp. The beach looked like a four-lane highway. There were dune buggies, all terrain vehicles, and people everywhere. Laurie got comfortable with a blanket and a book. She blatantly told me that the book was only a disguise so she could do some boy watching.

I busied myself at the back of the van, cooking shrimp on a camp stove. Boiling water took longer than I had anticipated. This wasn't like cooking on my stove at home. When I called Laurie, she was sleeping and redder than the shrimp.

"Wake up, Puddin, you are really burnt." I said in alarm. "I don't think we should have done that. This isn't going to heal anytime soon."

We ate our shrimp with Laurie standing up, then I put things away in a hurry and we headed out to find a drug store. We bought pain killers, lotion and burn ointment. We even tried Ole-Vera leaves. Nothing helped. The lady pharmacist said...

"Fifteen minutes in our sun, is like two hours of Wis-cawn-sin sun."

Laurie had close to third degree burns on the back of both legs, and she had to spend her time on her stomach in the back of the van. Sitting was too painful. Even the sun coming in the windows made her skin burn, so the curtains had to stay closed. We decided to head North and hit as many garage sales as we could find on our way home. Our route home went through Iowa and Illinois where we stopped to say howdy to my Bray cousins. Laurie never knew how many cousins she had. Then we went on to Fennimore.

By the time we reached Mom's, Laurie was feeling much better, though still not one-hundred percent. The three of us ordered in a pizza, got into our pajamas, and had a sleep-over. I had forgotten how good it felt to spend a quiet evening, not arguing, with people that you love.

Cyle in his fatigues

Chapter Fourteen

Cyle came home from basic training in California. He looked so handsome in his uniform, but like most Marines, he was so hyped up on the corps, that's all he would talk about. Julie and her parents had the wedding all arranged. Cyle and Julie had a large church wedding, reception, and a dance. Two days later Cyle had to report back, to be shipped to Hawaii, where Julie would join him in three weeks. That would be a dreamy way to start out married life.

My flower gardens all needed tending. Spring planting would be here in no time and I hadn't even pulled last year's plants out yet. I was just making some head way on them, when the 'bug' pulled in the drive and Laurie and her red headed friend, Diana, came giggling up the path.

"We found an apartment, Mom, it's in Monona, close to both of our jobs." Laurie said. "We can move in this week end."

"What?" I shouted. She's the last of my kids, and I really didn't want her to go. "How come now? Graduation isn't for another month. Aren't you going to stick around until you find out if you made it?"

"Yah, sure, Mom." She said. "Will you haul my things if we load and unload them? One trip in your van should do it."

Saturday morning Diana and two other girls came to help. We all started carrying things down when I caught a scent that started my stomach churning.

"Damn it, Laurie, who's got licorice?" I yelled.

Laurie was snickering, "Sorry, Mom. I forgot. We're all chewing this new gum."

"You can let me know when the loading is done and my house is aired out." I crabbed. "My van won't move an inch until I can't smell that stuff." Then added. "I'll be out in my flower gardens when you're ready."

Her moving meant Brenda and Holly could each have their own room. I had lost interest, regardless. They wouldn't clean their room, I refused to, and Carl just didn't care.

Graduation was held outside. The weather had been unseasonably hot. Tag's oldest daughter, Connie, who was also graduating this year, surprised Laurie by coming all the way from Fennimore for her party.

My children were all out of school now and gone from home. I would be forty on my next birthday. Lately I had been irritable and moody, even more so than my natural, bitchy, self.

My doctor said, "Many times, when the last child leaves home, it can cause the change of life to start." Then he laughed. "Or was it, that the change of life makes the last child want to leave home?" Anyway, I had it, or it had me, and there wasn't a blamed thing I could do. I was getting old.

*   *   *   *   *   *

I started doing some oil painting. I was no Picasso, but my paintings weren't too bad. The space to hang or store them was my problem after a while. Carl had a solution…

"Either sell some of them or quit painting."

I should have said, "If you don't get paid to sing and play, you have to quit," but I didn't. He accomplished what he wanted. I quit painting. It had been a nice escape for a while.

We stopped at a bar in town one afternoon when Holly was with us. I was talking to some acquaintances at one of the tables when a commotion broke out by the bar. Carl had taken a swing at a young fellow. It seems he said something to Holly that Carl didn't like. Carl missed the guy's chin and hit his shoulder instead. The shoulder was fine, but Carl's wrist was a mess.

"Mr. Regent," said the doctor, "you are going to be in a cast for months, if not permanently."

Carl could still move his fingers to play his guitar, and he didn't seem upset at all.

"I have plenty of sick leave coming," he said, "and I have some things I've been wanting to do."

Now what's he got planned? Must be another part of his life I don't need to know about?

Margaret had remarried and moved away from Madison. It was not too far away to still call us though. It just cost more to call so it didn't happen as often. Now it was a game to see how long we could keep her on the line. Her new husband must have appreciated the phone bills. She was still drinking.

Carl took several trips to Northern Wisconsin during the next few weeks. He brought home realtor pamphlets and newspapers from all over that area. Finally he broke the ice about his plans.

"How would you like to buy a resort, Sarah?" He asked, just as nonchalantly, as if he were asking me if I wanted a cup of coffee.

"What?" I shrieked. "What are you talking about?"

"A resort up North." He explained further. "The North is full of lakes. It would be a perfect place to retire when the time comes."

"No." I said. "I've never even thought about moving. I like it here, but I know you've been planning something. I suppose you've already found something. I hope you didn't buy anything." It would be just like Carl to buy something and tell me later, or not at all.

"Not really." He said. "There are several I'd like to look at though. Want to go looking with me this week end?"

"All of us?" I asked.

"No." He hesitated. "Maybe the girls can stay with Peg for a couple of days."

"I don't know about looking at resorts, but I really need some time away from this house, work, and the girls," I answered.

We drove all over Northern Wisconsin, not just that week end, but for several. What we found was, most of the resorts were selling off each individual cabin and closing shop. People were opting for the motor-in type vacations. They wanted pools, saunas, and whirlpools. Carl wasn't giving up. He kept looking.

I had a woman working for me now. Adele was really interested in the upholstery business. When she heard what, Carl had in mind, she made me a proposition. She would work for no wages if I would teach her the trade. Then, when and if, we decided to move, she would buy my business. In the five years since I started upholstering my reputation had spread. If she was going to take over, I wanted her to do a good job. I didn't have any idea when Carl would find what he was looking for but I agreed to start training her immediately.

Carl was cleaning the car. "I have a few places to look at this week end. Do you want to go along?" He asked.

"No, Carl, I don't think so," I said, "all the drinking we do on these trips really wears me out. I have work piling up and I need to get some rest. Why don't you take the girls along and give me a break?"

"I guess I can do that." He said, then with the next breath he got defensive. "Are you sure you don't have some other plans and just want us out of your way?"

He knew better, but this was his way of laying a guilt trip on me, and clearing his conscience, for anything he might do. I just gave him a nasty look.

"Can you at least pack some things for the girls?" He asked.

"Carl," I said, "you haven't been working. You have a lot of free time, and you know how to pack for them. You do it yourself."

"You don't have to get nasty." He said. "I know you've been busy, and your Granny problem doesn't help. Okay, I'll get their stuff ready."

"Good idea." I snapped back at him. We hardly spoke the rest of the evening.

They left early the next morning. God, was it nice to have some peace and quiet. I drank my coffee alone and caught up on my correspondence to Cyle and Julie. They had written that they were expecting a child. The letter was ten pages long before I finished. There was a lot to tell them. Laurie was going steady with Dwight and they seemed quite serious. I hadn't seen much of Arron, but told them where he was at and what car he was driving now. The resort thing and selling my business to Adele took two pages.

When that was finished, I took a long, hot, shower and put on some fresh old beaters. Buck and I went for a romp in the yard, with Nuffers a few steps behind. Buck was now half as big as a horse, and Nuffers was a huge, sleek, black, tomcat.

Sarah Ann Bray

I sat in the sun with them until I heard the phone.

"Sarah's Sewing Service." I answered.

"Hi, Mom, can we get together and talk?" This was a surprise. Arron hadn't been out to my house since he and Carl had fought.

"Sure, come on out, Arron." I said. "I have the house to myself for a couple of days."

"I know. I saw them drive through town this morning. We'll be right out." He said. Then he hung up, leaving me wondering who 'we' were.

They were there in ten minutes. He and a tiny little blonde, who he introduced as Bridget, but he called her Birdie.

I hugged him and said "Hi" to Bridget. "It's been too long, Arron." I said. "It doesn't have to be this way."

"I'd just as soon not be around Carl," he said, in a tone I knew was not open for discussion.

"What we wanted to talk to you about, Mom, is a wedding dress. Birdie is so small," he said, "they suggested we'd be better off getting one custom made. Of coarse, you know who came to mind." Birdie never said a word. Just stood there smiling at Arron.

"I can see the problem." I put my hands around Bridget's waist. "When is the wedding?"

"We haven't set the date yet." He said. "We didn't know how long the dress might take?"

"I'm not sure either." I said. "I have a lot of work piled up downstairs."

"May I use your bathroom, Mrs Regent?" Birdie asked

While I had Arron alone, I asked. "Do you want Carl at the wedding?"

He said. "What I'm sure of, Mom, is that I want you there. If Carl comes, and I'm sure he will, he'll have to behave. He wouldn't let you go all the way to Wausau to have a good time without him. If he acts up, I won't be responsible for what happens. All of my buddies will be there."

The dress and head piece she wanted were elaborate, had much hand sewing, and a lot of lace and beadwork. For the best part of the next three months, I juggled staple guns and seed pearls, tack hammers and lace, fittings and deliveries, trying to appease both ends of my work. Luckily, Arron and Carl didn't cross paths, and Adele was worth her weight in gold. She turned out to be a very adept student and her work improved in leaps and bounds.

Carl knew that refusing to go to the wedding with me would be an open declaration of war. His being included on the invitation at all had to be Birdie's idea. Maybe a polite decline would have been the easiest way out, but Arron was my son. I wanted to be there when he got married, even if I had to go by myself.

142

Carl decided to go. Most of their wedding day was spent holding my breath, but Carl surprised me. He actually made drinking coffee look enjoyable while everyone else was living it up, and the day past without incident.

*   *   *   *   *   *

I pushed the door to the dress shop open, and Bobby ran in ahead of me.

"Ilky, Ilky. Where are you?" Bobby squealed

Stan was sitting up in the office doing book work. When we came in, he quickly put everything away and walked out. He nodded as he walked by.

Ilka poked her head out from behind a rack of dresses. "Hi Bobby." She greeted him. "You and Mommy must be out enjoying the sun today."

"Yep." Was all he said.

"It's about time the sun made an appearance, don't you think?' I asked.

"It's been a very busy day here." She said. "The first day people have wanted to get out for a while."

"Well, it's almost closing time. Can you get away for coffee or do you have to go right home?" I asked.

"I don't have to be home at all." She said. "Stan just left for work. I have two packages that have to go to the post office before it closes. Then maybe we can pick up something for a picnic in the park."

"You've been reading my mind. Bobby needs some fresh air." I said. "He'd enjoy going to the park."

"What have you been up to?" Ilka asked me.

"You know what I've been up to," I shrugged. "Heal and think. But yesterday I did manage to do our laundry. We don't have many clothes with us, but they all needed washing."

"At least the Laundromat isn't that far from the motel." She said.

"A good thing." I agreed. "Getting around without a car makes everything harder."

Ilka locked the front door, shut off the lights, and we each grabbed a package before heading out the back.

"Come on Bobby. We don't want to lock you in." I warned.

He scurried ahead. "Where we goin now?"

"We're going with Ilka to the post office," I said, "then we'll have a picnic, okay?"

"Yep." He said again.

After the mailing was done, we picked up food and found a table in the sun. Bobby ran off to play on the swings.

"How are your wounds healing, Sarah?" Ilka asked.

"They're doing fine. My ribs are still very tender, but that's to be expected." I gently rubbed my rib cage.

"And your other project, how's that coming?" She asked again.

"Great. I've been thinking about my older children," I said, "how they grew up, and why they all left home early."

"Why was that?" She asked.

"Carl." I said bluntly. "They disliked him from the start. Even thinking about my early relationship with him, makes me shiver. He more or less bull dozed me into moving up here and buying a bar. I could have been stronger then and saved myself a whole lot of grief."

"Was he nasty way back then?" She looked at me with disbelief.

"Yes," I said, "and I was so blind. If I had been able to admit the truth or had the good sense to listen to the kids, we never would have gotten married."

"Then we never would have met." She put her hand over mine and patted it.

"Ilka, I believe our being friends, was destiny. You didn't travel all the way from Germany so we would <u>not</u> meet." I joked.

"Stan never told me I was coming to America to meet you." She went along with the joke.

"That just goes to show you." I said. "Men don't know everything."

She laughed, "Sarah, you can make my day."

"Well, you have made more than one day for me, Ilka. Bobby and I are so lucky to have your friendship."

"You mentioned your other children. Have you talked with them?" She asked. "Do they know how badly you were beaten?"

"Laurie knows." I said. "Arron still keeps his distance."

"That's so sad." She said. "If I lost touch with Mickey it would kill me."

"It's Arron choice," I said, "but he'll do just fine. He has a lot of talent."

"What kind of talent?" She asked.

"He's a writer, a carpenter and is also very artistic." I bragged. "He's a cop, but he's also an all-around handyman."

"Wonder where he gets that?" She grinned.

"Bobby," I yelled, "you'd better come and eat before it gets cold." Food was the last thing on his mind. I didn't really care. We had been cooped up for too long in that room.

"Comin, Mommy." He squealed. He climbed onto the seat of the picnic table and ate a whole two bites before running off to the merry-go-round.

"It's okay," I said, "we can take it back to the motel and he can eat later."

"Before I forget," Ilka said, "thanks for the picnic, Sarah. Are you sure it won't cut you short?"

"We'll be okay," I said. "You've surely done enough for us."

"I didn't do anything I didn't want to." She said stubbornly.

"Good," I said. "When we go back to the motel, could we swing by the store? There's a couple of things I'd like to get."

"Sure." She agreed. "By the way, we should be going. It's getting dark."

"Bobby, let's go," I yelled. "I was enjoying the fresh air so much, I lost track of time, sorry."

"It's okay." She said. "I'm in no big rush."

She drove to the store and watched Bobby while I ran in. Later he gobbled two peanut butter sandwiches before dropping off to sleep, and then I slipped back into my memories...

*   *   *   *   *   *

I was showing Adele how to make smooth corners on the back of a chair before stapling, when Laurie came down the stairs to my shop.

"Hi, Mom. Hi, Adele." She said. "I see you have your nose back to the grindstone."

"About time, I'd say."

"Mom, you look more relaxed since Arron's wedding is over." She said.

"Having all that white wedding material out of the house is a relief." I said. "Any one of the dogs, cats or kids could have been a disaster with it around. How did I do it for so long before, Laurie?"

"We didn't have any house pets. Remember? And us kids were angels." She bragged.

"That's right. I forgot. All but the angels' part." I laughed. "How come your not working? You don't usually come to see me during the day."

"I don't have to be to work for a couple of hours, late shift today." She said. "Can you get away for a few minutes or are you two doing something important?" She asked.

"Adele can do this. It's a chair I'm getting ready for my auction. You don't mind if I leave for a minute, do you, Adele?" I asked

"If I can't handle this, I'd better forget about buying the business." She shushed us with her hand. "Go on, enjoy yourselves. Bring me some coffee when you're done."

Laurie and I went up to the kitchen. I poured two coffees, and we went out into the family room to be more comfortable.

"Adele seems like a nice lady. She looks like she enjoys the work." Laurie was skirting.

"She does. What's on your mind?" I asked. "I know it's not my work, or Adele's."

"I almost hate to tell you after what you said about white, wedding material." She looked at me and grinned. "I'm your next victim, Mom."

145

"You're getting married? I knew that Dwight was trouble." I pretended to be mad.

"Yep." She said. "Your last chick is leaving the nest."

She was so happy, but I couldn't let her know she was breaking my heart. Get over it, old girl, Puddin has grown up. And she doesn't need you any more, except...

"Do you know what kind of dress you want?" I asked.

"I know exactly what I want." She said boldly. "Mine won't take as long as Birdie's. I want a plain, white, satin, A-line dress, with a stand up collar and long sleeves."

"That sounds easy enough." I said.

"You haven't heard the rest." She held her hand up. "My head dress will be the train and it will be trimmed all around with tiny yellow rosebuds."

"Beautiful." My mind was already picturing what she would look like as a bride.

"Then you think we can do it?" She asked.

"Of coarse we can." I boasted. "Have I ever let you down?"

"There's more, Mom." She hesitated. "I want Brenda and Holly to be in my wedding party."

"They'll love that." I said. "What are they going to wear?"

"I'm having five attendants, all in yellow, with see through flowered capes. The dresses, we'll buy. Do you think you can make the capes?" She asked.

"Not a problem." I said. "Have you looked at material?"

"No, not yet." She said. "I thought maybe you and I could do that, and find a pattern for my dress too."

"I won't say anything to the girls." I suggested. "You can tell them. They've never been in a wedding. I don't think."

"Well, Mom, I'd better get going. Don't forget Adele's coffee." As she walked out the door she looked back and grinned again."This will give you something to think about in your free time." She knew how little of that I had.

The night of practice we drove from Madison to Stevens Point with two wheels off in the gravel because of an ice storm. We were late, which was no disaster just for practice, but we had to make it there. I had most of the wedding attire in my van.

Her bouquet was made up of yellow roses. Laurie was a radiant bride. My three little munchkins are all grown up and married. Can that be? Where did the time go? What have I done with my life?

At the reception I sat watching Jake act like 'the big man'. He always seemed to be there for the good times. I was feeling kind of blue when Arron came to our table...

146

"Carl," Arron said. I held my breath... "Can I have this dance with your wife?"

He didn't wait for an answer, but took my hand. "Come on, Mom, teach me how to two-step."

It only took a few minutes and he had it down pat. It was Laurie's wedding, but for this one dance, whirling around the floor with my son, I was queen of the ball.

*　*　*　*　*　*

Carl's search continued as soon as the weather warmed in the spring. He had already located three places he wanted to look at.

"Come along with me this time," he said. "We'll take the fishing gear and do some casting for Muskie in the evening."

I had cabin fever from the long winter of working in my shop. Adele was doing well and she could get along without me for a couple of days. Casting for hungry Muskie might be just what I need.

"I'll take my camera along." I said, letting him know I was willing. "I love this time of year."

Dropping the girls off at Peg's gave me a chance to play with the grand babies. Then Carl and I headed North.

We never talked much on these long drives. He was a little hard of hearing and repeating things got tedious. I usually took along a book or a sketch pad. I never knew what topics were safe to talk about, anyhow. As we pulled in the drive to the first place on his list, he turned and said...

"This is a bar, supper club, and dance hall, all in one. Do you think we could handle something like that?"

"I thought we were looking for a resort, not a bar." I said a little snappy.

"Resorts are on their way out." He said. "We'd just be buying a pig in a poke."

"Well, I certainly, don't want a bar." I protested. "I've been down that road before and don't care to repeat history."

"Let's go in and take a look anyway, as long as we're here." He insisted.

We walked through the front door and my first instinct was to turn and run. Carl walked over and started talking to the two men at the bar. The one behind the bar, was undoubtably the owner. He was already drinking, looked like he had slept in his clothes, and had forgotten how to shave.

When Carl came back to where I was standing, he had a huge grin on his face.

"He says we should walk around and look things over." Carl relayed the message.

"So far everything I've seen is so covered with nicotine," I said. "I can't distinguish any color. It's like looking at the world through gold colored glasses, dark gold."

We walked and the sand gritted under our shoes. "Wonder how long it's been since he swept?" I whispered.

"I like the size of this barroom, Sarah." Carl was oblivious to me. "You could easily fit a hundred party goers in here."

"Let's look at the kitchen." I figured that's where I would be stuck if we bought this place.

There was litter laying on everything except the top of an old domestic stove, and it wasn't clean. The owner noticed we were in the kitchen. He stuck his head through a door at the front end and shouted.

"I've never opened the kitchen. It was condemned when the last owner's were here. I only use it to fix a few meals for myself. But keep looking, you've only started. If you want to see the living quarters, give me a holler. It's a big ole kitchen, isn't it?"

I went to the back end of the kitchen, where the dishwashing area was. The big sinks were full of empty cans and bottles. No one had done dishes in those sinks for many moons.

"This is kind of depressing," Carl whispered. Then said, "Let's go and look at the dance hall."

The stench of stale beer and dirty ash trays permeated the air in the hall. There were tables and chairs scattered, in no particular order. Each table was covered with empty cans, bottles, and ash trays that overflowed onto the tables.

"I can just imagine us backing a truck up and shoveling again, Carl." I grimaced.

The grin on his face told me he had been thinking the same thing. "But just try to imagine this room without the litter, Sarah, it's great."

He was right. You had to step down one step. A short wall ran half way crossed the room on your left, partitioning off the dance hall bar from the rest of the room. There was a stage at the far end, and I do mean far. This was a huge hall.

"I love the barn boards on the walls, Carl." I said. "Someone put a lot of work in here."

There were cutouts on the far wall with a sun porch, and more tables, running the full length of the hall.

I gasped, "Look at this view, it takes your breath away."

Carl walked out to the sun porch, and just stood, looking. Windows ran the full length and on one end, overlooking a lake. Even with the filthy windows, it was breathtaking. Sparkling water lapped the shoreline. A row of white pines, trimmed over head high stood along the shoreline. The breeze whispering through them was like a ghost of Grandma Leighy's pines.

"You want to see the living quarters?" Carl asked.

"We may as well, as long as we're here." I couldn't take my eyes off the lake.

Carl motioned for the owner. "I guess we want to see the rest."

The man unlocked the door. "You have to understand," he said, "these are bachelor quarters and I'm no housekeeper."

That was immediately evident, the place was just quarters, not a home. It smelled like animal quarters though, with this man's personals thrown everywhere. I felt very uncomfortable.

We weren't in there long, when I said, "I've seen enough."

The owner re locked the door, and went back to the bar area.

I whispered, "Carl, it's beautiful, but what a mess, and I still don't want another bar."

"Well, Sarah," he said, "it's not like we haven't waded through a mess before." He had only heard what he wanted to hear. My objections to owning a bar went right over his head.

"The place has lots of potential. The building looks solid, but we're going to have to do lots of thinking before jumping into this. I do not want a bar." I reiterated.

"What's your bottom dollar?" Carl asked the owner, who was starting to look like his own best customer.

"I'm asking ninety thou." The man said.

"How long have you had it for sale?" Carl asked.

"Two years." He replied.

"We may stop back tomorrow." Carl said. "Will you be here?"

"Yep." He said. "I never get very far away."

The other man at the bar nodded his head in agreement at that statement.

"Let's go, Sarah, we have a lot more driving to do." Carl said.

We drove farther North. The next place was a lodge on another lake. They had vacancies so we decided to spend the night. We ate supper and took a boat out to fish until dark.

"This place is more to my liking." I said. The sun felt warm and the lake so calm. I was almost ready to doze off.

"They don't even know we're looking. There is no pressure that way." Carl said as he gazed all around.

"It is sure out in the boon docks." I said. "Without advertisements, no one could find the place."

"That's what would make it nice. You wouldn't have many tourists coming in off the highway." He made a motion like he was casting, and added. "More time to fish."

"That's good thinking, if you want to go broke. Someone would have to stay on shore to do the work." My mind raced back to Werley, and who got left at home with the work.

Carl was rowing toward shore. "Let's go snoop around some more."

We put the tackle away, washed off, and walked over to the main lodge, where we discovered this place also had a bar. The bartender, a young man with a full head of curly black hair and a beard to match, mixed our first Manhattan with whiskey. I almost puked. It had been our fault. Perfect Manhattans are made that way. Our new friend, who reminded me of 'Grizzly Adams', even joined us in a couple, beings we were his only customers.

"What are they asking for this place?" I asked. "Sure is big."

"It's got a price to match, two-hundred-fifty-thousand." He said.

"You're right." I said. "Do you think they'll get that?"

"Oh sure, this place has changed hands many times." He winked. "The only ones making any money here are me and the realtor."

I excused myself. This was way out of our league. I was tired and could tell Carl had no intention of quitting. My leaving early would serve another purpose. If I was asleep there would be no chance of saying something that might set off a tangent... my plan worked.

"Let's get going, sleepy head." I shook Carl's shoulder in the morning. "We've got a lot more miles to travel, and one more place to see."

He showered quickly and we headed out. The terrain was mile after mile of pines and sand, and lakes in every direction. A fisherman's dreams come true. This fisherman would have to wait. The price on that place was way too high.

Our reality was back, south of Madison. The kids, a buckskin dog, three cats, and a business. We turned the car around and headed home.

Chapter Fifteen

I made some phone calls to the Board of Health and found out what had to be done to reopen the kitchen. We had talked the owner of the first place we looked at, down to sixty-five-thousand.

It meant I'd have to sell my place. Carl would have to sell the home he had purchased for his parents to live in. His Mom had gone into a nursing home, two months ago and Dad had found a room, close to the nursing home, so now the house was sitting there, empty. Carl listed his place with a realtor.

"I'm going to sell my house myself." I said. "There is no sense giving the realtor a big chunk."

"How do you plan on doing that?" Carl asked.

I handed him some cards I'd already made up. They had a large 'FOR SALE' on top and all the pertinent information below. "I'll put these in places I know have bulletin boards."

"What about all the paper work involved with selling it?" He asked.

"The realtor in town says they can do it for a price." I said.

"How much?" He asked. "Is, for a price?"

"Close to five-thousand," I hesitated for effect, "if they sell the house. Not even three-hundred for the paper work."

"Quite a difference." He agreed. "Go for it."

"I plan on it." I said. "I do have a mind of my own."

My house sold on the second day. The papers took a few more days, but an offer was made and accepted. My business had been sold and moved out earlier. I wrote letters to all of my former customers, introducing Adele.

The basement seemed so big and empty without the cutting table, piles of material, and equipment. I swept the floor and dug out my old roller skates. Many nights I had wakened from a dream of skating smooth and gracefully around the rink. My aching body told me this was no dream. My wheels stopped on some small obstruction on the floor. When my butt hit the cement, I decided to put the skates back in storage.

The move North was a real challenge. The furniture and all the boxes were loaded in a moving van. Carl drove the old pick-up we used for running trap line, complete with one big Buckskin colored dog and all the stuff from the stable. My van was loaded with two aquariums, three cats, two girls and a houseful of plants. It resembled a jungle with an occasional head peeking out of the foliage. The old truck led the way, in case they had any motor problems. Buck rode with his head out of the window of the truck and never took his eyes off of me.

Patches and Nuffers were Mousey's kittens from two separate litters. Ordinarily, she wouldn't give them a side ways glance. On this trip, she hunted them down in the van and gave them each a bath like we were getting ready for church, while the girls and I watched in amazement. Animals do have their own way of loving.

Getting there was the easy part. Cleaning the gigantic building took months. The previous owner had agreed to get the carpets shampooed. He did it himself, and when we walked in they sloshed. He must have thought the smell would go away if he drowned it. It didn't. Drying the rugs took the better part of two months with fans running full blast.

I cleaned enough of the kitchen to prepare our meals. The health inspector was to go through it with me to see what we could use and what we should throw. That kitchen was seventy-five feet long and ten feet wide. Seemed like whatever I needed was at the other end.

"You know, Carl, by the time I finish a day in the kitchen," I said. "I will have run a marathon."

Mousey, our mama cat

"Just the opposite at the bar." Carl related. "I can wait on everyone just standing in one spot and spinning around. By the time my day is done, I feel like I've unscrewed my knees."

"How long do you think, our legs will last?" I asked.

Later that evening, after the girls were in bed, I took a cup of coffee into the house to think. Seemed like I hadn't had a moment to myself since we walked through these doors.

What have I gotten myself into? I'm not a kid anymore. I hate bars. Did I think about this long enough? My home in the country was just the way I wanted it. And my business, it took years before I had it just right. Too late now. They're both gone. I signed my name on those papers. Dear God, I signed my name on those papers.

* * * * * *

When the health inspector arrived I was in for a surprise.

"Barney? Barney Herpel? You're the health inspector?" I asked with delight. "I didn't pay much attention to the name they gave me over the phone. I surely never expected someone from Fennimore."

"For gosh sakes, Little Sarah Bray." He laughed, "I don't think I'm considered from Fennimore any more. After twenty-three years I believe I'm a bonafide citizen of LaCrosse.

"Well, I'm not Little Sarah Bray any more either, so we're even." I said. "I'm glad you're here, anyhow. I need you to go through this kitchen with me. It's a mess. You can tell me which things to pitch before I start cleaning."

"Well, let's have at it." He glanced at his watch. "I have another appointment in just a short while."

We walked the length of the kitchen. I tried to be quiet, and he kept jotting things on his clipboard. When he finished, he summarized it for me.

"The walls are white, fire resistant, scrub able material. They are fine. The stainless-steel work counters are fine. Wooden dish racks will be okay, but don't put paper liner on them like they have now. Leave them bare. They're much easier to keep clean. The commercial stoves are in bad need of attention, but if you can get them clean, their fine. The domestic stove is all right for your own use right now, but when you open to the public, it has to go, along with the three domestic refrigerators. You need to get UPC labeled refrigerator and freezer units. The ovens need thermometers and the cold units need temperature gauges. The floor tile is fine. The stainless sinks are good. Here, I'll give you a list of cleaning supplies you can and cannot have in the kitchen." He handed me pamphlets and a copy of his report. "All the things I said were fine, will only pass if they are spotless, you know."

"I figured that." I said. "Thanks for going through it with me, Barney."

"When you get all finished, let me know." He said. "I'll come and give you the go-ahead." As he walked out, he said, "I'll tell Sherry I saw you, Sarah. Good luck."

"Thanks again." It had been nice to talk to someone from home.

Carl had made himself scarce during the inspection. Now he came through the door, "One of your old boyfriends?"

"Don't be ridiculous." I threw up my hands in disgust. "Barney was several years ahead of me in school. His sister, Sherry, was a classmate and friend of mine."

"Ya, I know why all the guys from Fennimore stop by." Carl sneered.

Fact was, and he knew it, I had taken out adds in the Fennimore and Oregon newspapers. I invited anyone coming to our neck of the woods to stop by and say hello. Ours was a new business in a popular vacation area. You have to advertize.

I could have saved myself the time and money...Several acquaintances, men and women, stopped by to wish us well. Each time, he made stupid accusations, right to their faces. Few ever came back for a second visit. He was doing the same with my family.

Laurie's husband, Dwight, was a business manager. He had several years of training. When they came to visit, I tried to get as many pointers as possible on pricing and profit margins from him. Carl argued about everything. Dwight was disgusted and angry by the time they left. Laurie came by herself for a while, then she stopped coming too. She said she couldn't stand the way Carl was treating me.

"Sarah, some <u>man</u> on the phone for you," Carl yelled.

"Hello." I said into the phone.

"Sarah, hello, this is your health inspector." Barney said. "I have some information that might interest you."

"What's that?" I asked.

"There is a restaurant not far from you that is closing." He said. "The building has been sold for a Laundromat. They won't be needing their refrigerator units. I'll give you the number if you're interested."

"Great, thanks, Barney. That solves a big problem for me." I said.

I called the number to get more information. The place was close by, so I went to look at the equipment. Promising to get them moved immediately, allowed for haggling on the price. There were two freezer units and a large refrigerator unit. They also threw in some shelving they needed to remove, and we needed the shelves.

"I really stole the equipment, Carl, the stuff was in their way," I told him, "but we have to move it right away." Then I told him the price.

"Moving it won't be a problem. You must have had to lay down good for them, to get it for that price. Was your health inspector there?"

"My God, Carl, why do you have to say those terrible things?" I asked. "I was dealing with the people who owned the café that closed, and no, he wasn't there."

Why was I defending myself? I haven't done anything wrong. He seems to be trying to make me feel small and dirty.

By the time we had the kitchen open for business, Brenda and Holly were preparing for the start of school. They had made friends at the swimming pool during the summer months. That should make it easier for them beings they were the new kids on the block.

When we purchased the bar, it came fully equipped with two regular bartenders, who both wanted to stay if we wanted them to. Ann was a girl about twenty-seven, a little on the chunky side, who was raising three children alone. She was a fun person, a hard worker, and a good bartender. She helped me scrub down the kitchen and clean those big stoves. The oven cleaner singed her hair when she crawled into the big oven. Her comment...

"Don't worry about it, Sarah, I needed a haircut anyway."

Deno Martinez, the other bartender, was an older man with a large family of boys and one girl.

"When you get the kitchen going and start having receptions, my three oldest boys have worked here before, and they're always willing. They enjoy tending the back bar."

Now we had a pool of extra help and the kitchen passed inspection. We decided to have a salad bar in the dining room. My days were spent making things to fill it, making soup and chile, and home made Lefse, which was a must for my salad bar. Instead of rolls, I served small loaves of bread at each table, on a small cutting board. Each Tuesday night I would make seventy-two loaves of bread. (Grandma's Therapy) This was for our regular menu.

My van was sold to do some needed repairs to the roof. We were now down to one car. Carl lorded it over me every time I had to use his car, so I had another set of keys made. At least I wouldn't have to grovel to do my grocery shopping for the kitchen.

The receptions started. Standard food for them was ham sandwiches, baked beans, cole slaw, potato salad and punch. This was set up in the hall for most occasions.

Once the newness wore off, I started running 'specials' every night except Monday. We closed on Monday to do book work, shop, and get some fresh air, usually with a fishing pole. The dining room was getting busier all the time. Hiring waitresses is another story. To make it short though, some were good, others were bad, but most I just put up with. Cooking and waiting would have been too much for one person.

When the back bar was open, it added to my seventy-five foot dashes, as the ice machine was way up front and I had to keep the back bar supplied with ice.

On one occasion, not just a reception, but the wedding took place in the hall. The crowd was so large that I had to set the food tables in the dining room. The food line started to diminish so I used the break to run a pail of ice to the back bar. When I entered the back door of the hall, Carl and the table hop were the only ones at the bar. The bride and groom were by the stage opening gifts and the crowd was watching them.

Carl was sitting on the first stool. The girl was sitting on the next seat with her legs up on Carl's lap. His cast wasn't getting in the way of him inspecting her credentials.

Heat flooded over my body and without thinking I dumped the ice on the floor.

"You Asshole!" I said.

I turned and went back to the kitchen. Work would help me cool off. He didn't bother coming around with an excuse. Later, he was so drunk, saying anything would have gotten me a beating, so I kept quiet.

Next morning, like every morning, I took a pail of water and some dog food and headed out to feed Buck. He wasn't there, only his chain. I ran back inside.

Shaking Carl's shoulder revolted me, but ..."Carl, where is Buck? He's not on his chain."

"Waa...what? Oh, I put him in the basement yesterday." He said. "The gnats were eating his ears so bad, they were bleeding."

"There's rat poison down there." I screamed. "Did you pick it up?"

"I never thought about it." He was slipping on his pants frantically.

We both ran to the basement, only to find my big buckskin colored friend laying in a pool of blood. He was still alive. The pain in his eyes as he looked at me for help was killing me. A trip to the veterinarian, only helped to put him out of his misery. We brought him home to bury outside my kitchen window. Nuffers searched everywhere for his friend.

Space. I needed some space. Carl Regent was here and I needed to be as far from him as I could get. A large thermos of coffee and a pair of ham sandwiches left over from last night would get me by. I literally ran to the car, stopping only briefly to grab Nuffers. He laid in the passenger seat and purred while I drove to a quiet, out of the way flowage, where I could be alone to think.

How could this happen to me? My family and friends are all alienated. Burdening Mom, Tag or Jane isn't something I could do. A loveless marriage? Carl can't love me and do the things he does.

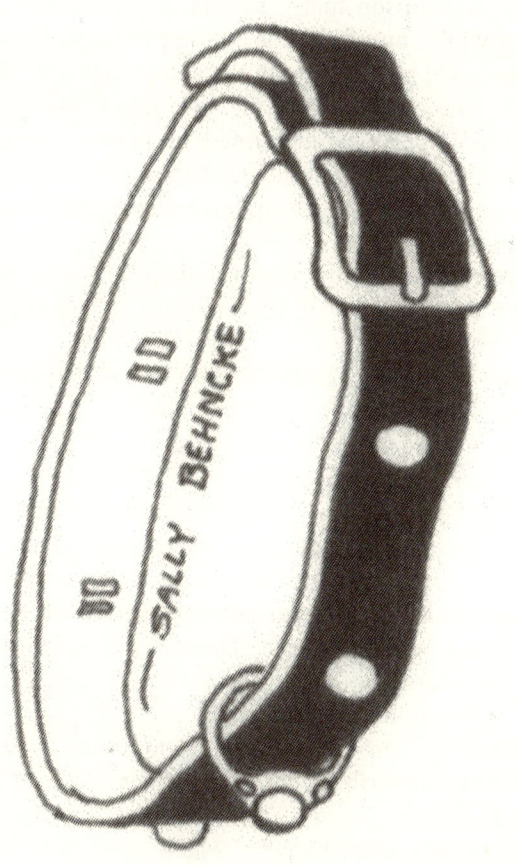

Nuffer's collar with my pinky ring

He accuses me of infidelity, when he's the one who was screwing around. I'm not sure if I love him or hate him. Everything I worked for is tied up in this miserable place. Even my vehicle is gone. I have nothing and nowhere to go. I'm trapped. Yet I know, when it's five o'clock, I'll be in the kitchen cooking, cause that's who I am.

"Nuffers," I said, "nothing's going to happen to you." I drove to the nicest section of Summit, slipped a pinky ring from my finger and put it on his tiny red collar, held him close for a moment, then opened the door and said, "Goodbye."

* * * * * *

The company in Madison that Carl had worked for was down sizing. This worried him for a while, but the union pushed through the clause for thirty and out, in their contract. He had been with the company for thirty-one years, so now he was officially retired instead of on sick leave. He would have company insurance for four more years, which turned out to be a blessing.

My breasts had been unusually tender lately. Of coarse my first thought was cancer. I was in constant fear of getting bumped while tending the bar, so Doctor Bradley ran some tests…

When he gave me the results, I was shaken. "But I've been going through my change of life for a couple of years now. I didn't know this was possible anymore."

"It's the most dangerous time for pregnancy, Sarah. Your body is all confused." He put his hand on my shoulder. "Don't you want to be pregnant?"

"Carl's always wanted a son," I said, "but I thought I was too old."

"How old are you?" He asked

"Forty-three." I replied.

"That's not too old." He said. "I have another patient now who is forty-three and pregnant. My youngest daughter was born two years ago when my wife was forty-three." He was rifling through some booklets. "I'll have to get you an appointment for your amniocentesis. These will explain the procedure." He handed me some literature.

"What is an amniocentesis for?" I asked.

"With this test they can determine if there is any problem with the baby, Down Syndrome or other birth defects common in older pregnancies. The test is essential." He said.

"Can they tell the sex of the baby?" I asked.

"Yes, but only if you ask." He replied.

"At my age, I want to know." I said. "Why buy pink if it's going to be a boy? I don't exactly have a lot of baby things lying around anymore."

"You'll have to go to Madison for the test," he said. "And it has to be done before thirteen weeks. Just in case they have to abort the fetus, after that it's too late."

"I don't believe in abortions, at least not for me. Besides, I want this baby."

"It would only be in case of birth defects. You're going to be quite old before this baby is an adult."

"All right, you can set it up. Just let me know when." I said. "Mondays are best for us, because we're closed."

I wasn't at all sure how Carl was going to react to this news. In order to delay facing him, I stopped in the dry goods store. I'd been wanting to get some soft material for a new housecoat. When I walked in, I was the only costumer. The clerk was very attractive, but was way overweight. As she got close, I caught a whiff of her beautiful perfume

"Can I help you?" She said, with a very strong accent.

"Sure," I said, "but I have to ask you two questions first. What part of Germany are you from?" I inhaled deeply. "What is that heavenly scent?"

"It' Taboo." She laughed. "How did you know I was from Germany?"

"My Grandparents came from there. I'd recognize that accent anywhere."

We talked for over an hour about everything. My fear of cancer, and her bout with it. She'd had a mastectomy, and the weight problem was because of the treatments. When I told her about my being pregnant she shivered and said.

"You've got more nerve than I would have." She said. "One was enough for me, and I had Mickey when I was young. We must be close to the same age. I'm forty-three."

I somehow felt I could talk to her about anything, even Carl. She didn't open up on that subject, but from her reaction, I felt she knew what I was going through, from first hand experience. By the time I left she had sold me five yards of Jade green velour and I had made a friend. Her name was Ilka.

* * * * * *

Brenda was now a junior in high school. She was dating Mike Martinez, one of Deno's sons, and they were getting a little more serious than Carl and I wanted.

"I'm quitting school." She announced one day.

"What?" Carl shouted.

"I said I'm quitting school." She repeated.

"I heard what you said." He yelled. "What's it supposed to mean? You think I'll just sit still while you quit school?"

"Mike and I are going to Florida." She said as she flipped her hair. "Nancy quit at my age."

"Just like that, huh?" Carl said. "Nancy also had a baby. Are you going to try that too?"

"If you try to stop us, we'll run away anyhow." She flipped her long hair again and strutted off to her room.

* * * * * *

Within two days Brenda and Mike were gone. Carl didn't even attempt to stop them. Holly was lost without her sister, but she was excited about the trip to

159

Madison. She was going to be allowed to skip a day of school to go along. It had been a long time since she had seen the other girls.

It was a bright morning as we headed toward Madison, and the sun was right in our eyes. Holly took along a book. She knew we didn't talk much on the road.

"Let's stop at the Dell's for breakfast." Carl said. He seemed to be in an exceptionally good mood.

"We don't dare take to long." I said. "These tests were sure set up for an early hour."

"Are you scared, Sarah?" Holly asked.

"Not really scared, Holly." I said. "Nervous is more like it. You know how you feel when you're doing something for the first time? I've never done this before."

"You didn't have to do this with your other kids?" She asked.

"No." I said, "and, I wasn't forty-three then either."

` When we reached the hospital, people shuffled me all over, ran several blood tests, filled out form after form, finally they got to the big event. I was sweating. Guess I was more scared than I thought. It was painful. I won't lie. When they put that large needle in my abdomen, it felt and sounded like they punctured the skin of a basketball. The hardest part of the test was that my baby was kicking already and wouldn't lay still. It didn't last long, and then we were free to go. They would let us know the results in two weeks.

We drove to Peg's. The beach hadn't changed much since we left. Peg had let the other girls know we were coming so they were at her house. Holly hung on each of them. Peg motioned me aside after a short time.

She whispered, "Why is Holly acting like a little kid?"

"I can't tell you, Peg. She's been acting like that around her Dad lately too." I said. "Maybe it has something to do with Brenda leaving, but I think she's just taking her last fling of being the baby of the family."

Peg said, "You might be right, anyhow, Nancy and Brandy noticed it too."

"I wouldn't worry about it." I said. "She's been the baby for a long time."

"I ran into Cyle and Julie last week. They have a cute little boy. They said they're living in McFarland now. Have you been over there?" Peg asked.

"Peggy, I haven't seen any of my kids. Both boys have boys of their own now. I don't know either of my grandchildren." I said. "We don't have a life anymore, just a bar."

"Hi! All," Rick said as he came in from work.

"Hope you remembered the pizza." Peg called from the kitchen.

"Sure thing." Rick entered the room like a ballerina, with three stacked pizzas above his head

Everyone scurried around to sit at the table. After polishing off all but small scraps, Rick smiled at Carl.

"Care to join me in a cocktail, Sir?"

"I thought you'd never ask." Carl said, with a huge smile.

After the third one, I knew I'd better get Carl on the road, or the forth would lead to the fifth and so on. "Carl," I said, "we have a long ride ahead of us."

"Guess I have to go, a man doesn't stand a chance around all these women," Carl complained to Rick.

*   *   *   *   *   *

Carl said he was headed home but this wasn't the way out of Madison.

"Where are you going, Carl?" I asked.

"Never mind." He snapped. "You got to go where you wanted to. Now it's my turn. I'm going to my old watering hole." He pulled up in front of a bar, jumped out, and disappeared through the door. Holly and I tried several times to talk to him. Each time he'd just order another round. By ten o'clock he was smashed and belligerent. He was willing to go, but wouldn't relinquish the car keys. In the first six miles he was in the ditch four times, once knocking over several fence posts. I was crying but it was Holly's screaming that finally convinced him to let me drive. As soon as I took over the wheel he passed out. Holly eventually fell asleep. I don't think a barrel of tranquilizers could have made me close my eyes. When we arrived at home, I woke Holly but let Carl stay where he was.

*   *   *   *   *   *

Two weeks later, after the groceries were all put away, good time for me to put my feet up and recuperate from lugging in all those bags. Carl was busy with the bookkeeper. As I walked past the men, Carl raised his head.

"Madison called, it's healthy and it's a boy." He said. He kept right on with what he was doing. Then he added, "But it's breech."

I thought he'd be pleased about the baby being a boy. He wouldn't even take a minute off to tell me the news.

Most all of the bars were closed on Monday, so the Tavern League's monthly meetings were held on the second Monday of each month. Tonight's meeting was at a bar a half mile from ours.

"I should have stayed home tonight, Carl, I can't drink, and I can't get comfortable." I said.

"Then why the hell didn't you?" He grabbed his drink and walked away.

One of the other wives leaned toward me and whispered, "What's the matter with your husband? He's been acting like a real prick lately, everyone's noticed."

"I really don't know. It scares me when he's like this." I admitted.

161

As the evening progressed and the business part of the meeting ended, Carl drank faster and faster. It seemed like he wasn't able to get enough.

"Can we go, Carl? I don't feel well." I lied, but I knew he was drinking way too much.

"You know what you can do?" He screamed. "You can get rid of the little bastard."

The people standing close all turned and looked at him. Then, like he had invented something new …He stood up on his toes and bellered so everyone could hear…

"Get rid of the little bastard."

"Get rid of the little bastard. Did everyone hear?"

I shrank, inside. I wished I could disappear. Making it to the back door, I walked home devastated. Holly was at a sleep over, so I went down to her room, curled up in a fetal position and cried myself to sleep. I didn't hear him, when and if he ever came home.

Chapter Sixteen

The sun was shining, so I decided to sit my expanding body on the steps outside the kitchen door and soak in a little sunshine, when a bright yellow van pulled in. A lady climbed out, walked over, and sat down beside me.

"Are you hiring at all?" She sighed. "I'll be honest with you, I'm over fifty. No one seems to want older people anymore."

Her eyes were the same soft blue as Grandma Bray's. I liked her right off.

"Come to think of it," I said, "I could use some help in the kitchen. Do you cook?"

"I can do whatever needs to be done, but I don't want to serve drinks." She said.

"We don't need any more help in the bar anyway." I told her. "How many hours do you want?"

"Well, my husband and I farm and I work nights in the Lefse plant, so a few hours during the day, I guess." She already looked tired and she still wanted more work.

"You're hired. What's your name?" I held out my hand to her.

"Mary, Mary Rumple." She said, taking my hand.

She came each day dressed to work in the kitchen but always brought along extra clothing, for whatever I needed her to do.

Mary and I cooked, cleaned, laid floor tile, painted walls and raked lawn. Whatever the chore was, she was game to help me. At fifty-five, she and Darrell, her husband, had never lived anywhere but his home farm. They married late in life because of World War II, but they had two daughters, who were ready to start college. She and Darrell had never been out to eat, never. Unbelievable. Mary talked about her family as we worked. She described them so lovingly that I felt I knew them personally. I don't believe she had a mean bone in her body. She didn't complain of being tired, but worried overtime about me.

I found a young gal, Cheryl, who said she would take over the kitchen while I was in the hospital. I had been training her for three weeks. Mary even helped with this. We had to make sure Cheryl knew how to put food away safely in the cooling units, keep the salad bar fresh, and how to reheat my bread loaves just right. One problem she had was cooking steaks to the proper degree of doneness. Mary had the patience of a saint. She didn't get upset when Cheryl seemed to forget everything she had been told. Carl's presence made Cheryl nervous. He griped constantly about paying someone to do my work, he did it very loud and always made sure that Cheryl was within earshot. Sometimes I wondered if she would ever be able to handle the kitchen if Mary and I weren't there, and she would have to contend with Carl on her own.

The cramping started in the sixth month. I doubled over in pain and couldn't stand up straight until it quit.

"You go lay down, Sarah," Mary said. "I'll get everything ready for the supper hour crowd before I leave."

I knew she'd be late getting home, but I had no choice.

Two times I went to the hospital with false labor, way too early. They stopped it both times, but the last time Doctor Bradley told me.

"Sarah, you need complete bed rest if you want to carry this baby to term."

"I don't know if that's possible but I'll try." I told him.

It took all my courage to tell Carl. I was afraid he'd explode. "Dr. Bradley wants me to stay off my feet until the baby comes, Carl. I don't know if Cheryl can handle it."

"Too bad," he smirked. "Your little cooky called today and quit."

I felt like the wind had gone out of me. What could I do? I couldn't get anyone else trained in time, so I worked, and the cramping continued. Lately I'd been having trouble with a lump in my throat that made it hard to breathe or swallow. Dr. Bradley assured me it was caused by stress. Stress he had said. Now where in the world would I, Sarah Ann Bray Regent, get any stress?

Mary stayed some days to wait on tables so I wouldn't have to, even though she was worn out and had other places she was supposed to be.

On October twenty-fourth, still a month early, the labor was for real. There wasn't a surgeon at the hospital when we arrived. The ambulance driver, John, a young man I recognized from the bar, stood in the doorway of my hospital room waiting to transport me to LaCrosse.

"You may as well send John away." I said. "No way are you putting me in an ambulance. You want to send me sixty miles with a nurse and an ambulance driver, while I'm trying to give birth to a breech baby? This is a hospital. Get the doctor here." There were people all over me. Nurses sticking me with needles, others poking me with an IV. The anesthetist introduced himself, for all the good that was going to do me. Carl was over in the corner looking helpless. Sarah Bray's will power wasn't this powerful. I was experiencing pain that I didn't know was possible. Bring on the anesthesia. From then on, I only remember bits and pieces. I had signed a paper earlier in my pregnancy for them to do a tubal ligation. Some dumb ass kept asking me, as I swam in and out of consciousness, whether or not I was sure about having my tubes tied. I wanted this baby, but I sure didn't want any more. Why did they keep asking?

I remember wishing Puddin could be here with me, and praying that her pregnancy was nothing like mine. Then I caught a faint whiff of Taboo. Was Ilka here? No, she wouldn't be at the hospital. Oh God, when is this going to be over? I don't want any more of that stuff. There's still a baby in me. Here I go again. When will this end?

After six hours of labor, the baby was half way into this world in the wrong direction and stopped. Baby boy was in distress and turning blue before the doctor arrived. There were more people around me now than before. During the C-section, they had to pull the baby back through the birth canal. Neither the baby nor I was in very good shape. I could hear them talking, like I wasn't even there. With all the kicking, while I was carrying him, the baby had pulled himself almost free of the placenta. Please, don't let me lose him. Another inch and I would have lost him. The cramps were from the tearing. It must be over. I can't hear anyone anymore. It's so peaceful.

They brought Robert Andrew Regent into my room in an incubator, for a few short minutes before they transferred him to LaCrosse, to the infant trauma center. He was small, but perfect. He weighed only four pounds, eight ounces. His color was back to normal, but they wanted to be on the safe side. I ached to hold him, but had no strength left. He's so b e a u t i f u l.

It was the next morning and I had been knocked out since they took the baby yesterday. As I tried to wake, I could hear my Mom and Aunt Dora talking. My body was going back into labor. No, it wasn't another baby. My body was trying to finish the job it started, and the labor pains were just as hard. They gave me another shot, and knocked me out again. Around noon it happened again. I was able to stay alert long enough to tell Mom to go out and see Carl until later. At four o'clock they came for a short visit before heading home. Mom didn't need to see me like this anyhow. From the straining, I had two black eyes and I looked like the walking dead.

Carl stopped by on his way to the post office. He looked almost as bad as I did.

"I couldn't stay in the room with you last night." He said. "You were straining so hard, I thought your eye balls were going to pop right out of their sockets. I wasn't much help, seeing you in all that pain."

"So, what did you do?" I asked. I already knew the answer.

"I guess I went home and got drunk." He said. "I really don't remember. Every time the phone rang I was afraid they were going to say that neither one of you made it."

I thought, any excuse is a good one. I should know. I've been there too.

Robert (Bobby) was back the next day. My breasts were overfull so my pleasure in seeing him was twofold. He was doing fine. He was a fighter, and he was hungry. If my appetite was any sign, I was on the mend as well.

That afternoon the florist brought a bouquet of nine red roses, with a card that read, "Thanks for the son," signed, "Love Carl." He explained later, a rose for each kid. A nurse supplied me with some paper and a pencil so I could draw, to break the monotony of inactivity. This vacation was a big change from being

165

on my feet all my waking hours. I drew a picture of the bouquet and card. The flowers wouldn't last forever, but a picture could.

Bobby's basket in my kitchen, 1979

I left the hospital alone on the forth day. Bobby had to be under blue lights for jaundice, so he had to stay two additional days. Using the breast pump and delivering milk to the hospital gave me a chance to visit my baby often.

By the time I was healed enough to reopen the kitchen, Bobby was home with me, but he seldom slept. It was like he didn't want to miss anything. Mary was back during the day. We fixed a basket so Bobby could be in the kitchen with us.

*   *   *   *   *   *

Holly, well that girl was another story. She had been acting strange since I returned, sneaky is the word. I knew something was going on so I did a little investigation.

"Holly," I asked, "where did all these new clothes come from?" I found several new outfits in her bedroom.

"They're not new." She protested.

"They are so. The bags from the stores are right here, and some of them still have tags on." I held up the evidence.

"Those bags are from a long time ago." She was lying through her teeth.

"I do all the laundry," I said, "I'd surely know if they were old."

Taking the bags, I went to the phone and called the stores. Then I went to Carl.

"You have to talk to Holly, Carl. She has been bringing clothes home on approval, wearing them to school, and returning them to the store." I was very irritated.

He smiled, "Neat trick."

"You've got to be kidding me." I said, angrily. "You can't let her do that. These clothes are expensive. What she's doing is illegal. If you won't stop it, I will. What kind of father are you?"

He just filled his coffee cup, walked back to the bar, and started talking to one of his cronies.

Next day, I rounded up all of the new clothing, bundled Bobby up, and made a round of all the shops. The clothing that she had obviously worn, I paid for. The others I just returned. At each shop, I explained what had happened and made them agree not to let her bring any more items' home on approval. If she wanted something, she could try it on at the shop and pay for it before bringing it home. I purposely left Ilka's shop until last so I could show off my baby and visit for a minute.

"Oh, Sarah, I've forgotten how little they are." Ilka said. "Can I hold him?"

I handed the baby over to her, then explained what I had at the other shops.

"I'm glad you told me and I'm sure the other shops are too," she said, "this happens more than you know and it costs the shop keepers a lot of money each year."

"God, I'm glad you said that. I was feeling guilty about doing this to Holly."

"You shouldn't." She insisted. "Parents are the ones that should know what their kids are doing. How are you feeling now? I heard you had a rough time having the baby."

"I did. The body can take a lot and still heal. I'm fine now. My back still bothers at times, but I can live with that. It's good to see you again, but I see you have some other costumers, so I'd better let you go." She just stood there admiring Bobby. "Can I have my baby back?" I asked.

"You mean I can't keep him?" She grinned.

"Not now. Some day I'll probably wished I had left him with you, but right now I can't get enough of him." I said. "Gotta go now."

She hugged me and Bobby like one big bundle. Her hug felt so good, I wished for a minute I didn't have to go home. Who knew what was waiting for me there?

*   *   *   *   *   *

Holly flew in the door after school, "Well, did you turn me into a criminal, today?"

"Holly, I simply returned the clothing that you hadn't worn, paid for the ones you did, and ask them not to let you have things on approval. You can still shop. Just pay for what you want."

"I won't be able to show my face in any dress shop." She cried. "I'm not a criminal."

"You can call what you did anything you want." I said. "You did it to yourself. Don't put the blame on me. You got a couple of outfits anyhow and that's more than you deserve."

From that day, she refused to do anything. She wouldn't make her bed, clean her room, or put away the laundry I had done for her. All she did was talk on the phone for hours on end, until one day. There was a terrible thunder storm and I ran in to check the windows. I couldn't get past her.

"Get off the phone. It's lightning out." I ordered.

The earpiece was no sooner back on the receiver when a ball of fire knocked the phone off the wall and shot crossed the room. Holly just stood there with her mouth open, unable to talk.

"Are you all right?" I asked.

She just nodded her head.

"Now aren't you glad that wasn't your head?" I said smugly.

This little prima-donna's attitude was really starting to piss me off. Carl's attitude toward the problem ran true to all the other problems he had with his daughters. He buried his head in the sand, so to speak. If he didn't see it, it would go away. Anything I tried to do with Holly meant nothing, if he didn't back me up. He did nothing but ignore me. The lump in my throat that, by now felt like a baseball behind my Adam's Apple got continuously worse. It was getting harder to swallow or breath with each passing day. The only way I could get the lump to relax was to drink. So I drank almost every night. In the morning the lump would be worse. I was trapped in a never-ending puzzle. It was kind of like the chicken and the egg. There was no apparent answer, so I stayed in the kitchen and did what I was supposed to do. When that was done, I drank.

*   *   *   *   *   *

"Mary," I said, "you've been a godsend. I don't know how I'd get through a day in this place without you."

"Thank you, Sarah." She said, never missing a lick with the potato peeler. "You've been good to me too. If I could help you in any way with Holly, I would, you know. I just haven't thought of a way. You're like the sister I never had. You and I can talk about anything."

She was wrong. I hadn't been able to talk to her about Carl's abuse. I didn't want to alienate her from him. She was the only female Carl openly admired without an ulterior motive. His physical abuse had stopped since I had gotten pregnant. The verbal abuse continued but not in Mary's presence.

She called me from home early on Tuesday morning, "I won't be able to come in this week, Sarah. Darrell died yesterday." She choked up and couldn't say any more...

I interrupted the silence. "I'm sorry, Mary. Don't worry about anything here. Are the girls with you?"

She recovered her composer enough to answer. "Yes. They found their Dad in the barn when they went to help with chores."

"Do you have the arrangements made?" I asked.

"Almost, the funeral will be in York, on Thursday, at the Lutheran church, at two o'clock. The wake is Wednesday evening, seven til nine."

"We'll see you Thursday, Mary. Is there anything we can do?"

"No," She said. "The girls and I can manage for now."

"I'm so sorry," I said again. "You let me know if you need anything, Mary."

Carl and I attended the funeral. We had only met Darrell once, but it felt like I knew him through Mary. She was such a dear friend. I wanted to be with her in her grief. She stayed home an additional week. Managing the farm alone and her other job was next too impossible. I was selfish enough to hope she wouldn't quit working for me. She didn't, but she cut back on her hours. When she did come in, she looked all worn out.

"Mary, you've got to slow down." I warned. "You're ruining your health."

"You're a good one to talk." She huffed.

"But if your health gives out, then what will the girls do?" I asked.

"Our girls are very capable of doing the farm work. They're very independent. Eighties-Ladies, Darrell used to call them." Her eyes filled with tears. Both of her girls were in college part time. I knew the reason she worked so hard was to get them through school.

She finished mixing the dressing she was working on. "Can Holly come out to the farm to visit this week end?" She asked. "I'll come and get her. It'll give you a little break."

"You can ask her, but I'm sure she'd love to." I answered her, knowing full well why she had asked in the first place. A break from Holly was just what I needed.

Holly was tickled about the upcoming visit and had her bag packed way in advance.

Friday evening, just before Mary was expected, a phone call came from Rilla, Mary's oldest daughter.

"Sarah, I have some bad news. Mom was killed by our bull sometime Wednesday or Thursday. We don't know exactly how it happened, yet, but Amy and I found her when we came home from school this afternoon." She was having trouble talking. "I know she was coming to get your daughter tonight, but...

"My God, Rilla, I don't know what to say. I'm so sorry for you girls. Twice in such a short time." I was overwhelmed with grief and couldn't talk anymore. Then, "I'll have to call you back later, Rilla. I'm sorry, your mother was one of the dearest people I ever knew."

She said, "Mom loved you too, Sarah."

Next morning I called her back. We were both able to talk a little better. She told me more details and when the funeral was to be held. Holly was upset too. Her last memory of Mary, was planning a visit that never could be.

I missed her so much in the months following the funeral. My work in the kitchen didn't seem the same without her. It was almost like someone had severed my right arm at the elbow. Tears came to my eyes every time I thought about Mary lying in that pasture, at the mercy of a bull she had raised from a calf. According to the coroner she had laid out there for at least twenty-four hours before she expired. During that time the bull had ravaged her repeatedly.

If anyone was ever to tell me that Mary Rumpel had ever done a bad thing, I wouldn't believe them. She didn't have a mean bone in her body. If overwork was a sin, then she had one strike against her. I never heard her complain about anything. Mary will always be one of my guiding Angels.

Chapter Seventeen

Alone! Who said I wanted to be alone? Not this way. When the judge said Carl could have Bobby every other week end, he didn't give me instructions on how to not go crazy while my son was gone. Will Carl drink tonight while Bobby's there? Will Bobby be safe? Would Carl dare to strike a little boy? I've got to get out of here! I need some air!

I walked street after street. Thank God, the rain had stopped. Those lonely streets went on for miles and miles, until it started to get dark. I don't want a drink. I don't want a drink…Go to a meeting. The next street over led me right to the meeting hall. Tonight's topic? Acceptance!

> God, grant me the serenity to accept the things I cannot change,
> The courage to change the things I can,
> And the Wisdom to know the difference.

Talking was out of the question tonight. Listening is what I needed. Acceptance was my big problem right now, tonight. Even listening tonight was a problem. All I could think about was Bobby.

I stopped for a large coffee and then returned to the motel, alone. If Carl could see me now, he would be pleased. He has reduced me to a blithering idiot. He knew just how to do it too, my son. The son he always wanted and then never wanted at all. Now, because it will cause me pain, he wants him again. My mind races to all of the 'every other week ends' to come, when this will happen all over again. Tonight, I just have to get through tonight.

I sat staring out of the door at car after car driving past. Before I realized it, it was daylight, and Colleen was leaving all dressed for church. My coffee was still sitting on the table, cold and untouched.

Here comes Ilka. How did she know I needed her?

"Sarah, are you okay?" Ilka asked as she burst through the open door.

"Not really." I whimpered. "How will I stand him going twice a month, overnight, to his Dad's? Carl has never loved anyone, and he has never shown Bobby much love. He's just using the visitation to hurt me more."

"There must be something you can do." She tried to assure me.

"There isn't. Once the judge gave him visitations, that's it." I shook my head.

"But that was only your preliminary hearing." Ilka said. "Your attorney can surely request a different visitation schedule."

"Why are you here today, anyhow, Ilka?" I asked. "I hope you don't think you have to babysit me."

171

"Colleen called. Said you'd been sitting, watching the road all night." She admitted.

"Not all night, I wasn't. I went to an A.A. meeting." I boasted. "I had a choice. Either go to a meeting or get drunk."

"Well, that's a step in the right direction anyhow." She said. "At least you didn't drink."

"He doesn't want Bobby out there, Ilka." I said. "He can't smack me around anymore, but he can hurt me worse this way."

"You better talk to an attorney and see what can be done." She warned. "You can't go through this every time Bobby goes there. I'm going to walk next door for some hot coffee and donuts. I'll be right back."

While she was gone, I splashed some water on my face. When I saw my reflection in the mirror, I cringed. He really had made a mess out of my life and my face. "Tomorrow I'll fight back."

Ilka returned and we shared her treat while I told her my plans.

"You had better go home to Stan, Ilka. Don't let my problems cause problems for you."

"I suppose I'd better get back." She said. "Then you're sure, you're okay?"

"I'm sure." I said. "You're the only one around here who cares at all, and I appreciate everything you do for me. Without your friendship I'd be lost."

She hugged me. "Let me know how you come out tomorrow."

After she left, I sipped the coffee and my mind drifted back once again...

*　*　*　*　*　*

Finding a sitter for Bobby turned out to be a constant hassle. Holly would play with him and listen for him after I put him to bed, but wanted no part of taking care of him. It was just as well. I couldn't really trust her to keep an eye on her brother, when all she seemed to care about was talking on the phone.

Millie and Paul Gasch were middle-aged costumers of ours. They were a matched set, both very short and stout. Never being able to have any children of their own, they took a shine to Bobby. Paul would pinch hit as a bartender if we needed him. Millie, as a rule, accompanied her husband to the bar, but drank nothing but soda or orange juice.

"I'd love to watch Bobby for you." Millie commented one day, after hearing me complain about not being able to find a good sitter. "But you'd have to bring him downtown to our house, because I don't drive."

"That sure would help out, Millie." I sighed. "Since he's started trying to walk, it's too dangerous for him around all of the hot things in the kitchen. He's into, and touches everything."

172

Millie watched Bobby for close to a year. She bought a stroller just for him, and seeing the two of them out walking became a common sight for the town's people in Summit.

On Christmas Eve, because of his build, Paul usually dressed up as santa for several families. He thrilled Bobby with his masquerade and then Millie and Paul left for their next stop, where she took ill. They canceled the remaining appearances and went home to bed. Millie past away in her sleep that night. She was buried with a rose from Bobby.

After that a neighbor acrossed the road who had recently lost her husband too, thought taking care of Bobby would fill some of her lonely time. I was almost afraid to hire Minnie, after Mary and Millie, but she was a good sitter, her and her dog, Fritz. Bobby was walking now, and we used the trip to Minnie's for fresh air and exercise. It was convenient to have a sitter so close by.

Carl didn't seem to care what I did with Bobby, as long as I kept him out of the bar and out of his way. My scampi, young, escape, artist had ideas of his own. He could always find a way to sneak into the bar. He made friends with everyone but was also picking up some bad habits. One evening he was playing in the tub while I fixed my hair for work…

"Mommy." He said.

"What, Honey?" I asked.

"F___ you, Mom." He said boldly.

My mouth flew open and I dropped my hair brush. I sat down on the stool to catch my breath. How was I going to handle this? How would you impress on a four-year-old that a word all the bar patron used in great frequency was not a nice word? Were Carl and I bad parents? No, that wasn't the right question. I already knew what kind of a parent Carl was. Was I a bad mother? Heck, I wasn't even a good grandmother. I now had six natural grandchildren, who didn't even know who I was. Their parents wouldn't come here on a bet, and I couldn't get away from here.

"Come on, Bobby, let's get you dried off." I said, as I grabbed a towel and picked him out of the tub. As I got him into his pajamas, I kept talking softly, because he listened better that way.

"Bobby, that word you said to Mommy wasn't a nice word." I repeated the word so he would know which one I meant.

"Don't be mad at me, Mommy." He sniffled.

"I'm not mad at you, Bobby." I said as I hugged him. "I just don't want you to say that word again, please. Mommy doesn't like that word."

"Okay, Mommy." He said.

As we waited for his present night sitter to show up, I rocked him and read a story. The time I got to spend with him between a day sitter and night sitter, was so short, I wanted to savor it.

When the phone started ringing I didn't even get up. I knew Carl would answer out in the bar or Holly would soon be flying up the stairs to get it. It didn't ring a second time, so I knew Carl had picked it up. Then I heard his footsteps coming toward the living quarters. It must be for Holly. The door opened…

Carl hollered. "Holly, get the phone." He turned and left without a word to me and Bobby.

When she came bounding up the steps, I said…

"Holly, please take the phone into the next room and close the door so we don't have to listen to your conversation. I'm reading to Bobby."

She gave a deep, disgusted sigh. "Then I'll have to stand up to talk."

"One time isn't going to kill you. I said.

She disappeared through the door and slammed it hard on the phone cord. I could feel my throat tightening.

"Bobby," I said, "I don't know how I'm going to do it, yet, but I'm going to escape from this trap I'm in." He didn't understand what I was saying. It didn't matter though, I did. I realized now that selling my house was only a way for Carl to get what he wanted. This bar. Once he had it, I became cook, dishwasher, waitress, cleaning lady, bartender and then brood mare for a son he didn't even want. And I was doing all of this for no wages. I call that slavery. This was Carl's bar. It was Carl's car, and Carl's money. I no longer existed except to work. Just how I was going to do it wasn't clear yet, but at least now I had a goal.

"Hi, Sarah. Hi, Bobby," the sitter said as she came in. "Sorry I'm late, but I had to stop for gas."

"It's okay. I was enjoying my visit with Bobby." I said. "But I do have to go to work now. "Kids, what do you want for supper?"

"Can we have a pizza?" She asked.

"It's okay with me," I said, "but stick your head through that door and ask Holly if that's what she wants."

"Okay." She opened the door and Holly agreed to a pizza.

"By, Honey," I said to Bobby. "I'll be in when suppers ready. You mind the sitter now."

"By, Mommy," he said. I didn't want to leave. I wished we had a normal life and I could spend the night with my baby.

Walking through the dining room, I stopped to admire my salad bar. Earlier I had picked some fresh parsley to garnish between the salads and Lefse. It looked inviting.

While the pizza was baking, I thought about the bank account I had opened in Bobby's name shortly after he was born. All of my tip money and what I gleaned from aluminum cans went into his account. The account wasn't large, but now I had a purpose. I had to get out of here or die trying. Somehow I felt that's where I was headed anyhow, if I didn't get away.

Beings I was not only cooking, but waiting tables now as well, there would be more tips. When customers came in, from then on, they got my best service, extra coffee refills, and a very pleasant country smile.

*   *   *   *   *   *

Holly didn't get off the school bus, she must have gone to some friend's house. She'd probably call and tell her Dad where she was, only she didn't. At eight o'clock I called her best friend, Mary.

"Mary," I said, "is Holly at your house?"

"No, Mrs. Regent," She answered, "Holly isn't here. She left school at noon and caught a bus to her mother's in Milwaukee. Didn't you know she was going?"

"No, we didn't know." I said. "Did she tell you why or for how long she was going?"

"She hasn't told me anything for quite some time." Mary said. "I know she just broke up with her boyfriend. Holly hasn't been hanging around with me and my friends for months. Something was bothering her and she never wanted to talk about it."

"Thanks, Mary," I said. "Sorry I had to call. I'm sure we'll hear from her."

After ten o'clock, Holly called...Carl answered.

"Dad, please, just put my things in boxes. We'll be up Saturday morning to get them." Then she hung the phone up before he could answer.

Carl was furious. There was no one at the bar right now. He grabbed a handful of plastic bags and took off for her room. He shoved everything she owned into bags. Clothing still on the hangers, make up, shoes, toys and games, school books, everything got shoved in together. There were five garbage bags full.

Saturday morning he sat them out on the steps and covered them with a tarp. When the car pulled in, there were five people in it. Where were they planning to put everything? They backed up to the pile, ripped the bags open, took what they wanted, and threw the rest all over the yard and parking lot. After they left, Carl shoved it all into fresh garbage bags, threw it in the car, and took off for the dump.

*   *   *   *   *   *

After trying several unreliable nighttime sitters, I finally found Katy. She was a jewel. She was an honor student, no less. She lived two miles away, but the school bus would drop her off here at the bar. She studied while watching Bobby. I'd take their supper into them, and at ten I'd drive her home.

I never drank until I got Katy home safe [Rule # One], but I could catch up in no time while tending the bar. My drinking was out of hand. Very few nights I didn't pour myself into bed. After the third drink the lump in my throat seemed to go away. Some nights I didn't remember going to bed, but would wake up with a black eye, broken teeth or my body hurting from being beaten on. Other nights when I wasn't wasted enough, I felt every blow he made. Our pool table was the old style with a real slate top that weighed a ton. This was his favorite weapon. He swung me around and threw me at it. It wasn't going to break. I was. Only God knew how I hated this place.

At closing time if Carl was drinking with a friend, he shut down the lights, grabbed a bottle, and the two of them would polish it off. Those nights I'd sneak off and be asleep before he came in.

If it was he and I, he'd put on our favorite Ray Price tape, 'For the Good Times', and we'd sit down with a drink. These nights started out all cozy, but at some point he'd change and start smacking me around. Most of the time it started with the mention of any of the kids.

Halloween and a paper bag mask

*   *   *   *   *   *

My mind had been on the menus for the upcoming deer season and I hadn't given any thought to Halloween until the kids came around to the kitchen door and knocked. Katy had painted a face on a brown paper bag and cut eyes, nose, and mouth out of it. Bobby was so cute. The eye holes were so big I could see most of his face peeking out. Katy took him to Minnie's and the other close neighbors. My little guy was growing up too fast, and I was missing most of his life. He was going from one sitter to the next.

"Carl," I argued, "we've got to get out of here, even if it's just for a few days of fishing."

"We can't afford to close." He was adamant. "And I'm not going to hire someone to come in and rob us blind while we're gone."

"Then let's close for a few days." I persisted. "We both need a break from this place. It's fall and Muskies are hungry. Come on, Honey, Hayward's not that far." I thought the lure of Muskie fishing might tempt him.

"I said no!" He bellered. "You wanted this place. Now you're stuck with it."

Turning away, I walked back to the kitchen. I hadn't wanted this place, but I knew talking to Carl was like talking to my stove. If I gave it too much gas, it would blow up too. Maybe if I quit drinking, I could protect myself. Easier said than done. The only way I could tend the bar was to drink. The lump in my throat wasn't getting any better.

Deer season was coming and that was always a busy time. I ran specials each night for the hunters and served turkey and ham with all the trimmings for Thanksgiving, which fell during deer season. We had a group of our regulars that came out to mingle with the hunters. Some had become good friends over the years. Then there were some local women who came out, simply because the place was full of deer hunters.

Opening week end came and went with the usual hullabaloo. Because of deer season, we didn't close on Monday. Tuesday, I had just finished making my second kettle of chile for the day and was on my way to deliver two bowls to a couple at the bar when the phone rang.

"Sarah, phone." Carl motioned to me to hurry. "It's Laurie and she sounds really upset."

"Will you grab some crackers for Evy and Doc?" I asked as I walked toward him.

"Sure thing." He replied.

I took the phone. "Hi, Laurie."

"Mom." She was having trouble talking.

"What's the matter, Laurie?" My mind was racing, but she couldn't answer. Finally...

She said. "Cyle was in a car accident."

"Did he get hurt?" I asked.

"He's dead, Mom." She cried.

"NOOooooo!" I screamed, I threw the phone against the wall and ran into the house. I sat on the floor in a corner and curled into a ball. "Not Cyle, God, Not Cyle." My throat was so tight I couldn't breathe. I thought I would choke. Can't I set time back so this will go away? My children aren't supposed to die before me. I was dying inside and for the first time since the aspirins, I wanted to be dead.

Carl came in a few minutes later and handed me a large glass of Brandy. He said nothing, didn't touch me, just turned around and left. I stared at that damned Brandy for what seemed like hours. The first swallow cut through the lump in my throat like a razor. The remainder of the glass and the second and third just followed the beaten path. I needed to get as far away from Sarah Bray as I could get. She wanted to die. I needed to find a reason to live...Bobby. He was with the sitter.

Next morning when I thought I might be able to hold it together, I called Julie, Cyle's wife. She seemed to be doing better than I. She told me Cyle had made a will when they were living in Hawaii. He wanted to be cremated. There would be no wake, casket or showing. Only a memorial service.

"Carl," I said. "I can't let him go without some closure. Otherwise I'll never believe he's gone."

"You want to go to the funeral parlor?" He asked.

"Yes, I have to." I said.

Carl threw up his hands. "Get ready then, we'll go."

His car wouldn't start. Someone, I can't even tell you who, pushed us for miles to no avail. They finally got us to an auto repair shop. I was completely coming apart. I couldn't stop shaking. The alternator was shot. I went through two hours of hell until they got us on the road.

We made a long, quiet trip to Stoughton where Cyle was being kept until cremation. Quiet except for my sobbing. Bobby was unusually quiet. He knew something was wrong with his Mommy. Bless his heart.

The undertaker warned, "It isn't a good idea for you to see the body, Mrs. Regent. Your son had been driving home from deer hunting. He was sitting at a stop sign when a semi truck coming the opposite direction missed his stop sign, slammed on his brakes, and jack-knifed. The semi tipped over on your son's pick up." Then he explained further. "There weren't any broken bones, but the steering column had pierced the boy's heart. When they removed him from the column, the blood rushed through his bruised body making him dark all over. I think it best that you don't see him that way."

"I don't care." I said. "He was once a part of my body. I have to be sure it's him, and if it is, say 'good-bye'."

"As long as you know what to expect." He shrugged.

"I'll be all right." I assured him.

The room they had him in was cold. They pulled back the sheet covering Cyle. He was dark all over. They hadn't even cleaned the blood from his nose, eyes and lips very well. I kissed him and brushed the hair from his eyes.

"Good-bye, Cyle, I Love You."

All the past experience I had with death did not prepare me for this. There was a loss that tore so deep inside, and it would never be possible to be a complete person again. With all my faults, I had always had one constant. The love for my children never wavered. A portion of the target for my love had been wrenched away. No person, nor a hundred, million could ever fill that void within me. I left a part of me behind as we left the room.

We swung by McFarland to see Julie and the two boys, J. C., and Mickey. The boys were too young to fully understand what had happened. Julie was being brave for them. How could this happen? Death is so damn final.

The day of the service we arrived to a church full to overflowing. Cyle had been an active church member and everyone that knew him loved this friendly giant of a guy. My heart was breaking and I couldn't stop weeping. Part of me was gone forever.

I avoided the news on television and newspapers. Seeing my sons death broadcast to the public would be more than I could bare. I never heard the truck drivers name, nor did I ever want to.

I thanked the good Lord for all the work waiting for me at home. My work and Bobby were all that kept me sane.

Chapter Eighteen

After Cyle's death I put an earnest effort into curbing my intake of alcohol. With the addition of some new specials, business was better than ever. People we had never seen were coming out to eat. Pidge and Daniel Cappin started coming on a regular basis. The four of us hit it off from the first. He had cancer and wasn't doing well, so when he wanted to drink, it was hard to refuse. We would meet them on Monday nights for a night on the town or just go out to their house for a quiet meal and movies. The nights they came to our bar, were the occasions I slipped back into my old ways. One morning after such a night, I received a phone call…

"Mrs. Regent, this is Amy, from last night. We made our reception plans with you. We need to make some changes in our plans. Nothing major, but we want to add some things to the menu for our reception."

"I'm sorry, Amy," I said. "I have to apologize. I don't remember talking to you, at all."

"Then it's a good thing I wrote everything down." She said. "I'll stop out this afternoon with a copy of what we agreed on and the prices you gave me."

She came out at three o'clock. The paper she brought me was right on target. Even drunk, I had tended to business. It scared me. I was completely blacked out and still functioning. She was a complete stranger.

I felt so bad, I said. "Tell you what, Amy, I'll take 10 per cent off of the price of your food and throw in two bottles of good champagne. Only don't offer me any of it. This is really embarrassing."

Daniel passed away in his sleep the end of November. Pidge went to pieces, and after my recent loss, I could relate. When she was at home, she would call at any hour of the day or night for consolation. The tinkle of ice told me that she was using my method of drowning her grief. Carl and I included her in our Monday shopping trips to wherever we were headed. Sometimes it was an evening of bowling or just going out to eat. Instead of us being a couple, we were now a foursome, Carl, me, Bobby, and Pidge. One night we had been shopping in Eau Claire and had one or two too many at the Rwanda Inn, so we decided to stay over instead of driving home. Carl reserved a room, with two double beds. Carl and I had one bed and Bobby and Pidge had the other one. She wasn't the least bit shy in just her undies as we retired for the night. I was glad she could be so relaxed. I wouldn't have been, no matter how good of friends we were.

When Christmas neared…

"Why don't we invite Pidge for our holiday dinner? She'll be all alone otherwise." Carl asked.

"I had kind of planned on it." I said. "A big dinner for just you, I, and Bobby would be ridiculous. None of our family will make the trip to eat with us. I wish things were different, Carl. Christmas doesn't seem the same without my kids around."

"If they don't want to be part of our lives, that's tough." He snapped.

None of the kids, his or mine, would make the trip to be verbally abused, and I didn't blame them. Carl seemed to feel that since this was 'his' place, he could say or do anything he pleased and everyone should know that.

Bobby, playing pool where the action is

After an unceremonious meal, post holiday blues set in. For all anyone cared, I could have fixed hotdogs. I once again tried to find happiness through the amber glow of brandy. Nights were spent trying to anesthesize myself, and days filled with regret for what I'd done the night before.

I have to pull myself together. If Social Service ever catches wind of how things are out here, I could lose my son. Maybe if I go talk to Ilka. She seems to be the one person who keeps me anchored to the world. She's never seen me drunk, Thank God.

I went after Bobby left for school and Carl was still sleeping. Luckily, her shop was empty.

"Ilka," I said, "I need help. My world is falling apart. Alcohol is what gets me through the day, and I know it's my worst enemy. Carl acts like he hates me. The only time he touches me anymore is when he's pounding on me, and now he's taken to leaving after we close and staying gone all night." The tears filled my eyes and words choked up behind the lump in my throat.

She put her arm around my shoulder and we walked to the back of the store. She said, "There is a lady that comes in quite often, who is a recovering alcoholic. Would you talk to her?"

"I'm ready to try anything. Bobby deserves more than this." I sobbed.

"You need to do this for yourself." Ilka said. "I don't want to lose you as a friend."

Ilka looked around, behind me. "Where is Bobby today?" She asked.

"He's in a kinder garden now, Ilka. Now he will be with children his own age. Maybe he'll have a chance to learn something besides cuss words." I grabbed a tissue and wiped my eyes. "How do I reach this lady?"

"I'll give you her number." She looked through the phone book and jotted a number down on a slip of paper. "Please, give her a call, Sarah. Her name is Pearl. She works, but I think she's home after four."

I talked to Pearl for a long time that evening and she told me all about the Alcohol Anonymous meetings. The Summit group had thirteen meetings a week. Some were early morning, some afternoon meetings, but most were in the evening, six-thirty to eight. You never had to wait very long for a meeting. On April first, scared stiff, I walked out of my kitchen, drove Carl's car to town, and walked down the stairs to my first A.A. meeting.

*　　*　　*　　*　　*　　*

After I once started going, if we had a slow supper hour, I just walked out and went to a meeting.

The group Carl had been hanging out with since I got sober, thought my meetings were a joke.

"How many meetings do you have to go to before you're not an alcoholic?" or "How many alcoholics does it take to screw in a lightbulb?" They would ask. Little minds live in little people. They even poured booze in my coffee, if I walked away from it. The smell was a dead giveaway, though, and I never drank it.

I'd been in A.A. for almost three months and was due to receive my three month medallion. I was proud of myself. Carl had tried every trick he knew to get me back drinking. When I walked into the bar area, he and his friends all got silent. When I'd walk out to the kitchen, they started snickering. I owned half of this terrible place and tonight I felt like an outsider. His tricks were working. I'll show the son of a b!

I had three sinks full of dirty dishes to do before I could run Katy home. I mixed myself a double, downed it and another while finishing my work and then drove Katy home. I broke [Rule # One] I felt guilty, and I had let myself down. Now I'd have to start all over from day one. He was having such a good time, he could tend the bar alone tonight, or maybe his friends will help him. I walked into the house and went to bed.

Waking early, I had Bobby ready for the school bus, except for his breakfast, when Carl slammed through the door with a drink in his hand.

"You ain't sending him to school today." He slurred his words. "I'm taking him to Madison with me."

I knew he hadn't come to bed, but he'd been drinking all night and he was still at it. I wasn't going to let him take Bobby anywhere. I started toward the kitchen, and said I was going to fix Bobby's breakfast, and I did, but I also called the sheriff's office. Bobby ate his oatmeal and toast. Then an officer showed up and stood guard while our son got on the school bus.

Carl took his drink outside and staggered around swearing and calling me vulgar names, while the children on the bus laughed at the drunk. The cop just looked disgusted.

After the bus left... The officer nodded at me, "You want me to give you a ride somewhere?"

"No. Just let me grab a sweater and my purse. I'll walk. I need some fresh air."

I had no idea what would happen next. Would Carl keep drinking? Would he try to drive to Madison in this shape? Where would Bobby and I go when school was out?

The walk to town was long but the sun felt good. I wanted to talk to Ilka. When I reached the bridge, I couldn't cross it. Each year my fear of heights gets worse. Even the thought of crossing that bridge on foot made me ill. Turning around and started back to a neighbor's house. When I passed the bar, the car was gone. All the sudden, it dawned on me, Carl might go to school and get Bobby. I started shaking all over.

I ran as fast as I could to the neighbors and knocked

Lotty answered the door. "This is a surprise, Sarah, come on in for coffee."

The tears started and I explained my bazaar situation and why I was a total wreck.

"Don't worry." She said. "Let's go to school and check on Bobby."

She drove to the school only to see Carl's car sitting in front, so she drove around to the back entrance. I knew where his class room was. I bundled him into the car and we drove away as a patrol car was pulling up. The school must have called them.

"You want me to take you home?" Lotty asked.

"Can you wait a minute?" I asked. "Let me find out if they're going to hold him?"

"I don't mind at all." She said.

We were safe. Mr. Regent wasn't going to be released for twenty-four hours. Bobby and I spent a quiet night alone reading books, drawing pictures and watching television.

Lotty offered us a ride to town in the morning to bail Carl out of jail and I apologized to her for all the trouble.

Carl wouldn't speak to us. His time in jail, the two-hundred dollar fine, and the fifty to get the car out of impound was all my fault.

*　　*　　*　　*　　*　　*

I didn't care a whole lot about the crowd Carl was running with, but their being at the bar constantly kept our situation at a boiling point. I felt like an outsider, in my own place. Dan and Dede weren't married. He was married but not to her. Addy and Tim weren't married either, but lived together on a farm right next to Pidge. She had been hanging with them lately. I guess they were more fun to be with. The five of them might just as well bring sleeping bags, they never seemed to leave.

The vending machine service man showed up in the afternoon on his weekly rounds.

"I've got good news," he said. "I finally found 'For the Good Times' for your juke box." He slipped the switch twice for free plays and closed the machine. The song started playing.

"Don't look so sad, I know it's over...

I braved the crowd and asked. "Carl, can I have this dance?"

"No," he snapped. "My feet hurt." He snickered and his friends joined him. How could I be so stupid? Could I have thought for one minute that I had a place in his world anymore?

"It's just as well." I said, trying to hide my humiliation. "I have to go to the store before the supper hour, anyhow."

As I left, they were having a good laugh at my expense. I noticed the gas gauge in the car was on E so I stopped to fill it, before going to the market. When I finally returned to the bar with my groceries, Carl's gang was having a rip-roaring good time. He was out on the floor dancing with Pidge, then took turns with the other ladies. His feet didn't hurt now. I made myself scarce. My kitchen was a good hiding place.

At closing time he went out to start the car so it could warm up while he counted the til. He had been leaving each night with his friends. He was already drunk and still drinking. The drinks were straight booze, going down like water.

"You must be planning on leaving, huh?" I remarked.

He started in my direction, "Why in hell, do you care?"

I didn't see it coming, but when he got acrossed the bar from where I was sitting, he doubled his fist, swung, and hit me in the mouth. My teeth snapped and flew from my face. My stool went over backwards and I heard my ribs crack as I hit the edge of the pool table. He staggered into the house and passed out. I went in and curled up beside Bobby.

Early in the morning Bobby woke up hungry. We reached the kitchen to a strange noise. It sounded like someone was gunning a car engine outside the kitchen door. It was our car, engine running full blast, with no one in it. I raced out to try to shut it off. The car door was so hot I had to get a hot pad to open it. The interior was like an oven. Using the hot pad, I turned off the key but the engine kept running. The windows were starting to cloud over from the heat. The gearshift just flopped around, all the gears had melted. I ran in and shook Carl.

"Carl, You left the car running last night, and I can't shut it off." I screamed. "You'd better see what you can do."

He jumped up and ran toward the kitchen. Just as he reached the car, it quit. It had burned up that whole tank of gas. Mr. Regent wasn't so smart now. He had no car to run in.

I was in pain and felt ridiculous without my teeth.

"This time, Carl," I said. "I'm not working without my teeth."

"Well, I sure as hell ain't gonna run that damned kitchen." He yelled.

"Then leave the damned kitchen closed." I yelled back. I took Bobby's hand and started toward the living quarters. "Maybe you can get your friends to help you."

*　　*　　*　　*　　*　　*

Ilka took me to Dr. Bradley's office.

"Your in luck, Sarah, your ribs are only cracked. I'd better take a look at your lip though, it may need some stitches." He decided on no stitches but advised, "Next time you'd better step out of the way of the truck that hit you."

The dentist said it would take a week for the needed repairs on my plate. Katy could take some time off. I stayed in the house with Bobby, the kitchen stayed closed, and Carl was on his own tending bar. The worst part of each day was when Bobby was in school.

Carl's friends were present all week, circling like vultures, waiting for bits and pieces of me. Whatever kind of fireworks they were waiting for, I did my best to avoid. Fixing food or getting coffee was the only reason I went out into the bar at all. Carl left with them every night. I didn't know, nor care, where he went.

Friday night I could hear his loud voice and knew he was getting extremely drunk. His friends left without him. I figured he was even too drunk for them to enjoy.

After locking the front door of the bar, he came into the living quarters, silent for a change. I was sitting in a chair reading. I looked up and seen a hatred in his eyes that froze my blood. He never made a sound, just grabbed me by the hair and yanked me out into the bar and pulled the door closed behind him. Now his loud maniacal bellowing started. Time after time his fist hit my face. He threw me against the wall, the pool table, and then the wall, again. The last thing I remember seeing was the corner in the hall by the front entrance. If I hit that corner, something was going to break. I wasn't doing too good a job of protecting myself by staying sober. My chest and face hit that corner full force.

When I came to, I vaguely remembered the pool of blood I was lying in, crawling to unlock the door, and calling 911.

Chapter Nineteen

When Carl's car pulled up, in front of the motel room and Bobby jumped out, I was so relieved that tears filled my eyes, but I didn't want Bobby to see them so I grabbed a tissue. The first thing Bobby said was…

"Daddy says I'm not suppose to tell you anything, Mommy."

"That's fine, Honey. Let's get you in the shower. You have school tomorrow." I didn't want to know anything about Carl or that bar anyway, but Carl had already started his brand of poison. If I had let it get to me, it would have eaten me alive and I couldn't let that happen. As soon as Bobby dozed off it was my turn for a long hot shower, a rub down with baby oil and a much needed nights sleep.

*　　*　　*　　*　　*　　*

The next morning I walked Bobby to school and made a beeline for down town, and to the café for a cup of Jo while I waited for the attorney's office to open. His door was visible from my booth. When I saw him arrive I decided not to pounce on him until he had time to settle in, so I waited through a half an hour and a second cup of coffee.

His receptionist looked up when I said, "I'd like an appointment for a divorce."

"He should be able to see you right away." She said. "Please, just have a seat."

I sat while she took a folder and walked into his office. She immediately came back out.

"He'll see you now." She said.

After introductions, I explained to him about Carl's violent temper when he drank. The evidence of my beating was still very clear. "My main concern is my son's safety." I explained. "I'm afraid if he is out there over night, he'll be in danger."

"I know you're hurting and I understand your situation," the attorney said, "but I have to advise against taking this back in front of the judge too soon. It would be like a slap in the face to him, like you were questioning his original decision. It might just backfire."

"What do you mean, backfire?" I asked.

"He might turn around and give your husband a whole week's visitation, every other week." He explained. "And I don't think you want that."

"My God, no." I said. "Leave it the way it is for now. What happens if he hurts my son?"

z"Then we could do something about it." He said.

"And that's justice?" I spat back at him.

"I'm sorry," He looked at me over his glasses, "But that's the way it is."

"Well," I said, "the way it is stinks."

He filled out all the necessary papers and told me what his cost for a divorce would be. Man. I should be an attorney.

"Where can I reach you?" He asked.

"You can't, right now." I said. "There's no phone in the motel room. I'll stop back to check with you often until I get a phone."

"Fine," he said, "but right now I need to know what you want in this divorce."

"I know he has to pay support for Bobby." I said. "Other than that I want my name off of that liquor license and my maiden name back. I just want to be free of him."

He stood up and shook my hand "Good luck, Sarah. Drop by in a couple of days, just in case I have any questions."

I stopped by Ilka's shop and told her what I'd done, and that I couldn't change the visitation order. She might have to help me through a whole lot more bad week ends.

"At least you've taken the first step, Sarah. That should make you feel better." She said. "Tomorrow Stan and I are leaving on a buying trip for the store. I'll be gone for three days. I'd feel better if I knew what's happening with you." She looked so sad and concerned that I was afraid worrying about us would spoil her trip.

"We'll be fine, Ilka. You have a good trip and buy lots of pretty things. You never can tell, one of these days I may want a new outfit to put on this gorgeous body of mine." I laughed. "No kidding though, Ilka, Bobby and I have plans to make. Our time at the motel is just about over."

After I gave her a hug I hurried out the door before she could tell how much her leaving bothered me right now. The sky was looking ominous and I had no doubt I'd need the umbrella to get Bobby from school. I took a deep breath and hurried up the hill.

*   *   *   *   *   *

There was an ad in the shopper for a trailer house that we could afford. One month rent plus a deposit would leave us with enough to shop for an old beater of a car. The car had to be first or we couldn't even get out to see the trailer. The mobile home park was out of town, three miles. Even the car I found was in the country. Ilka was out of town so as much as it went against my grain, I dialed Pidge's number.

"Hello." She answered.

"Pidge, it's Sarah. Could you possibly give us a ride to look at a car?" I pleaded.

She hesitated for a few uncomfortable seconds, then said, "Where is it?"

"I think it's out in your neck of the woods somewhere." I told her the name of the farmer who owned the car and she knew where he lived. "He said he'll be there doing chores for a couple of hours, if I can make it out."

"I'll be there in thirty minutes." She said.   When she pulled in, I remembered, I hadn't even told her where we were. I wondered how she knew, but she had probably heard rumors at the bar. Her car was nothing but the best. She acted like we might get it dirty and spread a blanket for us to sit on. I thought a ride wasn't asking too much, but I was beginning to regret having made the request.

The roads were wet from all the rain and she made it obvious she didn't want to be there, by sighing and complaining over every little pothole or puddle.

The car I was looking at was actually an old brown station wagon with a board for a back window. There was a small section with Plex-I-glass so it was legal, it ran good, and the price was right, so we made a deal. Pidge watched the transaction with disgust.

"Thanks for the ride, Pidge." I said as I waved good-by to her.

"Yea.," was the only reply she made.

She slammed the door and pealed out of the drive, probably headed straight for the carwash.

A call to the landlord got me an immediate appointment to look at the trailer. It wasn't much, but what could I expect? We'd have a place to sleep. It was empty, and we could move in right away.

*   *   *   *   *   *

Bobby picked out a coloring book to keep him busy in the back of the hall so I could attend a meeting. I really needed one. This was one place that you could get anything off your chest. So far I hadn't succeeded in talking, without choking up. That's okay too. If you do break down and cry, chances are, everyone will cry with you. It's all right to just listen if you aren't able to talk.

At the bar I hadn't been able to get through my grief after Cyle's death. People don't come to a bar to listen to the bartenders problems. You are expected to listen to their problems for hours on end. This one's wife treats him badly. That one is getting screwed at work, another's sauerkraut turned out badly. Some times, you hear the same story over, and over, and over again. My A. A. meetings were a complete change of the pace. At fifty, I finally found out there can be life without alcohol. Maybe I'll have the courage to change the things I can.

Two of my new friends from A.A., Curt and Dan, offered to help me pack my things and move, so I mustered enough courage to call Carl…

"Will I be able to get my things from the bar?" I asked.

"If I say no," He said. "You'll just run to your buddies in the police department."

I replied, "It doesn't have to be so difficult, Carl, all I want are my things."

"Well, I have things to take care of on Monday and Tuesday." He said. "Can you get your stuff out in two days?"

"I think so. Will you leave a key?" I asked.

"I'll leave it where we always did. You can leave it there when you're done." He said, then added, "I'll be taking all the money, so don't even bother looking for any."

I couldn't believe his gall. "I'll leave the key." I said, then hung up quickly before I said something I might regret.

I was soon thankful for my old wagon. It took several loads just to get enough boxes around. The two guys had trucks, so I would pack boxes until we had a load, for either the trailer, or the storage unit, and then they'd go unload.

I kept an eye out over my shoulder all the time we were there, for fear Carl would return and raise his kind of hell in front of my new friends. I hated being in this place, and all of the misery I'd seen here. Family men came in, cashed their paychecks, and then left later, almost broke. Cheaters arrived in all shapes and sizes. Heartbreak would unfold with you as an unwilling partner.

Taking off was not like Carl. At least not when he knew I wasn't opening the place for business as usual. After all the times I had begged him to get away, now he was taking time off, locking the doors, and closing for business.

"Are you going to pack or daydream?" Curt said.

"Sorry, Curt, guess I'm being a slacker. I hate this place so much, but it still seems strange actually packing to move out."

"Well, don't change your mind now. We're almost finished."

"Not a chance." I said. "There's only one more closet, but no packing. The things in there are still in boxes. They're the tools of my trade. I never unpacked them."

"What is your trade?" He asked.

"I had an upholstery shop before we bought this nightmare. Being cooped up with the same person twenty-four seven for eight years has been torture. I don't know how I stood it this long. In my shop I usually worked alone and I prefer it that way."

"Where do you want them to go, storage or trailer?" He asked.

"I'm taking them with me to the trailer. Carl has all my other tools locked in the basement. I'll have to wait for them."

"Usually the man of the house has the tools. Doesn't he have any?"

"Not enough to mention. We bought a few after we got married, mostly garage sale junk." I stood up and shook myself off. "Let's get out of this place."

Although I knew there were rough roads ahead, I was relieved. I was free of Carl. As I drove away from the bar, I couldn't help remembering two other times I had driven away, one time from Werley, and once from the Beach. Maybe it was from the lack of sleep or from all the turmoil in my life, but I started laughing out loud as a weird thought went through my head. Perhaps this was a sign. A sign that I should have been a race driver, where I could leave all the macho men behind, eating my dust. Right then and there I made up my mind. Never again would anyone take possession of my personal space. From now on I'd go it alone. That has to be better than what I've been through.

Chapter Twenty

The mobile home had all of the usual amenities of 'boxed living' cubical's. I was thankful for the stove and refrigerator that were furnished. Mine had been sold when we bought the bar. Bobby and I had gotten used to cuddling at bedtime during our stray at the motel, so we used the small bedroom to store unopened boxes and Bobby shared my big waterbed. The previous tenants had been drinkers also, and had punched several holes in the doors to the bath and one bedroom during their feuds. I used my tools to cut out plywood maple leaves, to cover the holes. As I made the repairs, I asked myself, why do people claim to love each other, and then do something like this? Nice people can turn into animals, just by adding booze.

"It's a hot day out," I said to Bobby, "let's fill your wading pool. Maybe the other children can come and play in it with you. It'll be a good way to get acquainted."

"Where is it, Mommy?" He asked. "I don't know where it's at." Although he seemed to be enjoying the new surroundings, he had been yanked around a lot lately.

"I slid it under the trailer, Hon." I said.

We got the pool and the hose out and by the time we had finished filling it several kids had collected in our little patch of grass. One boy who was maybe eleven or twelve had been standing two trailers away, watching.

"Do you want to join in?" I hollered to him.

"Sure." He answered.

It only took five minutes before I changed my mind and asked him to leave. Pushing the little kids around was not my idea of fun. After that day, he made a vendetta out of getting even. Running out from behind a trailer and pushing Bobby off his bike on the blacktop, or standing in my next door neighbor's yard while flipping me the crow was his way of retaliating. He had me on such an edge, I started being sharp with the person I loved the most.

"Do you know what you sound like, when you're mad at your little boy?" The lady from the next trailer asked me.

"No. I didn't know I was being so loud that you could hear me." I apologized. "I'm sorry, and it won't happen again."

"Good. You've been waking our baby." She griped.

I must have scared Bobby too. He had heard enough bellering from his father, and he didn't need to hear it from me.

After the neighbor brought my shameful behavior to my attention, we started going for rides when Bobby arrived home from school. We went to visit the dogs at the pound, or berry picking. Sometimes we'd stop for coffee at Ilka's. When it got dark, we'd return home, have supper, and go right to bed. Each day was the same old, same old. That monstrous kid was relentless.

*   *   *   *   *   *

One Friday afternoon there was a knock on the door. It was the owner of a supper club close to the trailer park. I had met him and his wife at the Tavern League meetings.

"Hi, Sarah, I heard you had moved out here." He said. "Do you think you could possibly fill in for our cook tonight?" He looked a little frazzled. "She has been out sick. My wife usually fills in for her, but there's been a death in our family and she had to go to Chicago this morning, leaving me in a real bind."

"I can try." I said. "It's been over a month since I ran a kitchen, but I'll give it my best shot."

"Can you be there by five?" He asked.

"That will cut it really close. I'd have to take Bobby to the sitter's house. Tell you what," I said. "I'll see what I can arrange and call you in an hour."

I called Vicky and asked if she would mind watching Bobby.

"Are you kidding? Of coarse I don't mind." She said. "We've missed him being around. You'll be working late, so why don't you just plan on him spending the night." She suggested.

"That's a good idea, Vicky." I said. "I'm glad you thought of it. No telling how late I'll be."

"Will it be for just one night?" She asked.

"I'll know more about Saturday night later." I said. "I'll call in the morning when I know for sure."

I finally found some work clothes after rifling through several boxes, then cleaned up, and called the man back.

Bobby was happy to see Katy and the other girls, so I was able to sneak off and get to the supper club forty-five minutes early. A new kitchen would be a challenge. No, it would be crazy, they had equipment I'd never even seen before, and I knew how busy they got on Friday night.

We served mountains of fish, quantities of chicken, steak, lobster and shrimp. It was quite an experience, but I didn't burn the place down, so it was okay. I was exhausted when it was over. They had a dishwasher or I never would have gotten home. Then I had to do it all over again on Saturday night. Sunday and Monday they would be closed and his wife would be back by Tuesday. The extra money would sure come in handy.

Sunday evening Laurie called. "Hi, Mom, how are you doing?"

I told her about my wild week end in a strange kitchen, and we laughed about it, then she got quiet.

"Mom," She said. "Did you know that Carl has a girlfriend?"

The blood all rushed to my head and my heart was beating in my temples. He hadn't been on my mind for a couple of days now and it felt good that way. When she mentioned his name, it all came boiling back, like a lava rush during an eruption, and my face flushed.

"No," I admitted, "but I suspected he did."

"He's had her for some time." She said. "They were down to see Nancy and Brandy a couple of months ago."

"I was still at the bar then, Laurie." I said. "How did you find out?"

"I ran into Nancy when I was in Madison." Laurie said. "She said her Dad and the woman both had plenty to drink when they came to visit. Carl actually asked the girls if they were getting their ashes hauled often enough. The girls finally had to ask them to leave."

I knew he had no respect for women, but this was disgusting, talking to his own girls that way.

"Did they say who she was?" I asked.

"They said the name," Laurie hesitated, "but I can't remember it."

"Pidge?" I said bluntly.

"That's it." She squealed. "How did you know?"

I said, "The pieces of the puzzle just fell into place."

"The way Nancy talked, they've been together for several months." Laurie said. "Did you know all along?"

"No, but I should have." So that's where he went. Come to think of it, when he disappeared so did she.

"You know her, Mom?" Laurie asked.

"She was supposed to be a good friend of mine." I said. "Now I feel like a real fool. They were shacking up already when I cooked Christmas dinner for her."

"Why did you cook for her?" She asked.

"It was Carl's idea." I said. "He said she'd be spending the holiday alone. I guess he would know."

After we hung up, I called one of the bartenders I was still on good terms with, and the call earned me a very good education. After paying for half of that dump, eight years of slaving in a kitchen, taking a beating whenever he had the urge, giving birth to his son, helping him raise his girls and all the other things I had done for him, that louse closed the bar for a week and took Pidge on my vacation.

*   *   *   *   *   *

195

While riding in the country, I noticed a 'For Sale' sign on a house I had always admired. I stopped at the bank and talked to Deloris Enga. She was a loan officer I had dealt with, in the past.

"The house is in bad shape, Sarah." She said

"Can I at least look at it?" I asked.

"Sure," she said, "but first let me warn you, the bank had to repossess the house some time ago and we're not in the realty business. The people who have been living there have made a mess, so don't expect too much."

"I've been in the house when it looked great." I told her. "If it's that bad how do they expect to sell it?"

"They probably won't." She replied. "At least not the way it is now. The bank will probably end up putting money in the house on repairs and raise the selling price."

"Do you think they might accept an offer, as is?" I asked

"You could try. Let's go take a look." She said. "You might not want it."

We drove out to the house in her car. The lawn needed mowing. It was mostly weeds anyhow. That's what grows best in this sand. Deloris had a key, which we didn't need as both entry locks were broken. The kitchen counter was all blistered, wallpaper hung like willow branches and holes were punched in two walls. Evidence of little furry inhabitants was everywhere. The bottom two panels of the sixteen-foot garage door were missing, but the house was solid and fixable, and hopefully mine. I went home and wrote:

I, Sarah Ann (Regent) Bray, am making an offer to purchase the property at #48A Hwy. C, Summit, WI. I will make a $500.00 down payment and would like the house to remain on a land contract until I have enough collateral to transfer the property to a regular mortgage loan. I want the house as is with the understanding that I make all needed repairs.

Sarah Ann (Regent) Bray

Putting Regent on anything galled me, but my divorce wasn't final and I couldn't legally use my maiden name, yet.

They accepted my offer. It would take all the ingenuity I could muster to scrape together five-hundred dollars. An acquaintance had shown an interest in my round oak table, and she was delighted when I told her the price. The 'For Sale' add I placed in the paper to sell my thirty-thirty deer rifle with scope was answered as soon as the paper came out. I had my down payment. It was all over but the paperwork.

I was ready to start rebuilding my life, again. Once again as a single parent, but this time would be different. This time I was sober, free of Mr. Regent, old enough and smart enough to avoid the temptations that had ruined my life before.

*   *   *   *   *   *

I had already gotten a puppy, to keep Bobby company. It was a brown and white hound, whose brown spots resembled chocolate pudding. Bobby named him Pudd. The pup went with us on our visits to the pound. One of the inmates had adopted Bobby and me as his new people. Wolfe, as we had named our new friend, would start talking when he heard our old wagon coming.

"Ar ur ur ur ur," he said. It sure sounded like he was talking.

"Ar ur ur ur ur," we'd answer, then laugh. This big, grey dog could actually make us laugh.

Wolfe was scheduled to be put to sleep. He had been at the pound too long. I couldn't ask the landlord to let me have him. He had already bent the rules for Pudd. So I pleaded with the keeper at the pound.

"I'm buying a house in the country. Is there any way you can keep Wolfe until the first of the month?" I pushed out my lower lip like I was pouting. "I couldn't stand it if you put him to sleep. He's a real charmer. He's stolen our hearts and he makes us laugh. We need that now."

"I'll have to charge you for his keep," the attendant said, "but I'll keep him until the first."

"That's all I'm asking. Thank you." I said gratefully.

*   *   *   *   *   *

Sunday morning three guys from A.A. pulled in with trucks to help us get moved to our new house. We arrived at the house with all my belongings, from the storage unit and the trailer. The people living in the house were just starting to load their things to move out. It was a warm, sunny day and it felt good to be outside. We spread blankets on the lawn and decided to have an impromptu A.A. meeting. Any time there are two or more alcoholics together you can have a meeting.

Now the fun started. Around the corner of the house came a Tom Turkey. He strutted around the trucks. Cal, one of the fellows helping, was scared stiff of that old Tom. Well, Tom zeroed in on Cal like a nail to a magnet. Time after time we chased him off. Back he'd come, and straight for Cal. We put Pudd on a leash and let him out of the truck. That should do the trick. "Wrong." Tom wanted a piece of the pup too. After one peck and a resounding yelp, Pudd went back in the truck.

197

The people moving out finally noticed what a pain Tom was being, and put him in his pen. Pudd was set free, and now the tables were turned. We laughed until our sides hurt at the pup running around Tom's pen acting like he was the conqueror.

We did, finally have our meeting. Cal was new to A.A., like me. The other two were veterans in the program. As we each related our stories, it was apparent that our problems were all quit similar. We were all just ordinary people who had tangled with a tiger. When we finished, we joined hands and recited the Lord's Prayer. It was amazing how well all of them were doing, now that they were sober. It was a great encouragement to hang in there, no matter how rough the going got.

"Come on, pup. You've punished Tom enough." I said. Tom wasn't the least bit interested.

I had prepared sandwiches and coffee, so we ate while they loaded their last load. Their truck finally pulled out of the drive with Tom in it, gobbling his final good-bye. The house was a mess, so we decided to sweep the garage and pile things in there until I could clean. After the guys left, I mustered up enough energy to sweep one room, where we could make up a bed for the night.

Monday we awoke to our first day in our new home. I hadn't made arrangements for the bus to pick Bobby up here, so I drove him to school. I stopped at the electric company to transfer the meter to my name and the phone office to arrange for a phone. Then I stopped at a pay phone, and dialed the number to the pound.

"Hello, Summit Humane Shelter." The lady answered

"Hi, this is Sarah Regent. We'll be out to pick up Wolfe when I get my son from school at three-fifteen. I thought I'd better let you know. Today is the first."

"You phoned just in time. We would have put him down today." She said. "Three-fifteen will be fine. See you then, Sarah. It's a good thing you called."

I returned to the house for a couple of hours of scrubbing cupboards, putting dishes away, and cleaning everything that got in my way. Any major repairs would have to wait until I could get the material. By afternoon the house was looking better, but my hands looked like prunes.

At two-forty-five I put Pudd in the car and headed for school a little early. I needed to go to the office and make bus arrangements for tomorrow. The sight in the hallways of the school amazed me. Children barely potty trained were using computers. Being born before 'computer' became a household word, I'd never had any interest in them, but these tykes were handling them like pros.

Bobby ran out, "Hi Mommy, Hi, Pudd." He hollered. "Are we going to get Wolfe?"

"You bet we are, Honey. I think he's been at the pound long enough."

"To long." Bobby agreed. "I hope he likes it at our house, Mommy."

Wolfe was waiting and started talking before we rounded the corner of the building.

"Ar ur ur ur." The dog said.

Bobby laughed and answered, "Ar ur ur ur. He's the first dog I ever heard talk, Mommy. What do you think he's saying?"

"Maybe when he's been with us for a while, we'll understand him. Don't you think?" I paid Wolf's bill and loaded him in the back seat with Pudd.

We tied him to a maple in the backyard that had the girth of easily six feet. That should hold a wolf. There was far too much traffic to let him run loose just yet. Perhaps someday he may protect the house the way old Tom did. We didn't have to worry about the pup. He never went any farther from Wolfe than he had to. They were pals right off.

Without a stove and refrigerator our menu was going to consist of peanut butter sandwiches until I could remedy that problem. We had two packages of venison left and they wouldn't keep any longer. I cooked ours on a small portable grill, and we ate it with bread, washed it down with warm pop. The other package I cut into chunks for the dogs, and we headed out the back door, where I gave half to Bobby.

I said. "You sit on the step and feed your puppy," then I walked over and reached out a big piece to Wolfe. "Chomp."

"Ow." He bit meat, hand and all. It hurt so badly it brought tears to my eyes. Then I started laughing. Bobby laughed too but I could see the confusion on his face.

"Did Wolfe bite you, Mommy?"

"Yes. Honey, don't ever try to feed a wolf raw bloody meat out of your hand."

Wolfe also looked confused. After that I made him reach the end of his chain where he could only lick the meat, then nibble to get more. He never bit me again.

The locks on both doors were still broken so we brought the dogs in at night. It made us feel safer. We all stretched out on the floor to watch television. Wolfe was longer than I was tall. His fur was shades of grey. It was long enough to lose your hand in, but so thick, you couldn't get to his skin.

"Behave yourself, Wolfe," I threatened, "or you'll make a beautiful throw rug."

Of coarse I was kidding. He was part of our little family, one little boy, two dogs, and a bitch.

Excuse me, a small bit of bitterness showing there.

Chapter Twenty One

Besides being a disaster both inside and out, the house was a ranch style home, ninety-three feet long, including the built in double garage on the South end. The lap siding on both ends was painted white. In the center, both front and back, was a twenty-foot section of redwood vertical siding, covered by permanent aluminum awnings. Under each awning were sliding glass patio doors. There was a cement walk in front that ran from the drive to the kitchen door, past the front set of patio doors. The back patio doors opened to a badly planned patio. They had installed the patio bricks below ground level, and each time it rained we had a pond.

The Summit ridge ran East-West on the South side of the valley our house sat in. The Northern property line was six rows of White Pines running from the road to the woods way behind the house. Local C.C. camps, during World War II had planted them as a wind break. They were now about sixty feet tall. Between our house and the pines was a thick row of aromatic cedars, covered with small blue berries. The birds loved the berries, but made purple streaks on any laundry I was brave enough to hang out. Our property was one and a half acres. Behind us was a Christmas tree plantation, a large wooded hill, and more holiday pines. Also in our yard was an older single garage and Tom's pen.

The trails they used, when pruning the trees, became a favorite haunt of ours. We spent many hours walking these trails. The dogs eagerly led the way. From the top of the hill where we had picnic lunches, we could overlook our property, the plantations, and the highways.

Interstate ninety ran South East/ North West past our house with highway C running parallel between the freeway and the house. The hum of traffic was always present. When Bobby took the dogs for a walk alone, I always told him…

"If you get lost, sit for a minute and listen for the sound of traffic, it will lead you home."

I didn't need to worry. In no time at all we both knew the valley like the backs of our hands. It was so peaceful out here in the country after living in that horrible bar. The tension was gone from the air and I could breathe this country air without that awful lump in my throat. If I was worried or upset the lump might return, but not for too long and not too often. I wondered if the change was due to the lack of the booze, or the absence of Carl. In A.A. we learned that you have to make some changes in your lifestyle. Well, I was making changes and they were working. Finding new friends was as easy as going to a meeting. Finances were slim and I knew there was a chance I would have to go on AFDC for a month or two until my shop was a reality instead of just a dream.

I was back sewing, and drawing in my free time. The trips to Fennimore were expensive, so we couldn't go often, but I was in contact with my family by phone, at least. Some had a hard time forgiving me for my indiscretions when I was drinking. Others, like Tag refused to believe I was an alcoholic. He had never seen me out of control. Janie had, at least once, when I was married to Donald, but I think she understood. She liked her Martinis too.

What a different life I was living now. The only trace of the bar after the past few months was panic time at five o'clock. After eight years of supper hour starting at five, it became a built in reflex. Instead of running seventy-five foot laps in that kitchen, my nights were spent quietly with Bobby.

We cleaned out the old single garage for the station wagon. I tore down what was left of the garage door on the house, and replaced it with a wall. The wall had an entry door and two picture windows. This was the front of my new sewing and upholstery shop. I dry walled the interior and installed a new wood burning furnace in the shop, and another in the house. The old oil furnace wasn't trust worthy. Chopping and stacking cord wood gave me plenty of exercise.

Social Service liked my idea of a group home for people who had a problem with alcohol. By cold weather I had two ladies working in my shop, three boarders in my group home, and I was no longer on Aid.

Chapter Twenty Two

"If you keep gobbling candy every time we have a coffee break," Ilka commented, "you're going to regain all of those pounds you've lost lately, plus a few more." I knew what she said was true. Dropping the extra weight I had been carrying around since my pregnancy really felt good, and I had no desire to gain it back. The urge to drink was gone, but it had been replaced by a constant craving for sugar. The sugar I used to get from the bottle

"This gnawing inside just won't stop." As I wrapped my arms around my own body and squeezed tight, actually being able to feel my ribs again after so long, was delightful. "Maybe I should just go hog wild, get the ingredients I need, and mix a stiff drink."

"God no, Sarah," she squealed. The look on her face was so alarming that I broke into a smile to let her know I was only joshing.

"You like to push my panic button. Or are you trying to give me a heart attack?"

"I wouldn't do that to my body again." I said, then added, "Being free of alcohol is the best thing that ever happened to me, Ilka. You know me well enough to know that. With a little time, I'm sure the craving will diminish. You know what? I don't even like the sweet taste. Give me a big old fat, juicy, dill pickle, any day. It's my body that screams for sugar."

"There would be less calories in a pickle." Ilka said, as she puckered her mouth and gave a little shiver.

"Enough about my food intake," I said. "I do have something I want to talk to you about, now that we have a little time alone." No sooner had the words been spoken, when Bobby ran into the house through the back door.

"Hi, Ilka. Mom, is it okay if I take the dogs for a walk?" He was in constant motion, grabbing cookies and a can of soda to take along. It was like having a small whirlwind suddenly invade the house.

"Don't be gone too long, Honey." I managed to get out before the door slammed shut behind him. He didn't want to hear my input anyway. This young man had a mind of his own, and was becoming an expert at using his father and I against each other to get whatever he wanted.

"He absolutely wears me out." I said as Ilka looked on silently.

"I can see why," she said. "It makes me tired, just watching him." She sipped her coffee. "You said you had something you wanted to talk to me about. Everything is quite now. Why don't you tell me what it is before we have another interruption?"

"I didn't mean to make it sound like an emergency, Ilka. It's something I've lived with for a long time now, and it may not ever get any better," I explained.

"I'm sure you've noticed that every once in a while when we're talking, I lose my train of thought."

"Sure I have," she said. "I thought it was simply because you have too many irons in the fire. You do have more going on in your life than anyone else I know."

"That's the way my life has always been, Ilka. Being busy keeps my mind off of the things I no longer want to think about."

"Like what?" she asked. "You always appear to be right on top of everything. All except your wardrobe. One of these days I'll get you out of those grubbies, and into something fashionable."

"Ilka, you're a good friend, but how I dress is off limits even to you. The last time I worried about my clothes was when Cyle died. I had to pull a ten-year-old dress from the back of the closet to wear to my son's funeral. After that, clothes mean nothing to me, as long as I'm covered." I poured more coffee and tried to get my mind back onto my problem. "What I wanted to talk to you about are the blank spots I've been having. Those times you noticed weren't normal. My mind just goes completely blank and for the life of me I can't remember what I was thinking of or saying when they happen." Even talking about those times made me anxious and upset.

She patted my hand. "I did notice there were times when you were disturbed about something. Do you know why it happens?'

"Sure," I laughed. "Burned out brain cells cause them. Too much alcohol does that, and the brain doesn't grow new ones to replace the ones that die."

"Is there anything you can do about it?" she asked. If I can do anything to help, I will."

"This is something I did to myself, by keeping my brain pickled for so many years. Usually when part of your body starts to die they amputate. I don't think even Dr. Bradley would dismember my brain." We both broke out in laughter. "Hey, maybe I can get a brain transplant."

"There is nothing wrong with what's left of your thinking process," Ilka said, pretty much like I figured she would. Then she asked, "What do you think you can do about it?"

"Well," I said, "What's gone is gone for good. That much is for certain. Beings people only utilize about twenty per-cent of their brain anyhow, I'm hoping I can train some of the unused part to take the place of what is dead and gone." I hoped I was making any kind of sense and that she could understand how much this bothered me.

"Leave it to you to think of that." She shook her head. "How do you intend to do it? You going back to school?"

"I don't need school," I insisted. "I'm going to start reading. If I cram enough into my noggin, maybe some of it will stick." I bonked my forehead with the heel of my hand.

"I have lots of books, Sarah. What do you like to read?"

"Anything. The more variety, the better, I figure. I want a little bit of everything."

"When I come out again, I'll bring you some reading material." She finished her coffee just as Bobby came in the door with two large bouquets of wild flowers.

"Here's one for you, Ilka," he said as he handed them over. "The woods is full of flowers and berries."

"Thanks, Sweetie," Ilka said. "You are awfully good to your Mommy and me." He was too busy looking for a vase to put the other flowers in to pay any more attention to us. Then he grabbed a plastic container and headed back to the woods. I knew we would be having berries for supper.

After Ilka left, it was time for me to get supper ready. Having talked my idea over with her seemed to give it more credence. I felt good about it, and even more anxious to put my plan into action.

After supper was finished and we had all enjoyed fresh berries on our ice cream, I cleaned up the kitchen. My work for today was done. Bobby was all wrapped up with a game. There was good lighting by the couch, so I curled up, grabbed a book, and started my re-education.

*   *   *   *   *   *

From then on, when I wasn't caring for the guys in the group home, working in my shop, making repairs on the house, weeding my flowers, or spending time with Bobby, I was reading. Reading, in fact, became an obsession. The 'Farmer's Almanac', historical novels, mysteries, sci-fi, and westerns were all consumed with vigor. The more I read, the more I want to read. If high school had been this versatile, I could have been an "A" student. Discovering his "Roots" with Alex Haley was a learning experience. Having grown up in South-West Wisconsin, I had never had much experience with black people, and never realized how much they had suffered. Then I grew up with the Lincoln and Ford families, helped to build the Frankenstien monster, and rode the range with many of Louis La mour's characters. Louis became one of my heros. My library grew to over three-thousand books as Bobby and I scoured the garage sales. At Christmas my gift to myself was the lumber to build some much needed book shelves. No way would they hold all of my books, but I had acquired some beautiful hard covered novels and an impressive array of reference books. These I enjoyed having in plain sight. The remainder were first absorbed, then put into storage.

Even when Bobby and I took an afternoon off to go fishing, I would take along a book. On these trips Bobby had a tendency to wander. There was always a better fishing spot farther down the shoreline. Then I would get out my book and let him run off all of his excess energy.

I still attended at least three A. A. meetings each week. Speaking got increasingly easier, as I became more comfortable with the other members and with my own affliction. Occasionally, I was invited to speak to other groups for their open meetings. My confidence was building, not only in myself, but in my ability to maybe help someone else with an alcohol problem.

One evening while I was sitting at the kitchen counter reading, Ilka's car pulled into the drive. As she walked through the door I put a bookmark in place, snapped my book shut, and grabbed two cups out of the cupboard. She grinned at me curiously.

"How is your plan working? She asked. As she put her jacket over the back of one of the dining room chairs, she looked over at me, waiting for an answer.

Bobby after a successful day

"What plan is that?" I asked

"Sarah, you haven't forgotten have you?" She still had that ridiculous grin. "The whole idea with all this reading was for you to fill your brain with new ideas to take the place of your burnt out brain cells."

"Ilka, you remembered that?" I gasped. "I completely forgot. Reading has gotten to be so much enjoyment for me that I forgot I had a purpose." I filled our cups, sat down, and lit both of our cigarettes.

"I can't believe you, Sarah." Ilka said with a smirk. "All those times I called or came out and caught you reading, I believed you had a driving force. You were just having fun."

"Now that you mentioned it, Ilka, that hasn't happened for months."

The blank outs had happened less and less, until I had indeed forgotten all about them. Reading had become an addiction in itself, but this was one habit I had no intention of trying to cure.

*   *   *   *   *   *

"Mom," Laurie said from the other end of the phone line, "How would you like some company?"

"Sure, Laurie," I replied happily, "you know your welcome anytime. When are you coming?"

"Just as fast as I can throw some clothes in a suitcase." She said.

"You must plan on staying a while" I said. "Don't the kids have school?"

"Chad and Jessica aren't coming, just me." She explained. "Dwight and I are having some problems and I need space. He says he'll watch the kids." She sounded really depressed.

"I've got lots of work piled up, Puddin, but you always were one of the best helpers I ever had. Maybe you can help me get caught up."

"It sounds great, Mom. Working with you again on furniture may be just what I need right now." She said. "I'll finish packing and see you in about three hours. Love You!"

She wasn't there by nine o'clock, and I was starting to worry.

"What took so long, Puddin?" I asked when she finally arrived.

"I had a flat by the Rapids, and had to change it myself. Danged cars." She sputtered.

"You'll have to remember to have the tire fixed, before you go too awfully far." I said.

"I don't want to go anywhere." She stated firmly.

"Well, put your bags in my room and grab a cup of coffee." I said. "I'm just glad you're here."

We talked that night until we got too tired to make sense anymore. Two days later she contacted a minister in Summit. She needed someone to talk to about her marriage. He agreed to see her. After getting ready she headed out the door. I raised my hand and was ready to say something, when she interrupted.

"Don't worry, Mom," she said, "I'll drop the tire off to be fixed."

After a while her visits to the minister seemed to be resolving some of her problems, so she asked Dwight to come down and talk to him, too. Seeing the kids made her cry, but Dwight's presents upset her, she definitely wasn't ready to go home. She kissed the kids good bye and waved as they drove away. I needed to think of something to get her mind off of the kids.

"Hey, Puddin," I said in a voice that even to me sounded falsely non-calanthe. "I ran crossed something when I was cleaning out my files. I was going to toss it, but saved it to show to you." I shuffled through some papers on my desk and handed her the letter. She started to read...

She said, "This is addressed to Mrs. Victor, Mom, that's a long time ago."

"Just keep reading." I said.

She was silent as she read the rest of the letter. I refilled our cups. Bobby was playing his new video game in the living room. He has such fast reflexes, and he can beat the game most of the time. He concentrates so hard, you hardly know he's in the house, except for occasional swear words, of which he has a full vocabulary, no matter how much I complain.

"How come you never told me, they ordered you to get rid of Nugget?" She asked.

"I honestly don't know." I said. "When I thought about it, you weren't around or it wasn't the right time. After a while I just forgot about it, until I ran acrossed this letter."

"You know, Mom," she sighed, "I've spent all these years thinking you got rid of her to get back at me for going to Dad's."

"I wouldn't do that, Laurie." I said indignantly.

"I didn't think you would, deep down, but you never told me about this." She waved the letter.

"I'm glad I saved it." I said. "Guess this is a good example of bad communications."

She stayed most of the summer and we turned out a lot of work, side by side. The sessions with the minister continued, Dwight and the children came down several times, until finally...

"I think I'll go home, Mom." She said half heartedly. "Things still aren't right, but I miss the kids too much. I guess I can put up with anything to be back with them. It's time for school to start, and I should be there."

"I'll miss you being here with me, Laurie, and I know you'll do what you can to improve things between you and Dwight, but I've got to warn you." I took a deep breath. "A long absence builds a wall that most time is too high to climb. I speak from experience, but you know that. Things can never go back and be the same as they were before. I wish you luck, Puddin, and if need be, I'll be here for you."

Laurie packed and left that night, and our house felt a little empty. She called often to let me know how they were. I could tell from what she didn't say that all wasn't well. I also knew how she felt about broken homes, so I knew she'd try her best to keep her family together.

As I sat that night, thinking about Laurie, my mind wandered back to the dreams I had when I was even younger than she. The dream of someday celebrating a fiftieth anniversary, gone. Of being a good mother with a close nit family, gone. My children were scattered to the wind. Cyle, of course, is gone from my life, but not my heart. Arron will talk to me when I call to wish him Happy Birthday, but shows no signs of wanting to be close. Bobby, well he's a handful. Laurie has problems of her own, but we are as close as two people can be.

I got up from my chair, shut off the lights, and said a prayer that Laurie would make better choices than I had.

* * * * * *

Ilka always dressed so well and her make up was flawless, just the opposite from me in my old beaters. I often wondered why she had chosen me for a friend, but I loved her dearly.

"You just pitch into whatever has to be done," she commented while watching me wall paper the dining room walls.

"Don't ever kid yourself, Ilka, you can do it too." I said. "You're just as creative as I am, any day." I hadn't been ready to stop when she arrived, and she didn't mind watching.

"I always used to be," she said, "but Stan doesn't let me do anything. He makes all the repairs, balances the checkbook, mows the lawn, and everything else. He won't even let me paint a room."

"Sometimes I wish I had someone to help me with the work," I said, "but I can't imagine, not doing it. I wouldn't be happy if I wasn't busy."

Our coffee breaks were always a welcome treat. Gordon and Arlow, two of the guys I took care of enjoyed her company and sometimes we'd ask them to join us in a card game. They always complimented her on how nice she looked. Regardless of her weight, she was always dressed fit to kill.

"How can you afford all those expensive clothes, Ilka?" I asked one day.

"When the big companies are getting your order, it's surprising what a bargain you can get."

"I suppose so." I said. "That's kind of like blackmail. Isn't it?"

"No. That's business." She said. "By the way, Sarah, there won't be anymore buying trips. We sold the store. That new discount store opening up, is going to make it hard for the stores downtown. I just got out while the getting was good."

"Who bought it?" I asked in amazement.

"You remember the lady that owned the motel? Colleen. She's worked for me for years. She offered to buy it, out of the blue. Stan and I talked it over and decided we should sell."

"What will you do with all your time?" I asked.

"Colleen wants me to continue working there." She said. "Not as many hours, but that will keep me busy."

For weeks things went smoothly. She could stay longer on her visits, then suddenly she didn't come out at all. No phone calls, no nothing. She didn't answer the phone and hadn't been to the store to work. Colleen was in the dark too. Finally, really worried, I drove to her house. She didn't answer the door, but I didn't give up. Her car was there, so I pounded, knocked, banged on the door and yelled until she finally gave in and opened it. I was relieved. My imagination had been running wild. She had on no make up, wore old sweats, and looked like she hadn't slept since I'd seen her last.

"Ilka, what in the world is the matter?" I asked.

"I can't talk about it." Her body was shaking.

My mind immediately raced to cancer. "With me? Ilka, we can talk about anything."

"Oh, alright, Sarah, come on in." She relented.

"I've never seen you like this and it worries me." I said.

"I think I'm going crazy," she said, "I can't get things together."

"What brought this on?" I asked. "You looked great the last time I saw you."

"Stan ...," she was choking back tears, "he left me."

"After thirty-one years?" I asked. "You're kidding, When did this happen, hon.?"

"The last time I was at your house." She said.

"Because you were at my house?" I asked.

"No, Sarah," she said, "he's found a younger woman."

She was settling down a little. "I'll put some coffee on," I said, "You go in and splash some cold water on your face. We're going to have an all nighter. I'm not leaving until we talk it all out."

The guys had all had their supper, so I didn't have to worry about them. They would be glued to the television all night anyway, and Bobby was with his Dad.

209

"After we have a couple of pots of coffee and at least a pack of smokes," I said, "I want you to shower, put on your make up and fix your hair the way you always do."

She asked."You think that will help?"

"You bet it will. You know you're crying over spilled milk." I put my arm around her shoulder. "The serenity prayer says 'You have to accept the things you cannot change.' Tonight we'll do a little accepting."

"I haven't been here all the time, Sarah." She said. "I spent a couple of days in the hospital."

"Why didn't you call me?" I asked.

"I didn't want you disappointed in me. You always thought it was so great I had been married for so long." She covered her face with both hands. "I didn't want you to know I'd failed."

"This isn't your fault, Ilka, and Stan's not worth crying about." I thought for a minute. "None of them are."

"What am I going to do?" She asked. "I don't know how to do anything for myself."

"Boy, has he got you brainwashed." I said. "He wanted you to feel helpless. You're a German, just like me. Get your dander up and prove him wrong. After a few months, you won't even believe how strong you really are, and neither will he."

"You really think I can do this?" She asked.

"I know you can." I said firmly. "You go take a shower while I put on some more coffee. Why not put the sweats back on? They're more comfy than panty hose."

After forty-five minutes the old Ilka emerged from the bathroom, with make up, hair do and everything in place.

"You were right." She said. "I feel so much better. I couldn't stand to look at myself anymore."

"No more tears. This is the first day of the rest of your life, and we're going to make sure it's a great one." I said.

"I haven't been able to call Milwaukee and let Mickey know that his Dad has left." She pointed toward the phone.

"He should know. Do you feel like calling him now?" I asked.

"I can do it now," she said, "if you stay while I do?"

"I told you this was going to be an all nighter." I reminded her. "It's only ten o'clock. I don't plan on leaving until you fix me breakfast." I joked.

After she called him, we talked all night. In the morning I left in time to fix breakfast for the guys.

Ilka almost lived at my house for the next few months. The men and I watched an amazing metamorphous in our friend. She was getting stronger all the time, and was working on the second room she was completely redecorating. Stan's workshop was next. His things were going. She wanted to fill it with exercise equipment so she could lose some weight.

While I'm busy working, I think about her and smile. She has gotten so spunky, I don't think cancer even stands a chance, but I hope it never comes back to test my theory.

Chapter Twenty Three

Deer seasons have not been my favorite time of year since Cyle's death. Although it's been eight years, the pain never lessens. My only recourse is to schedule more work than it's possible to handle. Work keeps my mind occupied at least. The normal daily work doesn't count because it takes no thought to be a robot. I needed something challenging, but I was at a lose. Silently I asked God to send me something besides booze to help me make it through the anniversary of the worst day of my life. That evening the phone rang.

"Hello." I answered.

"Hi, Sis, how ya doin?" I'd recognize that question and voice any time.

"Tag. I'm so glad you called. I'm fine. I just said a prayer for something like you. How's Mom?" I asked.

"She's good, been keeping busy house cleaning. You know Mom. Everyone else is fine too. I don't know what you were praying for but I may have the answer." He said. "I did have a reason for calling. I saw something today and all I could think about was you, Sis."

"What was it?" He had my complete attention now.

"A carousel horse. Jim and I stopped at a shop today, in Dodgeville, where they had several of them. Jim got so excited, he bought a set of plans to build one. I knew it was something you would like so we picked up literature to send to you." He cleared his throat, "it's in the mail."

"I'm glad to know you think about me, even if we don't see each other very often." I said.

"I know you're busy with the home and all, but you've always loved to carve." He said. "This could be a real challenge for you." Why did he use my exact words? God works in mysterious ways.

He told me all about the horses and I could feel his excitement. So much so, it was contagious. By the time we finished talking my mind was racing. This was too much to be a coincidence. I honestly believe someone heard my prayers.

I put in an all nighter at the drawing table and by morning all the plans were drawn for my horse "Sidekick." I have never been one to follow anyone else's plans.

Just a few weeks earlier I had replaced my basement steps. The old ones were built out of rough cut lumber and I couldn't get them clean because of the rough surface. Never being able to throw something useful away, I still had the lumber piled in the basement. When the pamphlets came in the mail, I already had part of the boards cut and laminated. Bobby laughed at the big pile of boards glued and clamped on my workbench. Each night after feeding everyone and doing the dishes, I would disappear into the basement. In no time at all deer season was over, without a drink.

One evening after school, Bobby headed down to the basement to find his baseball bat. He came back upstairs. He was all excited.

"Mom, there's a horse coming out of that pile of wood."

"I know." I said. "He was there all the time. He just needed me to find him."

"That's great, Mom." He said "Can I help?"

Ilka came out almost daily to check on my progress. The stairs were a problem for her because of her weight, but she would go down three steps where she could peek at him. She had already lost a lot of weight. I was so proud of her. She claimed her recovery was mainly due to me. Well, the feeling was mutual. The saying goes, 'If you have one very true friend in your lifetime, you're lucky.' Well, I found mine.

One by one, Sidekick got his legs, tail, neck, head and mane. Now, I had to do the finishing touches. Saddle, bridle, saddlebags, reins and stirrups come next. Bobby helped me make the horseshoes out of copper tubing. I painted the horse like a buckskin with black mane and tail. The saddle was dark brown and he even had a bedroll and frying pan. He was not a traditional carousel horse. He looked more like a pony express horse at full speed. The finished length was eight feet from his nose to the tip of his tail, and he weighed roughly four hundred pounds.

The last thing was to give him eyes. I was told that once he had eyes he would take on a life of his own. It was true. After that, when we went to the basement, Sidekick watched our every move.

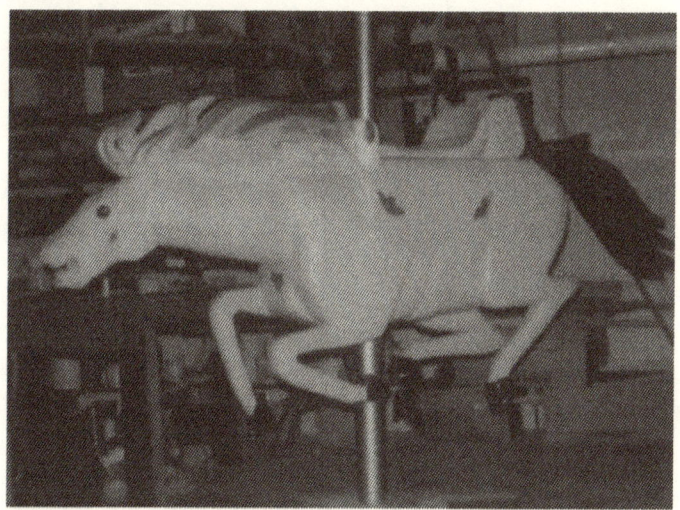

"Sidekick", my carousel horse

Sidekick was finished and so was the winter of eighty-nine. I had made it through one more year with my mind intact.

I took some time off from the group home in ninety to go back to school for my Certified Nursing Assistant certificate. I learned CPR, first aid, home health, nutrition, and fire safety. During this time I remodeled the sewing room (The original double garage) into six bedrooms, and the room I did upholstery in into a community room. I replaced the wood furnaces with natural gas, changed my target group, and now took care of veterans. The work was harder as some needed to be bathed, and I now had six people to care for besides Bobby.

Gordon had left and gone back to drinking. Arlow left also, but he was going to rent a room from Ilka. She hated being alone in her house. Stan's office in the basement would make a nice room for him. It was a load off my mind, knowing she wasn't in her house alone, and that Arlow had a nice place to live and was now working at a good job.

Chapter Twenty Four

Changing target groups also led to other changes. My old wagon was traded off for a conversion van. The men liked to pile in and go to town with me, and it made it easier to take them for their appointments at the VA. The common room was large, but it was a little confining. It had couches, television, cupboards and sink, tables and chairs, a refrigerator and a stackable washer and drier. I decided to add on a sunroom. My winter was spent drawing the plans and by spring I knew exactly how much lumber, sheeting, shingles, doors and windows I would need.

The summer started by sawing boards and pounding nails. The work was going so well, I decided to build another sun room on the front of our living quarters. I used the same plans only the second room was two feet longer. By cold weather both rooms were completed except for siding. I did a quick wrap with fifteen pound tar paper and lathes. The board and batten siding would have to wait for Spring. With all of the added sun from the porches, the house was warm and cozy. The men enjoyed sitting out where they could watch the finches, bluebirds, and hummingbirds as they came to my many feeders. Each year the flowers in my gardens increased. Every spring and summer the yard was a burst of ever-changing color. Last summer I planted three-hundred and fifty Blue Spruces as an eventual wind break, behind the house.

The spring of ninety-two came. With all the work in my gardens and trying to finish the siding, I had been out in the sun all morning. It began to feel like I'd had too much exposure. Some cool water splashed on my face and a coffee break would feel good. The water and the pain hit my face simultaneously

Something must be wrong with my teeth. Wrong, the pain was still there without them. Like most people do, I thought it was an isolated incident and wouldn't return. Wrong again.

I went through months of ex-rays, drawing blood, poking and prodding, prodding and poking. Trigeminal Neuralgia cannot be diagnosed. The only way they can detect it is to rule out any other reason for the pain. They finally wrote me out a prescription for <u>Tegretol.</u>

"You have to go on this gradually, Sarah." Dr. Bradley said. "One pill a day to start, and we'll work you up to three a day. Two-hundred milligrams a day is what you'll need."

The first pill put me in a state of drunkenness.

"I worked too hard to get away from alcohol," I told Dr. Bradley, "to go back under the influence of any drug this strong."

"You keep the prescription handy," Dr. Bradley said. "There have been many suicides from the pain of Tic De La Rou."

"What in the world is Tic De La Rou?"

"It's a cute little nick name for a terrible affliction."

I kept the prescription but lived with the pain for the next two years, and it changed my life. The mere thought of a shower or simply washing my face brought on fear. The touch of water felt like two-hundred-forty volts of electricity hitting the right side of my face. My first two or three bites of food brought on a similar reaction. If I could make it past that I was all right. Mealtimes were lonesome, as I didn't want anyone to have to endure watching my pain. Cold air or a slight breeze also brought on the pain. At the end of two years the pain was with me constantly, so I spent most of my time alone reading.

One evening, I had just gotten Bobby to bed, when the phone rang. I grabbed it quickly so it wouldn't wake him.

"Hello." I answered.

"Hellow, youshelf. I havnth talked to you in ages, Sharah."

This drunken woman stayed on that phone until three-thirty in the morning, while I sat listening in pain. Nothing I said made any difference. She hated Carl, or still loved him so much, she just went on and on and on about him. I fell asleep a couple of times, but when I woke she was still talking. I finally just hung up the phone and went to bed. My sleep was more important than listening to a drunk talk about a person that I detested. Thank goodness, that was the last time I ever heard from Maggie.

Finally, the pain was too much so I started the medication. It made the pain bearable but I was in la la land most of the time. I hated living this way. Like youngsters will, Bobby took advantage of my condition and did what he pleased. Not all bad, but not all good.

By nineteen-ninety-three I had to give up the group home. The men were like family, not just for us, but for each other. Most of them had to return to the VA hospital. All accept one. Willy wasn't a vet and had nowhere to go so he wanted to stay with us. I agreed. It would be a small income at least.

I was still doing some sewing and occasional art work. My functioning abilities weren't the best. My body wasn't accepting this drug very well. I needed to be near my family. Ilka had stuck by me through everything, but now I needed more.

Without all the men to haul around I decided a smaller car made more sense, so I purchased a small station wagon. Occasionally I could drive past a station without pulling in for gas. Bobby and I visited Mom, and looked at houses in Fennimore. Most were out of my price range. The bank in Fennimore was willing to give me a loan even though I hadn't sold my house in Summit yet.

I spotted a neat little house on the main street, but it was late, the realtor was closed, and we were on our way home. I remembered the realtor's number, by repeating it all the way home. I called and sat up an appointment for Saturday.

*   *   *   *   *   *

Friday night Bobby pleaded "Can't we leave now, Mom? The car's all loaded."

"I'm not able to drive when I'm this tired." I said. "I just need two hour's rest, then we'll leave."

"Oh, all right." He was disappointed, but I was tired. He busied himself with his video games, and I pulled the alarm and dozed off fully dressed. That way I could get up and go.

The alarm went off with a "Jangle."

"Come on, Mom," Bobby hollered to wake me, "let's go."

I was still so groggy. I couldn't believe I was still this tired. After I gulped a couple of cups of coffee, we headed out. Bobby dozed when the motor started humming. When I pulled into the station in the second town down the line, for coffee, I checked my watch. It was only ten-thirty. I hadn't laid down until nine. This kid has my number.

I shook him until he woke. "Wake up, you little twerp."

"Uh, uh, what, Mom. Where are we?" He mumbled.

"I stopped for coffee." I said. "What did you do back home? I didn't get two hours of sleep."

"I'm sorry, Mom." He apologized. "I was so excited to get going, when you fell asleep, I turned the clock ahead an hour."

"You little snot." I scolded him. "Well, I'm awake now. Go back to sleep. I'll wake you when we get to Grandma's." I didn't though. Instead of waking Mom at this hour, we slept in the car. She woke us when she got around in the morning.

Our appointment wasn't till later in the day so Mom and I decided to take Bobby to Woodman lake and try for some Bluegills. Mom loved a good batch of Bluegill fillets.

The house was just what we needed. I made an offer and we headed home.

"You said I could fish in the Wisconsin River, Mom." Bobby pleaded.

"You can," I said, "when we get there. I'm going to sleep while you fish."

I pulled into the boat dock at Boscobel, and backed the wagon to the far edge of the blacktop parking area. There were eight or nine other vehicles there, mostly four x fours with empty boat trailers. They must have been out on the river. Bobby grabbed his poles and tackle box. He came back for worms and a blanket to sit on. I rolled out the sleeping bag in the back, and locked the doors before I fell asleep. There were lots of people around, night fishing.

Bang, Bang, Bang. Someone was pounding on my car.

"Mrs. Bray," they yelled.

My heart almost stopped. Who knows my name? "What happened?"

217

The person said, "Your son has a big fish on and needs his landing hook."

I unlocked the door and climbed out so stiff I could hardly straighten up. When I had laid the seat down, I stuffed everything under it, and of coarse the hook was at the bottom. The blacktop hurt my stockinged feet. I can't get it from this side. I ran around to the other side. The door's locked. I went back through the other door. Damn, it's dark. I threw everything out on the ground. There is the hook, finally. I handed it to the couple who were standing there, waiting, watching me run around like a crazy person. They ran off with the hook. I was still half asleep.

I shoved the stuff back in the car, found my shoes, and ran over to the docking area where I could hear all the commotion.

"Look at my fish, Mom." Bobby squealed with delight.

"Wow, Bobby, he's huge." I said. Then I noticed the pole he had used.

"You caught that fish on my pole with my little number six hook. Does that mean he's half mine?" I joked.

"No," He bragged, "it means I'm a danged good fisherman."

The Northern weighed fifteen pounds, fourteen ounces, and was forty-four inches long. He had fought it for forty-five minutes.

"I can't believe I caught it." He kept repeating.

It did my heart good to see him so happy. Before we left for home, we found more ice for the cooler and waited for the newspaper office to open. They asked Bobby a lot of questions and then took a picture of a very big fish and a kid grinning from ear to ear

Chapter Twenty Five

I took possession of the house on the first of September, nineteen-ninety-four. It was a bungalow style house. The living room took the entire front half of the ground floor. Behind that were two bedrooms, a bath and a kitchen. Upstairs was one big room with lots of attic space. There was a full basement with a second bath and a hot-tub. It had a big shop area for all of my projects. Outside on the North end was a single garage with a cement driveway. The South end had an open porch with a roof over it. Out back was a large garden, even red raspberries. In front of the open porch was a thirty-foot Blue Spruce.

"Bobby," I said. "I think we have the biggest Christmas tree in town."

"I think so too. Are we going to decorate it?" He asked.

We did the first year, but I found it meant too many hours on a ladder, which I couldn't do.

The fall and winter of ninety-four were cold and windy, and I had to wrap my head like a mummy anytime I went out. In no time, they increased my medication to four-hundred milligrams, then six-hundred. It was harder for me to function all the time. They gave me disability because I couldn't work anymore.

Willy was an easy person to care for, Thank God. Most of my days were spent sitting in my recliner dozing off and on. He liked simple meals, cereal for breakfast, sandwiches for lunch. I made big suppers. Bobby even pitched in and made a meal now and then.

School started the day before we moved and I had quite a hassle getting Bobby enrolled in high school, but finally managed. I could have saved the effort. The principal had me on the phone constantly. Each time I tried to do anything, or would be sleeping, the phone rang, and rang, and rang. Bobby was an attention deficit child and I knew better than anyone, what a handful he could be. He gets bored easily and can't keep his attention on one thing, except maybe fishing. After a few weeks of this, the school notified me that he was failing all of his classes.

"I can't keep running up to school." I complained to the principal.

"Well, Mrs. Bray," he asked, "what do you suggest we do about your son?"

"I suggest you send him home." I told him. "I'll call Madison and withdraw him from the school system. He will be home schooled from now on."

"That's your choice." He said.

"Yes," I snapped, "that is my choice."

Bob, (He doesn't like Bobby anymore.) Was soon enrolled in a home school from the Chicago area, and was doing fine with his studies. I had given Bob my king-sized waterbed and he wanted his room in the basement where the hot-tub was. I managed to build a few partitions in the basement so he could have some privacy. He now had access to the back entry. This was an added burden on me, worrying about the comings and goings while I was sleeping, but the medication made me oblivious. I had to put my faith in God, take my meds, and hope for the best.

*　*　*　*　*　*

One day, when I walked to the truck stop for coffee, I took my camera along and snapped pictures of some of the local people. When I got the pictures back, I drew portraits from them. The truck stop agreed to display them. I took pictures wherever I went of people doing whatever people do. Drinking coffee, working in a store, building a house, it made no difference. It kept everyone wondering, who would be next. The Library, two banks, and two clinics also agreed to display them. I changed the displays every two weeks. Twelve a month, and I was loving it, when I could stay awake.

Drawing the portraits were a source of enjoyment for me for a little over a year, but it was getting harder for me to concentrate on anything. They increased my medication to eight-hundred milligrams a day. Blood was being drawn constantly to make sure the pills weren't harming the rest of my body. Finally they increased it to one-thousand milligrams, and I was shaking too much to draw. Staying awake to fix Willy's supper, doing dishes, and the laundry, was all I could handle.

Dr. Gunther, my doctor in Fennimore, gave me some bad news.

"Sarah," He said, "the <u>Tegretol</u> isn't working any more. I want you to see a neurologist in Madison."

"For what?" I asked.

"We don't have any other options now." He said. "Surgery is your only hope."

"They can fix this?" I asked.

"There are no guarantees, Sarah." He said. "Brain surgery is always risky."

"If it works, will I still be on medication?" I asked.

"No," He said, "you won't have to take it anymore."

"I won't know how to live a normal life." I said. "I've lived like a zombie for so long."

"I know what you've been through has been terrible." He said. "Maybe it will all be over soon."

Maybe? That didn't sound good.

"Do you think you can drive to Madison?" He asked.

"Sure I can." I said. "When?"

"Hang in there a minute." He said. "I'll make a phone call and find out."

220

It dawned on me, sitting there, if this surgery is that risky, I'd better get my affairs in order. Maybe Tag will agree to take care of things if I don't survive. At Mom's age, I can't ask her.

The doctor came back in the room. "He can see you tomorrow at ten. They're still on the phone for your answer." He said with urgency.

"I'll make it." I replied. He left the room again. Maybe Mom can ride along with me. We can go out to Jane's afterward.

I stopped at the desk, picked up the appointment card for the clinic in Madison. That city has expanded so much since we moved from that area, but I can still find the clinic.

Mom agreed to go with me, but reminded me that it was supposed to snow that night. I'd better call Chet. He kept my walk and driveway clear of snow. A good thing I did. When I woke at four o'clock, there was at least six inches of new white stuff but it seemed to be all done snowing. Chet had everything pushed off the drive. By seven Mom and I were on our way to Dodgeville, where we planned to stop for breakfast. The plows had been out all night and the roads were in good shape. If you live in Wisconsin all your life, you're used to snow. The sun was another thing. Driving East at sunrise, the sun comes up over your hood ornament, and you're looking it right in the eye. By the time we ate the roads were melted off and the sun was high enough, not to be a problem.

We went to the neurology waiting room. As soon as I sat down, I fell asleep, which scared Mom. The nurse woke me when they were ready for me. I needed another MRI. Ironically, the technician was a Tic De La Rou survivor. He let me feel the hole in his skull from his surgery. It felt gross. When the tests were completed, the surgeon came to talk to me.

"Hello, Sarah," He said. "I'm Doctor Imhoff. I'll be doing your operation. I need to explain a few things first. There is a glitch in your brain stem where all the nerves are. I may have to cut the nerve to the right side of your face. I won't know until I get in there, how much damage there is."

"You mean I may lose the feeling on that side of my face?"

"That's right. If it comes to that, you'll need to be extra careful. If you bite your tongue, you won't feel it. If you get something in your eye, you won't know."

"I don't have any choice, do I?" I winced.

"No, you really don't." He explained. "You can't live with this pain."

"When are you doing the surgery?" I asked.

"The day after tomorrow." He said. "Don't plan to drive though. You won't be driving for several weeks."

"I can arrange a ride. Are you going to shave my head?" I asked.

"At least part of it." He answered.

221

"If you have to," I said, "shave the whole thing. It's a small price to pay to get rid of this pain."

"Do you have any more questions?" He asked.

"How long will I be in the hospital?" I asked.

Dr. Imhoff had apparently been through this high voltage question and answer session many times. The real question was not about my head being shaved or the length of my hospital stay, but, will I survive? Which was a question he couldn't answer. He knew that humor was the best way to deflate my anxiety.

"About five days, if you behave. The nurses get even if you don't."

*   *   *   *   *   *

The lights in the ICU were dimmed, so when I woke there were no glaring lights like there had been in surgery. I could feel my face so I knew he hadn't cut the nerve. For the first time in five years the pain was gone.

Laurie, Mom, Tag and Julie, Jane and Brad, were all waiting for me to come around. Laurie had been entertaining everyone with tales of our trip to Texas. They were all relieved that I was okay, but it was late so they didn't stay long. Laurie lagged behind after everyone else left.

"Mom," she said, "I know that you've suspected for some time, that things weren't going well for Dwight and me. We decided to call it quits. I didn't want to tell you because you've been so sick."

"You knew it was coming, Laurie." I said. "You only hurt each other and the kids by living in an unhappy relationship."

"I wished we lived closer, Mom." She pouted.

"I do too." I said, "but, you'll be fine, Laurie. You're one of the spunkiest people I've ever known."

"I'm glad you're okay, Mom," she said, "but I'm going to get on the road. It's a long drive home."

My recovery was so fast, they released me on the third day. Hospitals send you home as soon as you're able anymore, and I was glad to be home, pain free.

*   *   *   *   *   *

Our home in Fennimore, 1994

That summer, I spent most of my time outside. I could again enjoy the fresh air. I decided to build in the open porch. No one used it anyhow, the way it was. So I got busy drawing plans again, then ordered my lumber, rough cut from the saw mill. Mom and I made a trip to Dubuque pulling my two wheeled trailer. We picked up an entry and storm door, nine windows, flooring, electrical boxes, heat runs and dry wall. We had a full load. With all this and the lumber, my garage was full. The weather warmed but it wouldn't quit raining. I finally hung plastic around the porch and started my project.

By fall I had my drawing room, winterized and carpeted. This was now a part of my house, my favorite part. Sitting out there, drawing, was like being outside in my garden.

My feet were giving me problems. I had really tried not to use the ladder any more than I could help. The orthotics weren't helping my broken arches, so back to the podiatrist. The examination showed that my arches weren't my only problem. This meant another trip to Madison. I hade no circulation in my right foot. They did a bypass in my leg almost a year to the day of my last surgery. The abuse I did to my body for all these years was coming back to haunt me.

223

Chapter Twenty Six

The Fennimore City Council contacted me while I was recuperating and wanted me to attend their next meeting. They didn't say why.

The chairperson said, "Sarah, the city would like you to do a mural for the Sesquicentennial."

"What's a Sesquicentennial?" I asked. I felt stupid because I didn't know if I had even pronounced it right, and I sure didn't know what it meant.

"Wisconsin's one-hundred-fiftieth birthday." She explained.

"I never heard that word before." I told her.

"You're not alone." They assured me.

"In nineteen-ninety-eight Wisconsin will be one-hundred and fifty years' old. Would you like to do it for us?" asked another council member, impatiently.

I purposely took my time about answering. They started to look at each other with doubt.

"Heck no," I hesitated, "I'd love to."

The rest of the summer I divided my time between the flowers in my garden and the flowers in my mind, my sketches. In the fall they gave me the go ahead on the preliminary drawings. The drawings turn into pen and ink and transparencies, during the fall and winter. I wrote a one page story to accompany each drawing, and proposed that we print up coloring books as a fund raiser for the mural, and they liked the idea. The state gave us a grant for part of the expense and different organizations in Fennimore also donated funds.

Bob completed his schooling and received his diploma. He finished in three years instead of four. Learning wasn't his problem. He just hated being cooped up in that schoolhouse all day.

Painting the mural was done in the city hall, during the winter if ninety-seven, so we could hang it in time for the unveiling on May thirty-first. I was going to use all the local volunteers that wanted to help. The paint was ordered, aluminum panels were delivered, brushes purchased and we were off and running.

Digger, who worked for the city, built a ten by twelve-foot easel for us to work on. Each panel was four by ten foot and it took three for each picture, forty-seven total. The finished mural would be one-hundred-eighty-seven feet long and ten feet high, and would be placed on the long side of the lumber yard shed.

I practically lived at city hall for four months, but they didn't charge me rent. They gave me a key so I could come and go as I pleased. Many times I worked all night. I was in seventh heaven, doing what I should have been doing all my life.

Many people came to help paint. Some young, some old, tall and short, skinny and fat, all came to help with a piece of Fennimore's future history. There is a little artist in all of us. I made some lasting friendships as we painted side by side.

They had a big celebration planned. A parade, and ice cream social, a cake baking contest, live country music, and the unveiling. Now, you can't have an unveiling unless something is covered to start with. So now I had to plan a tarp large enough to cover the mural, and some kind of system so that when the time came the tarp would drop like it should. Putting almost two-hundred feet of heavy duty plastic through my sewing machine was a rassling match I never care to repeat.

The celebration was to be in eighteen-fifty's clothing so any time I didn't spend painting, I was sewing. Every woman in town was making period clothing. As for me, I made nine dresses complete with bonnets or hats, four shirts, three vests and at least a dozen extra bonnets. Sleep was the last thing on my mind.

The big day was finally here. Laurie was coming down for the doings and bringing her fiancee, Joe, with her. My Granddaughter, Jessica, was coming along and, her boyfriend, Chad. Both gals were baking cakes for the contest. I had eight people who would be getting dressed in their outfits at my house. Laurie and Joe surprised me with their news. They were getting married next week end. They wanted Mom, me, and Bob to come to their wedding. Maybe I'll be recuperated by then.

Mom was cutting the rope for the unveiling. She was the only living person depicted in the mural, and she was nervous. She was eighty-seven now, and because she was a little unsteady on her feet, Tag was going to walk up with her to cut the rope.

Four generations of my relation showed up, one-hundred-fifty of them. One of the cousins made name tags for all of us. My Grandma Leighy would have been proud.

Laurie won first place and Grand Champion with her Banana Split cake. Joe just beamed with pride.

My feet hadn't touched the ground for days, but they had better today. I had to give a speech.

Everything went like clockwork. The tarp came down as planned, helium balloons floated up, and Fennimore had a mural they should enjoy for years. We all sampled Laurie and Jessica's cakes, and a few others. We danced a little. My tired old feet even did a polka, and then we walked home.

Laurie's gang had to be on their way. They had a four-hour trip ahead of them, work tomorrow and a wedding next week.

225

After two years preparation and months of running on the momentum built up for this challenge, this day had finally come and gone. I now had only one goal in mind. I sat down in my old recliner, kicked off my shoes, and collapsed.

Mom cutting the rope for the mural unveiling, May 31, 1998

Mural painted for the Sesquicentennial

Mural painted for the Sesquicentennial

Chapter Twenty Seven

On the twenty-forth of June I drove to Summit to receive my twelfth medallion from my home A.A.group. I had been waiting for this day for years. I planned a clock for my living room made with my medallions and I needed number twelve. Ilka went with me to the open meeting and then I stayed the night

The clock made from A. A. medallions

with her. We had a lot of talking to do. I only see her two or three times a year now. The next morning she was showing me her yard and the beautiful roses she and Arlow had planted when her neighbor came over to say 'hello'. She wanted Ilka to see an antique she had just purchased, and I was invited to tag along. We stepped in her back door and the two of them were examining the newly acquired piece. I was just enjoying the nice home, when I noticed something that immediately took my eye.

"Excuse me," I interrupted, "can I ask you about that tiny red collar in your china cabinet?"

"The cat collar?" The neighbor acted puzzled.

"Yes, could I see it?" I asked.

She lovingly took the collar from the case and handed it to me. There was my pinky ring. A tear filled my eyes as she told how a stray black tomcat had come to their house many years before. She wasn't sure of the cat's real age, but they had him as a beloved pet until he died of old age, three years ago.

"We tried to find the owner." She said. "They must have cared a lot, to give him this darling little ring. I've never had the heart to get rid of it."

Ilka and I returned to her yard and I told Ilka about Nuffers. She was free to tell the story to her neighbor later if she wanted to. It didn't matter. I was just happy to know Nuffers had found a loving home. Too bad Buck couldn't have been so lucky.

*   *   *   *   *   *

The remainder of the summer was spent hauling rocks from the country, load after load of rocks. They were piled everywhere. I had many curious onlookers who tried to guess what I was up too now. I just kept collecting rocks. Big ones, flat ones, round ones, red ones and brown ones, they piled up all over my lawn. Enough yet? No. Not quite. I kept collecting. Finally I reached a point where I ran out of space, so then I started removing the sod right behind my drawing room. I dug an area about fifteen feet square so it was below ground level roughly six inches. I went for a trailer load of sand and spread it two inches thick. When it was tamped down very hard, I laid the rocks in leaving, maybe an inch between them. I mixed mortar and carefully filled in between the rocks. My patio was ready to set up. I waited for over a week, until it was well cured before I continued with my project.

Now comes the fun part. In my mind's eye, I drew a design and started laying up row after row of rock and mortar, the way I'd seen my father do, carefully putting in wire at regular intervals. When I reached eighteen inches, I put overflow tubes in and continued the rock to twenty-four inches. I had saved the big flat rocks for the top row. Now this had to cure. So, I, not so patiently, waited. I lined the inside with chicken wire fastened to the walls with the wire I had laid between the rocks. Mixing mortar like crazy, in my little wash tub, I covered the wire completely. My fish pond was all finished but the waterfall. For that I needed lots of slow planning so the water would fall just right. Tag furnished me with a pair if cement drill cores. When I incorporated them into my plans it made the waterfall look like an old ruins. On the top I formed a bird bath, so the water entered the bath and overflowed down the falls. The plastic tubing was installed and the water pump was ready. I let the lining cure for another week, painted the interior with baby blue, waterproof paint, then filled it with water. No leaks, so I started the pump.

*   *   *   *   *   *

"You are supposed to call Judy at the newspaper office, Mom." Bob yelled at me from the house.

I walked in the back door. "I wonder what the paper wants?" I said, more to myself than anyone else.

"Well, call her back and find out." Bob said grumpily.

I dialed the phone. I was tired and it was time to fix supper.

"Hello," from the other end.

"Judy? This is Sarah Bray. My son told me that you called."

"Sarah," She said. "I have some good news. The people of Fennimore have elected you 'Female Citizen of the Year'."

Tears came to my eyes and I couldn't talk. I managed a feeble, "You've got to be kidding."

She continued, "You will be riding in a convertible in the parade, along with the man who was elected the 'Male Citizen of the Year'. There will be a ceremony in the park where they will present you both with plaques." By then I had regained my composure enough to talk.

"Thank you for calling, Judy." I said. "I'm sorry I couldn't talk more. I'm just a little overwhelmed."

"You don't have to apologize, Sarah." She said. "I understand." Then she added, "Let me be the first to congratulate you."

The waterfall and birdbath on the pond

Did she really understand? Could anyone understand? Some could, at least partly. Those who have been to the bottom of despair and crawled back out, one second, one minute, one hour, one day at a time. They know. They understand the feeling of being free of their demon. But this? This was a feeling I didn't know if I would ever really comprehend. Twelve years ago, beaten, broke, and alone with my small son, I had wondered if I could make it through the day. I did though. I made it through twelve years of days, one day at a time. Today they elected me 'Female Citizen of the Year'. Unbelievable!

$$* \quad * \quad * \quad * \quad * \quad *$$

Looking through my mementoes in my dresser drawer, I can easily return to my days of reckoning in a small motel room more than a dozen years ago.

Here is the broken harmonica my father dropped when I threw him out of my home. It's still in two pieces.

A heart shaped, antique, jewelry box where I've always kept my medallions from A.A.

Three wedding bands that were promises of the future, all promises broken.

A mother's ring with three gems. Arron, Cyle and Laurie gave it to me the Christmas we left the Beach.

Four locks of hair, tied with ribbon, from my children's first haircuts.

Photos of my life, some happy, some sad.

A little velvet pouch full of rose petals and a note saying, "Thanks for the son," Love, Carl.

Sea shells from Texas, and, Bobby's baby teeth.

$$* \quad * \quad * \quad * \quad * \quad *$$

Saying "I can't" has never been my way. Challenges have kept my life interesting, and if they were enjoyable experiences, I went back for a second helping. I wouldn't have wanted to miss any part of my life, with the exception of the last day I spent with my father.

During the quiet hours of dusk I let my computer rest and go sit by the pond, my own little sanctuary. Water trickling down the rocks of the falls, then cascading around a small figure of Christ who's walking in the water, caresses my mind, before falling once again to the pond to start its journey over.

Bobby at twenty-one

Each rock was beautiful, as a rock. Held together each has a place and a purpose, as they form the body of my pond. Just as the rocks along the path of my life each had a reason for being. Together they paved the way to where I am today, exactly where I'm supposed to be.

Most of my time I spend alone. A predicament with a bad, undeserved reputation. Happiness is a very personal thing. If you can be happy when you're alone, you can spread happiness as you walk among your peers. If you are unhappy, weather alone or with others, you spread only gloom.

My solitude is a sign of freedom. Freedom from abuse. Freedom from being someone else's possession. Free to use the gift that was given to me at birth. Free to be me, whoever I am. Most of all, freedom from alcohol.

My children are all grown now. I no longer have pain in my face. I can't walk too well, but I can draw pictures, …tell stories, …and…Soar Like an Eagle, One Day at a Time.

THE END

Life after the Battle

GOD sometimes chose not what I asked,

Rather, he gave what was needed,

To lead me to the perfect path,

To find the gift he had given long ago.

Sarah Bray

Sarah Ann Bray

About the Author

Sarah was born in Cuba City, Wisconsin and lived throughout the state her entire life. She had three children, two sons and a daughter, from her first marriage, none from the second and one son from the third. At the present time, she has six grandchildren; five boys and one girl who are all graduated.

She started drawing when she was old enough to hold a pencil. Her artwork was interrupted by alcoholism at a very young age. It wasn't until after she turned fifty that she began her struggle to escape alcohol.

During her life she has been an artist, cook, upholsterer, carpenter, caregiver, seamstress, tree trimmer, and mother. At fifty-five she went back to school for her Certified Nurses Assistance certificate. She even flipped burgers while going to classes. Hunting and fishing were her hobbies.

Because of health problems she returned to her hometown in 1994, and once again returned to artwork in earnest. Since then she has done over one thousand pencil portraits, many signs, and a one-hundred-eighty-seven-foot long mural. Any challenge was hard to resist, so at sixty-five she took on the new world and tackled the computer. While it is a handy tool to copy her artwork, she also found a new love. Writing.

While this story is fiction, it is based on Sarah's life. A resemblance to anyone is purely coincidental.

www.ingramcontent.com/pod-product-compliance
Lightning Source LLC
Chambersburg PA
CBHW030305290526
45785CB00001B/224